24273

Crow, Donna Fletcher

Elizabeth, Days of Loss and Hope

DATE DUE

SE 04 '96			
AG 16 '97			
JA 20 '98			
FE 11 '99			

DEMCO

Daughters of Courage

Elizabeth

DONNA FLETCHER CROW

CARMEL • NEW YORK 10512

For my parents,
Reta and Leonard Fletcher,
and
my special aunt and uncle,
Pauline and Lawrence Fletcher

This Guideposts edition is published by
special arrangement with Moody Press.

ISBN: 0-8024-4528-4

Printed in the United States of America

The Jayne Family

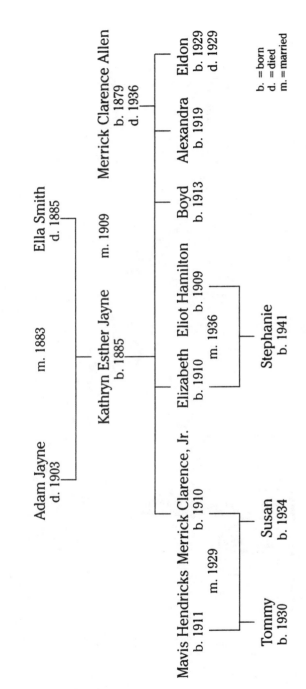

Adam Jayne
d. 1903

m. 1883

Ella Smith
d. 1885

Merrick Clarence Allen
b. 1879
d. 1936

Kathryn Esther Jayne
b. 1885

m. 1909

Boyd
b. 1913

Alexandra
b. 1919

Eldon
b. 1929
d. 1929

Mavis Hendricks
b. 1911

Merrick Clarence, Jr.
b. 1910

m. 1929

Elizabeth
b. 1910

Eliot Hamilton
b. 1909

m. 1936

Tommy
b. 1930

Susan
b. 1934

Stephanie
b. 1941

b. = born
d. = died
m. = married

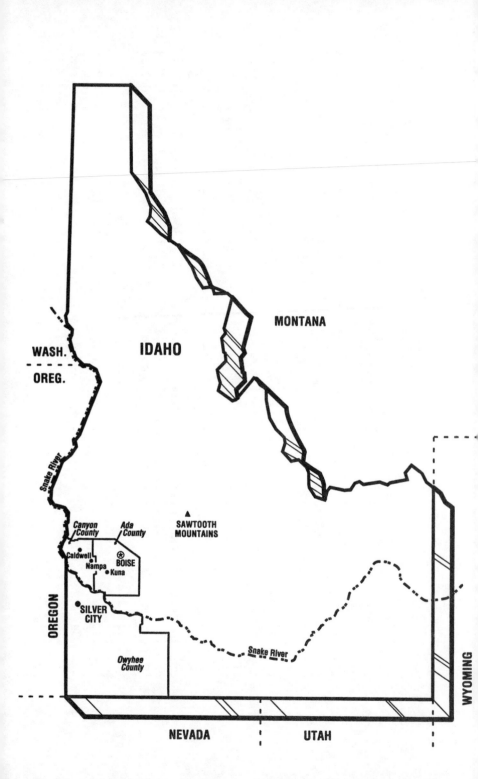

1

Elizabeth slipped out the back door of the farmhouse that had been home to her family for almost three generations now. The fresh morning hours were her favorite time of day, and May was her favorite month. She flung out her arms to embrace the dew-sparkled morning filled with birdsong.

Nothing could make her heart sing with more joy than the dawn chorus. No matter how full of hard work the day ahead loomed, she would have these moments to cherish. And in 1929 on a farm in Kuna, Idaho, hewn out of reclaimed sagebrush desert, with a large family—soon to be larger—the work never ceased.

She walked toward the big cottonwood tree in the corner of the yard. Her mother would be out in a minute. They would do a gardening chore, then hurry in to finish cooking breakfast, and the busy pace would begin. As the oldest daughter, Elizabeth had always been her mother's right-hand helper, just as Clarey, her twin brother, was their father's. An especially clear warble trilled above her head, and Elizabeth looked up into the thick, green branches, a smile at the corners of her usually firm mouth.

The screen door banged behind her, and she turned to extend her smile to her mother, walking across the grass in a flowered cotton housedress that was straining at the seams over her abdomen.

"Oh, Mother, how could you have lived here before there were birds?"

Kathryn smiled. "I was just seventeen—only a little younger than you are now when we came here, my dear, and we lacked so many things I don't think I even noticed there were no birds." Kathryn ran her hand through her soft brown hair, which was just graying at the temples. "As I remember, I missed the crickets at evening more than birds. Crickets came as soon as the water did in the spring of 1909, but we didn't get birds for a long time—not until the trees were big enough to shelter them. I don't know—they say someday we'll even have squirrels. I think I'd like that. I like watching the squirrels when we go into Boise."

Kathryn bent awkwardly to pick up a small plant, a ball of soil held around its roots with sacking.

Elizabeth took the shovel leaning against the porch. "How come we're planting this rosebush before the baby's born, Mama? I thought you did the others after we came."

"Yes, but I wanted to get it done before things get too busy with summer work, and it's better for the bush to plant it in the spring before it gets hot."

"Is this where you want it?" Elizabeth set her foot on the shovel.

"A little more to the right, closer to where your papa planted the pink one when Alex was born."

Elizabeth turned a shovel of the soil, rich with volcanic ash, that had been producing such fine crops since irrigation water came to Kuna twenty years before—whenever there wasn't a problem over water rights. "Trouble with planting early, Mama, you don't know whether you need a red bush or a pink one."

Elizabeth looked at the red moss roses sprouting new green leaves near the fence. They celebrated the birth of her twin, Merrick Clarence, Jr., and her sixteen-year-old

8

brother, Boyd. The small pink bushes for Elizabeth and ten-year-old Alexandra grew closer to the house.

Kathryn smiled, making her eyes crinkle at the corners. "Maybe that was part of why I wanted to plant it early. I wanted an excuse to plant a yellow rose." She set the root ball in the ground and held one green cane upright while Elizabeth filled the hole with water from a bucket and tamped in the dirt. "Thank you, my dear. Now you'd best hurry. With less than a month to graduation you don't want to spoil that fine record of yours."

Elizabeth started toward the house, then turned back. "I'll be home late today, Mother. I thought after school I'd go downtown and apply for a job." She bit her lower lip as she always did when she was nervous. "Mother, have you and Dad talked about this fall? If I can get a good job—I thought maybe at the pharmacy or the general store . . ."

Kathryn rubbed the soil off her hands before she patted her daughter on the shoulder. "Elizabeth, I know how much you want to go to college. And your papa and I think it's a fine ambition. But with all that money we borrowed to buy new equipment when prices were so good during the War—and then the bottom dropped out of everything . . ." She sighed. "It's been nine years now since we got a decent price for any of our crops—and costs just keep rising." Kathryn shook her head.

"I know—and the first rights to a college education are Clarey's because he's an hour older than I am, and he's a boy." She walked toward the house.

"If only we could send you both," Kathryn said to her back. "If we have a good harvest this fall . . ." But she didn't finish because Elizabeth had closed the screen door, very quietly.

Elizabeth dawdled on the small back sleeping porch she shared with Alex. She knew that Boyd and Alex would scramble to sit beside Clarey on the spring seat of the wagon as soon as they finished the breakfast dishes; then she

9

could sit alone in the less comfortable but more private back of the wagon bed.

Holding the dampened fingers of her left hand in the grooves of each wave of her rich, black hair, she smoothed every strand. When she and her best friend, Celia, had taken the plunge to have their hair bobbed three years ago, Elizabeth had chosen a mid-length style that stopped halfway between her ears and her shoulders, instead of the close crop at the back of the neck that most girls in her class wore. Elizabeth felt it was better for her since her eyebrows were heavy and her eyes dark—and since she was so tall. She was happy enough to have inherited her father's luxuriant hair, but why she had to have his strong bone structure at a time when all the popular girls were tiny, "five-foot two, with eyes of blue," like Celia—she sighed. Well, her mother had always told her life wasn't fair. Which took her right back to the matter of college.

She heard the screen door bang on the back porch, so turned to pick up her books. She mustn't make them late. Mr. Eastly, her history teacher, couldn't abide having students come in during the Pledge of Allegiance. "Goodbye, Mother," she called as she went out. She knew her father would be long in the barn by now—probably had the milking finished, since Clarey and Boyd had all the cows stanchioned and their share of the milking done before they ate breakfast, just as she and Alex had gathered the eggs and fed the chickens earlier that morning.

She sat on a box in the wagon as gracefully as her knee-length skirt and long legs would allow and looked at her brothers and sister in the front of the cart. Clarey—tall, broad-shouldered, with thick black curls spilling over his forehead. Mother never tired of recalling how that unruly hair and his dancing gray eyes reminded her of Merrick when she had married him, although in quiet moments she would admit that her husband had come much later to exhibit the gentleness that was so natural to Clarey.

Sixteen-year-old Boyd sitting beside him on the spring seat pulled off his cap and ran his fingers through his limp, brown hair, which their mother always said he inherited from her, much to her sorrow. Boyd showed little evidence that he would reach his big brother's height, but there was wiry strength and quickness in his slight frame that made it possible for him to outrun any boy on the school yard. Sometimes when Elizabeth watched him run she had the strangest feeling that he would simply keep running—his heels sprout wings and carry him on to the far horizons his blue eyes never quit scanning.

"Ouch! Clarey, you'll bounce me out!" Little Alex clung to the edge of the seat as Clarey guided the wagon over a rutted patch of road. Alexandra might be the smallest child in the fifth grade at Kuna Elementary, but she was not the most pliable. Alex could always be counted on to toss her blond curls and let people know what was wrong in her world. And once she had made up her mind, nothing could shake her.

The wagon gave a final lurch and settled into a smoother rut. Clarey clucked to their horse, fancifully named Rosie O'Day for her strawberry roan coloring, and Elizabeth returned to her earlier thoughts on a favorite theme—the unfairness of life.

She understood that a college education would be nice for Clarey, helpful even, now that they were starting to use so many machines on farms, developing new kinds of seeds, and so much bookkeeping was required—Elizabeth never tired of hearing her parents talk about how much had changed since they first came to Kuna and cleared the dry desert land of its virgin sagebrush. They had hauled all their water fifteen miles from the Snake River as soon as Indian Creek dried up in the early summers.

But one fact remained. Elizabeth kicked at a clod of dirt rolling across the wagon bed, then wished she hadn't when she saw the smudge it left on her black shoe. Still,

11

the fact was, one could be a farmer without a college education. And Clarey had never wanted to be anything but a farmer.

Clarey was every girl's dream of a brother: tall and handsome, always kind and helpful, fun and laughing. But he was not a scholar and not aggressive. Perfectly suited to quiet country life, he was happy enough to go to college since his parents thought he should, but it was not a major goal in his life. He wasn't the sort that set major goals and struggled toward them—he left that to his twin sister.

So what about her goals? One *could* farm without a college education, but one *couldn't* teach without at least a two-year normal school degree. And, as long as she was dreaming, it would be so wonderful to take a full four-year liberal arts degree. She thought of the catalog from Northwest Christian College she had on her dresser at home.

"Hi, Liz! Hurry up, or we'll all be late!" Her friend's voice and the jolting stop of the wagon ended her reverie.

Elizabeth looked up and waved, then jumped off the wagon when she saw that Celia Cottrell, accompanied as usual by at least three boys, was waiting for her at the bottom of the school yard. Elizabeth smiled absently, but didn't join in the lively chatter about an ice cream social at the Methodist Church next Friday, as they walked up the hill to the fine red brick building that replaced the school that had burned just four years earlier.

By the end of third period Elizabeth was glad to be released from her commercial class. The clattering of the typewriters was giving her a headache, and, as at the end of almost every typing class, she was close to tears of frustration over having all the keys stack up on her carriage when she tried to increase her speed.

But then three short blasts of the superintendent's buzzer brought all heads up.

"Well, it seems we are to have a surprise assembly today, class." It was impossible to tell whether the crisp

12

Miss Ponsonby approved of such goings-on. "You may take your books with you." She made it sound like a privilege.

"Maybe Mr. Oldham's giving the seniors the day off. I'd love to have a swim in Indian Creek!" Celia managed to talk to Elizabeth and bat her eyes at two different boys as they filed toward the study room, the only room in the building large enough to accommodate all 113 students and 6 faculty members that composed Kuna High School.

Elizabeth caught her breath. Maybe this was it. Had Mr. Oldham decided to present senior awards today? Now? Celia's thoughts didn't extend beyond time off school for flirting, but Elizabeth's flew straight to the goal that was never far out of her mind.

Many of the awards carried cash prizes—some as much as ten or fifteen dollars. If she could get one of the big ones it might be enough money to send her preregistration to the college.

As soon as the shuffling feet were stilled, Mr. Oldham cleared his throat, glanced at the gold pocket watch hanging from a heavy chain across his protruding vest, and cleared his throat again. "As you all know, graduation is just one month from today."

A murmur of enthusiastic agreement showed that little else was on his audience's mind. "In accord with this, I wish today to honor some outstanding graduates and to institute a new award to the outstanding member of the senior class."

Raised eyebrows on faculty faces showed that this surprise had been undertaken solely on the superintendent's initiative. But he proceeded first with the traditional awards: Five dollars to Whitmore Williams as best mathematician, ten dollars to Celia as outstanding musician. Elizabeth bit her lower lip. If the amounts increased, if she could win the top, could it possibly be as much as twenty-five dollars? She held her breath.

"And now, the new award—the Oldham Outstanding Senior Prize, which I shall award to a member of the graduating class who best represents the true ideals of character, leadership, and scholarship." He paused for effect while everyone looked around to try to pick out the winner. "The Senior Prize for the Class of 1929 is awarded to Elizabeth Allen for her positive approach, hard work, and success in her studies, in being captain of both the girls' volleyball and basketball teams, and soloist with the glee club."

Stunned, Elizabeth realized everyone was looking at her and clapping. Celia pushed her to her feet and gave her a shove toward the front of the room. She couldn't believe it. She had hoped so hard. It was really coming true. He hadn't yet mentioned how much the award was. She waited.

Mr. Oldham held up a heavy black cardigan. "Elizabeth Allen, this fine trophy sweater is yours to represent your hard work and success. Wear it with pride." Mr. Oldham put the sweater into her numb hands. "Congratulations, Miss Allen. We wish you every success after graduation. We know you'll make Kuna High proud of you."

She realized everyone was waiting for her response. "Thank you," she managed. "I hope—I—" she looked at the sweater "—I'll wear it at college." It was all she could think of to say, so she sat down.

After Celia's hugs, Clarey was the first to congratulate her when Mr. Oldham dismissed the assembly. "Good for you, little sister. If awards for hard work are going around you'll win every time. Then he said to the room in general, "Nobody works as hard as Elizabeth." Everyone laughed and applauded when he gave her a peck on the cheek.

"Bet he wishes that was Mavis," someone said from the back of the room.

Elizabeth smiled and returned everyone's congratulations and agreed to stop in Miss Spencer's room after school to have a photograph taken for the annual. But the rest of the day, even more than the satisfaction of winning and the disappointment of the prize not being money, two themes ran in her head: her own determined statement "I'll wear it at college" and the comment of her handsome, less ambitious brother, "Nobody works as hard as Elizabeth."

However appropriate it might be, it wasn't the image she would have chosen. She would rather be popular like Celia, or pretty like Mavis Hendricks, or sweet like Edith Renfro, but she was hard-working. And she supposed she'd have to make the most of that since it was the only way she knew to approach life.

As something of a talisman she wore her sweater that afternoon in spite of the heat. It was not easy for her to ask for anything, even for work, so the task of job-hunting she had set for herself was not one she looked forward to. The sweater gave her courage. Even if it wasn't cash, maybe it would help her earn the money she needed.

With her head up, her broad shoulders squared, her long legs striding forward, no one would have known she was quaking inside as she entered Janicke's Pharmacy. Bald-headed Mr. Janicke rubbed his hands on his white apron and leaned forward on the marble counter when she walked in. "Ah, now, what can I do for you, Miss Elizabeth?"

She hesitated.

He smiled encouragingly. "Is it an Oodles bar, then? Quite a spell since you've had one."

Elizabeth firmly shook her head. Her favorite treat was a big, gooey Oodles bar, all chocolate and caramel inside with chunky nuts outside. But they cost five cents. "No, Mr. Janicke, thank you. I've come to apply for a job."

"Oh, yes. Graduation just a month off. I expect lots of younguns'll be comin' around." He shook his head. "Sure wish I could help you. It's not that I couldn't use a hand with the work around here, and I know you'd be a fine, hard worker." As he talked he rubbed the counter with a towel, taking special care under each of the fountain heads where drips of fizzy phosphate had made pockmarks in the gray marble. "It's just that I can't afford to pay anyone else. A few years ago when farmers were getting $1.65 a bushel for their corn I had two assistants—but now they only get 50¢, and that means they only buy the necessities."

Elizabeth nodded as she backed toward the door. She knew all too well the truth of what he was saying. "Thank you anyway, Mr. Janicke."

She looked at the bank, thought of her difficulties with mathematics, and walked on down the street. The millinery and dressmaking shop seemed likely. She had been helping her mother sew since she was old enough to know which end of a needle was sharp, but Miss Simms's response was almost exactly the same as Mr. Janicke's except that Miss Simms quoted the price of alfalfa, that being what her father had raised.

Neither the general store, the hardware store, nor the bakery was any more encouraging. The woodworking shop and the barber shop seemed to require skills beyond her reach. That left the cafe. Surely they could use an extra pair of hands to make bread and wash dishes.

Mr. Parker, the manager, agreed they could, but they couldn't afford to pay those hands—although they would be glad to provide two hot meals a day for ten hours of work.

Elizabeth sighed. There was no shortage of food at home. She would be of more use staying there and helping her mother prepare meals for their family.

With dragging feet she turned the brass doorknob on Griswold's Printing Shop and newspaper office. A card in the window bore bright red letters, *The Kuna Times Weekly.*

Mr. Griswold wiped his inky fingers on a rag before he adjusted his small, round glasses. Surely it was the glasses that made his smile look like a leer, but Elizabeth couldn't help taking a step backward in spite of his friendly greeting.

"Well, well, well. It's Elizabeth Allen, isn't it? And what can I do for you, my dear?" His thick black hair and mustache were as shiny as the pot of ink beside his printing press. They made his skin seem even more startlingly white in the dim room.

Elizabeth wanted to flee, but she glanced down and saw the sweater she was wearing. If she was to wear it at college this fall, this was her last chance. She held out no hope for getting a job at the livery stable, feed mill, or blacksmith shop. "I've come to apply for a job. I need work for the summer."

Somehow she managed not to stammer. The fact that she was slightly taller than Mr. Griswold gave her a little confidence.

"A job?" He rubbed his hands together and considered, eyeing the stack of papers on his desk. "Can you type?"

Elizabeth nodded, ignoring her memory of tangled keys. "Yes. I'm taking a commercial course. We do typing and shorthand both."

"Fine. Suppose you start on those letters there right now. If I'm satisfied, you can work Saturdays until school's out, then three days a week."

She took a step toward the desk then hesitated.

Mr. Griswold seemed to read her mind. "I'll give you a ride home, my dear. It's no trouble. I go right by your front door."

Elizabeth was halfway through the first letter before she realized he had said nothing about how much he would pay her. But she did have a job! *If* she could get these letters done. Fortunately Mr. Griswold was busy setting type in the back of the shop so he didn't see how many sheets of paper she used up getting clean copies of his letters. She stuffed the ruined sheets in her book bag. She didn't want him to find the wastebasket full.

She was well into the third letter when he called from the back of the shop, "Oh, by the way, my dear, did I mention that I want two carbons of each letter? You'll find the carbon paper in the bottom desk drawer."

The wooden buildings of Main Street and the sagebrush bordering the road were making long shadows when Elizabeth was ushered from the building by her new employer. He didn't seem at all perturbed by her lack of typing speed, and he was effusively complimentary about her having caught two spelling errors of his.

He took her arm to help her into his little black Ford parked by the wooden sidewalk in front of the print shop. His hand felt warm even through the sleeve of her sweater. She put her books on the seat beside her and sat far to the outside. But as soon as they were started his hand cupped her right shoulder. "Better move over this way a bit, my dear. That door's none too reliable. Don't want my new typist landing in the dust."

His laughter was jovial, and she moved over two inches. What did she know about her employer? Mr. and Mrs. Griswold had lived on the farm next to the Allens for as long as she could remember. It must have been Mrs. Griswold's father's farm, because people still called it the Foley place. No one ever saw much of her. It was rumored that she was an invalid and that was why they had no children, but she managed to run the hired man with a firm hand while her husband escaped to his printing and newspaper publishing every day.

The discomfort Elizabeth felt with Mr. Griswold must be in her imagination, she told herself, because he was one of Kuna's leading citizens. A director of the Bank of Kuna, last year he'd been elected county commissioner.

But the truly overwhelming fact, the good news she couldn't wait to share with her family, the thing that made her hang onto her seat to keep from shouting as their farm came into view, was that she had an employer—no matter what he was like. She had a job! She ran a hand down the sleeve of her new sweater. She would wear it at college.

2

All the windows were open in the Methodist church that afternoon, but it was still stifling—unusually hot and dry for the end of May, even in the desert. Several of her classmates were fanning themselves with their commencement programs, but Elizabeth simply tried to ignore the discomfort as she listened to Rev. Brown's prolonged invocation. The high school orchestra, all eight members, played a Schubert serenade led by a clear note from Celia's violin.

Elizabeth bit her lip and ran her finger around one of the pink roses printed on the white voile dress her mother had made for her. Wearing such a beautiful dress—the prettiest she had ever owned—gave her courage.

And she needed it. For all her calm appearance, Elizabeth was quaking inside. *We look to the future with our heads held high and courage in our hearts. We are strong for whatever the days ahead may hold. . . . We look to the future with our heads held high . . .*

"We look to the future . . ." Suddenly she was on her feet, speaking aloud the words of the salutatory address she had practiced over and over in her head. It would have been the valedictory if she hadn't ended the year with a C in mathematics. Miss Ponsonby had taken pity on her and given her an A in commercial after all—probably for neatness, since it couldn't have been for speed.

". . . And so, as we look forward to prosperous times, building on the foundation that has been well laid here, we know we will never forget all that our high school years have given us in knowledge and friendships." Elizabeth sat down to resounding applause from her classmates and the audience.

Celia leaned across the dark-suited legs of the two boys between them. "You were super. How I wish I could speak like you—haven't a nerve in your body, have you?"

Elizabeth gave a tight smile. She was still far too nervous to reply.

The program continued through Whitmore's valedictory address and a speech by Mr. Oldham. Then it was time for the glee club selection. Now Elizabeth could relax. She truly enjoyed singing, especially in the anonymity of a twelve-voice choir.

"Beautiful dreamer, wake unto me, starlight and roses will come unto thee . . ." They were well into the second verse when a glance at her mother made Elizabeth miss a note. What was wrong with her mother? Just before giving her speech she had sought her mother's eye and drawn reassurance from her steady smile. On repeated glances at the pew halfway back on the left that was filled with Allens, just in front of the one occupied by their Jayne cousins and the Sperlins, her parents' best friends, Elizabeth had noticed the high flush on her mother's face—to be expected in this stuffy heat. Every face in the room was red and beaded with sweat. But now Kathryn was as white as the satin bow on her close-fitting black straw hat.

Then the song was over, and Elizabeth took her place to be presented to the chairman of the school board along with all her classmates who would be receiving diplomas. As she heard each name called, Elizabeth wondered how the brave words of her speech would apply to that individual. Did the future hold the bright prosperity she had spoken of so glowingly a few minutes before? Surely it did for Whitmore, who, as valedictorian, received his diploma first. He had won a fat scholarship to the University. With his brains for math he could probably rise to a job that paid $100 a month.

She glanced behind her at Edith and was answered with a dimpled smile. Edith was already engaged to a boy who had graduated two years before. Her future looked secure. Elizabeth looked on down the row. Walter Potter was already prosperous—his father owned three properties in town and most of the apple orchards west of town as well. Harold Matson with his suave good looks could charm his way to any success he set his heart on.

Millie Andrews stepped up for her diploma on her high-heeled shoes. With her Clara Bow lips and permed and peroxided hair, Millie never seemed to give a thought to the future as she skimmed through life. Elizabeth wished she could be more like that. Mavis, however, in spite of her frequent bright laugh, seemed more intense. The look her round dark eyes gave carefree, flame-haired Rudy Rudolphson as he received his diploma made Elizabeth worry about Mavis.

And what of herself? She sturdily pushed down her questions and doubts. Tonight was no time to give in to anxieties. She strode forward to receive her rolled white diploma with the black ribbon around it. She might have to work harder than most—it seemed that nothing ever just fell in her lap as things appeared to for other people—but she would live up to her own speech. She would succeed. She smiled back at her classmates, then at the applauding audience. Her mother had a little color in her cheeks now, but tension showed around her mouth even when she returned Elizabeth's smile.

And suddenly it was over, even the presentation of diplomas to the eighth graders, who had wiggled their way through the entire program on the pew behind the seniors. Everyone was hugging, laughing, crying, shaking hands.

Celia tugged at her sleeve and pulled her aside.

"Walter's dad just gave him the keys—that makes three cars, so we can all go!"

"Go? Where?"

"To Swan Falls—the picnic! What everyone's been talking about for ages. Now the whole class can go—we'll have a party we'll always remember!"

"Well, I don't know. . . ." She looked around for her family. Clarey was right behind her. "Are you going—to this picnic?"

"Of course. Everyone's going."

Nothing made Elizabeth feel more out of it than a scheme like this. She knew she always had her nose in a book or her mind on finishing one chore so she could get on to the next, but being told "everyone's been talking about it for ages" made her feel such an outsider.

And now her discomfort increased. This wasn't an official school function, and it hadn't been talked about for ages, or she would have heard—it had been whispered about. It even crossed her mind to wonder if the plans had been kept from her because she might raise an objection. But that was silly. What could there be to object to about a picnic? After all, they were adults now. They didn't need school sanction or adult chaperones for their parties.

"Well, I'll ask Mother. She might need me."

Kathryn, still pale but smiling brightly, assured her daughter that she must go to her class party.

"Are you sure, Mother? You look tired. Don't you need me?"

Kathryn nodded. "I am a little tired, dear. I do need to rest. But most of all I'm so very, very proud of you. Of you both," she added quickly as Clarey joined them. "My two graduates!" She kissed each of them on the cheek. "Now, Clarey, you take your sister to that party and have a good time."

Merrick, who had been visiting with Jules Sperlin, turned to second everything his wife had said, with a hug for his daughter and a handshake for his son. "Now you two go on. I'm taking your mother home to rest." He put his hand under Kathryn's elbow and led her through the crowd.

Elizabeth squeezed in beside Celia along with five others in Walter's little green roadster, and they set out with shrieking laughter over the rutted dirt road to the river.

The road ran straight out of town past greening fields of alfalfa, potatoes, and corn, south past Kuna Butte. Desert stretched in every direction, much of it still apparently untouched by human hand in spite of the continuing activities of homesteaders. Overhead a wide blue sky came down to meet the desert, making it appear that they could drive right into the clouds. A ground squirrel scurried across the road in front of the car.

Elizabeth started to comment that the newly graded and graveled road was an improvement over the dirt track she remembered from childhood, but her words were lost as Celia started them singing a popular song. Mavis, sitting on Rudy's lap in the back seat, turned around and waved a white chiffon hanky to their classmates in the car behind them, and Harold, at the wheel of his father's Model T, gave an answering toot on the horn.

Elizabeth relaxed and laughed with the others. Clarey was right. She did take life too seriously. This was great. And since it seemed she always had to have a goal for everything she did, she set a goal for the evening: to relax and have fun. "A party they'd always remember," Celia had said.

With increased intensity the sun was approaching the Owyhee Mountains to their right when they reached the rim of the Snake River Canyon and looked across at the craggy lava shapes. A prairie falcon swooped deep into the canyon, then rose again to his rocky perch. Even up here Elizabeth could hear the hum of the power plant that the legendary Colonel Dewey had sponsored at the turn of the century to provide power for his silver mines in Owyhee County on to the southwest. Now power lines ran up the

23

canyon and across the desert to the northeast—when the mining faded away electricity was needed to power the interurban railroad that ran from Boise to Nampa and Caldwell.

Elizabeth turned from thinking of the man-made structure to observing the steep drop at her feet and the narrow, winding road that led to the river. She put away her own fear of making that trek by thinking of her father and grandfather having made the same trip with horse and wagon during many summers to haul barrels of life-sustaining water for their families and cattle. She couldn't imagine what life must have been like for her mother in those days.

Dark shadows were already beginning to stretch across the canyon by the time they arrived at the bottom, where piles of lava boulders and sagebrush-covered sand sloped into the river. Elizabeth grimaced at the small sign warning of falling rock. Such admonition would be of little value should the great stack of lava decide to shift its position.

Green greasewood bushes and small willows bordered the river, a blessed greenness cutting through all the black and brown. There were even a few scraggly locust trees beside the dirt trail they followed along the canyon bottom, a small softness before the lava wall of the cliff looming five hundred feet above them.

"Here's a good spot!" Celia pointed to a willow-lined area sloping to the water, perhaps a hundred yards upstream from the largest of the islands that punctuated the river. Here they were far enough below the dam that the only sounds were the rush of the rapids and the overhead *kree* of soaring red-tailed hawks on the lookout for ground squirrels and jack rabbits to make a final evening feeding for the voracious appetites of their young.

One large hawk swooped near, making its high, whistling cry.

"*Kree, kree,*" Rudy called, in perfect imitation of the bird.

When the hawk called back to him, everyone broke into applause and delighted laughter.

The girls spread out blankets and unpacked hampers while the boys chopped sagebrush for a bonfire. Soon the blaze of the roaring pile was reflected far out in the river along with the last streaks of the sunset.

"Brr, it gets cold when the sun's gone." Mavis shuddered, making her black bobbed curls bounce, and snuggled up against Rudy, who gallantly removed his coat, then kept his arms around her after helping her on with it.

Elizabeth turned to take the top off a jar of lemonade just in time to catch Clarey's grim look. She ached for her brother. He had been fond of Mavis for so long, but she treated him so off-handedly.

"Naah! Who's afraid of a little cold?" Harold, apparently responding to a discussion of whether or not it was too early in the season to go swimming, pulled off his jacket and loosened his tie. "Last one in's a soggy biscuit!" He dashed for the bushes growing along the edge of the river to change into his bathing suit. Two of the other fellows followed him.

"Oh, come on, you guys, let's eat first," Celia called.

Rudy, always ready for anything, was already on his feet, but when Mavis seconded Celia's plea, the erstwhile swimmers did an about face to attack the food with as much enthusiasm as they had directed toward the lapping waters of the Snake River.

"Yeah, I'm starved!"

"What's in that basket?"

"Did anyone cut sticks to roast these marshmallows?"

Someone threw another armful of sagebrush on the fire, making the sparks shoot upward toward the stars just appearing in the sky.

"That's a mighty pretty dress, Elizabeth. Er—would you care for some chicken?"

Elizabeth smiled and took the plate Franklin Isaacs held out to her.

"Let's go sit by the river. I can't stand the smell of that fire."

Elizabeth let herself be led to a blanket a little apart from the others. She didn't want to be unkind, because poor Franklin always worked so hard at being polite, but Elizabeth never could entirely suppress her sense of humor whenever she looked at him—the similarities to Ichabod Crane were simply too startling: the big hands and feet at the ends of spindly arms and legs, and the big ears and nose protruding from a thin face always gave her the most wicked urge to start telling him ghost stories. She bit her tongue and struggled to make serious conversation. "It was a really nice graduation, wasn't it?"

A few comments about the commencement service and the activities of their classmates soon exhausted Franklin's powers of conversation, so Elizabeth took her turn. "What will you do now?"

"I'm going to Link's School of Business. Dad says if I want to work with him at the lumberyard I need to know business law and stuff. That's OK with me." Franklin turned his attention to his deviled egg.

Having no food left on her plate, Elizabeth was left with just sitting until one of them could think of something to say. To her relief, Walter picked up his ukelele and began strumming. Soon everyone was singing, "I'm coming, I'm coming, though my head is bending low. . . ."

Franklin licked his fingers, then put his arm around Elizabeth's shoulders. Since the air was turning chilly she let it stay there. She had determined to have fun. This seemed to be how the others did it.

Walter had shifted keys and begun another song when a cluster of boys on the far side of the group burst out laughing. "Hey, Millie, want some more lemonade?"

Interrupted in repairing her bright red lipstick, Millie jumped up with a giggle. "Sure, guys! I'm thirsty!" Soon the lemonade jars, surprisingly full at the end of the picnic, were passing from hand to hand.

"Here, give me your glass." Franklin reached across Elizabeth to where her empty glass sat in the sand.

"Just a little, I guess. I'm not very thirsty." She wasn't thirsty at all, but it was something to do. If she could just kid around with all the fellows as Celia was doing, or flirt like Mavis, she wouldn't always get stuck on the edge of things with someone as dull as Franklin.

Franklin returned and handed her a glass.

She took a sip, then spit it out. "That's sour!"

Franklin raised his glass. "That's gin."

"How could it be? It's illegal!" But even as she said it, she knew she was being naive. Prohibition just meant that people drank their liquor out of teacups and carried it in medicine jars like the one Walter was pulling out from under the seat of his car right now.

Elizabeth tipped her glass into the sand.

When Walter rejoined the group he picked up his ukelele and strummed out a twangy Charleston to which Millie and Mavis did a clowning act in the center of the group. Whitmore and Harold joined them, to much applause and laughter. When the number came to an end both girls kissed their partners on the lips.

Elizabeth looked at Clarey just in time to see the hurt look in his eyes before he lifted his lemonade glass.

"Who's for swimming?" Millie shrieked. She didn't even bother going into the bushes to slip out of her dress and reveal the daring bathing costume beneath it. Girls laughed and boys applauded as she ran for the river yelling, "Can't catch me!"

"Wanta go swimming?" Franklin looked at Elizabeth.

"You go ahead." She jumped to her feet. "I think I'll just go talk to Clarey." She didn't wait for a reply.

"Let's swim out to the island!" Walter was the first to splash into the water.

"I'll race you!" Harold was right behind him.

Those who had chosen to stay by the fire drew closer together, smiling over the antics of their more adventurous classmates.

"They'll all have pneumonia in the morning."

Clarey's prediction sounded almost hopeful, Elizabeth thought.

Then she turned to Celia, who sat down beside her. "You aren't swimming either?"

"Not in the dark. There's some strong currents in that river. Besides—" she sighed "—I've got a lot on my mind."

"Hmm?" Elizabeth looked at her friend with concern.

"I've got to make up my mind."

"About what?"

"Walter or Harold. What do you think, Liz? Walter's richer, but Harold's better looking. Which one would you marry?"

Elizabeth gasped. Was Celia serious? "Well, which one do you love?"

Celia burst out with the merry laugh that was her trademark. "Love? What's that got to do with it? I want security. I want a man who can give me a home and a family and a car. What else is there?"

Elizabeth was too shocked to answer. Instead she turned to Edith sitting quietly beside them. "You tell her, Edith. You love Rupert, don't you?"

Edith dimpled even when she wasn't smiling. "Oh, yes! I couldn't marry someone I didn't love."

"Well, sure." Celia shrugged. "But could you love him if he didn't have any money? I mean, you wouldn't marry a man who couldn't buy you a house, would you?"

"Well, we aren't going to get married until Rupert has all his land cleared and water on it."

Celia's triumphant reply was lost when Clarey jumped up to meet Mavis, stumbling up the slope from the river. "Oh, that water's so cold!" She fell into his arms with a sob.

Clarey picked up a discarded blanket and cuddled her in it. They disappeared around the far side of the fire.

Edith and Celia continued talking. In the background someone picked up Walter's abandoned ukelele and strummed "Red River Valley."

"From this valley they say you are going . . ." Soft voices blended with the shimmering gold fire, but Elizabeth didn't feel like singing. How could you go to school with people for your whole life and not really know them at all? What about the values she'd been confronted with tonight? Were these kids right? Were the love and hard work that had seemed a valid center for her parents' lives outmoded in this modern day? Would she have a better life if she worked and worried less, played more? Why not marry for money and give up the struggle for an education? After all, if she did reach her goal and wound up teaching school, how much money did rural elementary school teachers make? All she'd have to do would be to smile at Franklin and she could have him—and eventually his father's lumberyard. And weren't his family part owners of the orchards too? That would be security.

Her thoughts were interrupted by a commotion at the river.

"Where is he?"

"I can't see!"

"Somebody bring a light!"

Then a girl screamed. "There! Get him!"

Suddenly all was a rush of arms grabbing burning branches from the fire to serve as torches. People who had been swimming ran from the water. Those who had been sitting around the fire stripped off shoes and shirts to go in. Cries, shouts, and barked orders rang everywhere as the blazing torches slashed through the darkness, leaving trails of sparks behind them.

For a time Elizabeth sat frozen, trying to make sense out of it all. She wasn't a strong swimmer in the best of times, so there was no sense in her joining those who were attempting a rescue. Although no one was coherent, the facts seemed evident enough. Someone, probably with too much gin in him, had attempted to swim to the island in the icy, black water and been swept down the river, caught in a swirling current.

Elizabeth looked around her. How long had it been since she'd seen Clarey? Had he suddenly gone in with some idea of impressing Mavis? *Oh, Lord, don't let it be Clarey*. And then, having begun, she continued with her head bowed between her knees. *God, help these kids. Help them get whoever's in the river. Please. And please help me. I'm so confused.* Then she sat, head still bowed, with the crackling of the fire between her and the cries from the river filling the muffled blackness.

3

They didn't find the body until late the next day. Happy, carefree Rudy would be the life of no more parties. Rudy, the one who could make everyone laugh—especially Mavis—now made them all cry over his loss.

All they had wanted was to have a good time. Elizabeth had tried so hard. Why did things always twist and turn out bad?

Elizabeth was deeply saddened by the loss of her classmate. She attempted more than once to get a clear picture of what had happened. But when she questioned Clarey, he had less idea than she. As a matter of fact, when he and Mavis had stumbled back to the burned-down fire with some of the last of the would-be rescuers, he seemed confused, even surprised, to hear what had taken place. Once Elizabeth had asked sharply, "Where were you, Clarey?" But his vague reply was lost amid all the commotion.

And when they finally got home as dawn broke, another event had begun which pushed even Rudy's loss to the back of Elizabeth's mind.

"Is that Dr. Nolte's car?" Elizabeth was out of Walter's roadster and running toward the house before he had time to come to a full stop.

She burst into the front room to be confronted by three white faces with dark hollows under their eyes. Merrick came to meet her. "Is it Mother? Is she all right? Is the baby here?"

Merrick put his arm around her and led her to a chair. "Soon, we hope. Dr. Nolte's been with her all night."

"All night? You mean since Commencement? Why didn't someone come get me?—us?" she added as Clarey entered the room behind her.

"We got the doctor on our way home after graduation. But your mother was adamant. You weren't to be bothered. She wanted you to have a graduation night you'd remember."

Elizabeth nodded. Yes, she would remember it all right. "How is she?"

"Doctor says not much longer to wait." Alexandra spoke in a sleepy voice from a corner of the sofa.

In reply a thin, infant wail came from the next room. Merrick tried to hold Elizabeth back, but she rushed to the door. "Mother will want me."

She glanced at the tiny, red creature in the doctor's hands only long enough to see that she had a baby brother, then went straight to her mother. "Mama, are you all right?"

Kathryn was as white as the sheet she lay on. Her soft, gray-streaked hair was stringy and soaked with sweat, but her pale blue eyes were shining. "He's beautiful, isn't he?"

Elizabeth agreed without thinking about it. "But how are you, Mama?" She grasped her mother's hand that lay limp and white on the sheet.

"I'm fine. Just fine. But tired. I'm afraid I'm getting too old for this."

Elizabeth dipped a rag in a bowl of cool water and wiped Kathryn's forehead. Dr. Nolte placed the bathed and swaddled bundle in Kathryn's arms. Elizabeth helped adjust the pillows at her mother's back, then watched in fascination as she guided the tiny, searching mouth to the nipple that seemed far too large for it. Kathryn tickled the side of his cheek with one finger. "Come on, sleepyhead."

"Just like a kitten with closed eyes, isn't he?" Elizabeth laughed. Then Merrick came in, and Elizabeth slipped out of the room to leave her parents together.

Now Elizabeth was even busier than when she had been in school.

Kathryn, although Dr. Nolte seemed satisfied with her progress, regained her strength very slowly. "Of course, she isn't even to *think* of getting out of bed for a full two weeks. Then we'll see," he pronounced.

Aunt Nelly Jayne came over with food and large doses of her cheerful common sense as often as she could, but her own daughter, Vina Sperlin, who now lived on a farm near Nampa with her active brood of five children, had just had another baby, so Nelly spent much of her time traveling the other direction.

Kathryn's closest friend, Marie Sperlin, drove over from their farm to help out on the days Elizabeth worked in the printing office. Marie was married to Jules, older brother of Vina's husband, stories of whom never failed to delight Elizabeth—how he had once proposed to Kathryn, and had helped her clear Merrick of a murder charge by taking her spelunking in the Kuna Cave.

Elizabeth especially liked the times Marie would bring her daughter Grace with her and remain awhile after Elizabeth got home from work. Grace was younger than Elizabeth, but gifted with so much of her mother's charm and good sense that the girls seemed much the same age. And Grace shared Marie's talent for playing the organ. Taught from infancy by her mother, just as Marie had taught the young Kathryn, Grace always filled the tiny Allen house with music from Kathryn's old pump organ when she came. A sound they seldom heard, since Kathryn had so little time to play, and neither of her daughters shared her talent.

Elizabeth enjoyed her job. She had to. It was a job. Three days a week she drove Rosie O'Day into town, for, although Merrick had been one of the first in Kuna to buy a car, she had never driven it. Elizabeth left Rosie at the livery stable and spent her day coping with the mess on Mr. Griswold's desk.

On her third day there, the last Saturday in May, she had managed to type an entire letter without stacking up her keys and had to make only three erasures. Each time she remembered to erase the carbon copy first, then insert a piece of paper so she wouldn't smear the carbon while erasing the top sheet. She felt she was on her way to becoming a success as a secretary. She even managed to balance Griswold's account book. At least it looked all right to her. She didn't think she had forgotten to write anything in any of the columns of the wide ledger. She preferred adding the numbers herself, even if it meant counting on her fingers, rather than attempting to conquer the complicated adding machine.

But one piece of equipment she thoroughly loved was the telephone. It stood, a tall black cylinder, on her big oak desk with the receiver hanging on a little arm. It never failed to delight her when the bell jangled sharply over the clacking of her typewriter keys and the chugging of the printing press in the shop behind her.

"Hello, Griswold's Printing and the *Kuna Times,*" she now said loudly, leaning toward the mouthpiece.

"My husband, please," a sharp voice demanded.

The press, just geared up to print the front page of this week's edition, chugged its loudest. "Pardon?" Elizabeth yelled into the instrument.

"I want to speak to my husband, Cyrus Griswold. And don't tell me he isn't there."

"Just a minute, please, Mrs. Griswold." There was nothing about that woman's voice to suggest the invalid she was rumored to be. Elizabeth lay the receiver down and fetched her boss.

She picked up a sheaf of papers and pulled out a heavy wooden drawer of the file cabinet to work away from the desk while Mr. Griswold was at the phone. But she was still well within earshot as he yelled above the noise of the press.

"Yes, Phoebe. Yes, I know you need water . . . No, no, I have no intention of letting the orchards dry up . . . I'm a county commissioner, not a rainmaker. I'm doing what I can . . . Yes, Phoebe . . . Yes, of course . . ." There was a long silence at the print shop end before he hung up.

Elizabeth expected him to return immediately to his press, but instead he bent over the file drawer, seemingly intent on finding something while his arm and shoulder rubbed against Elizabeth in the small space. She crouched into the corner to make more room, and Griswold departed for his press, a manila folder in his ink-stained hand.

Elizabeth was happier than ever to get home that evening. She was especially glad to drive Rosie home after Mr. Griswold had offered her a ride.

"It's really very silly for you to drive in yourself and pay for stabling when I could so easily swing by for you."

Elizabeth had murmured something about this way she was freer to run errands for her mother and dashed out the door.

But it wasn't just getting away from his unwanted attentions that made her so happy to get home. Elizabeth was becoming ridiculously fond of her baby brother. They named him Eldon, and at only two weeks he seemed to recognize Elizabeth when she rocked him and sang to him. When the light hit his head, the golden fuzz covering it shone like the aureole of a lamp, and she couldn't resist running her hand over it.

It was easy to see that Eldon had won all their hearts, although Clarey, who was never afraid of anything, seemed strangely spooked by his infant brother. At least, Elizabeth assumed it was the baby that caused the worried frown on her twin's forehead every time he entered a room with the

35

baby in it. Of course, it could have been the continued dry weather. That was causing concern enough across the valley.

Boyd showed fond, if awkward, amusement in the baby's company, forever trying to tickle him or teasing him to grasp tightly to Boyd's rough, brown forefinger with his infant fist, always much to Alex's irritation. For Eldon was Alex's special charge.

When Elizabeth was home her attention was focused on helping Kathryn, out of bed only a few hours a day, and on running the house. Alexandra, almost eleven, however, had the luxury of being the one to bathe, change, and above all rock the baby. The only thing she ever complained about was the inconvenience of pumping and carrying the water from the yard and heating it on the wood stove.

"Wouldn't it be *lovely* to have running water like Aunt Nelly and the Cottrells?"

Elizabeth grinned. "We do have running water. It's just that we're the ones who do the running."

When Merrick, Clarey, and Boyd came in from the field, they washed up in the baby's leftover wash water, being sparing as everyone was now of the precious resource that was in too little supply.

"When you're all washed, be sure you dump the water on the roses," Kathryn called from her room.

Elizabeth took a supper tray in to her mother, who had just finished nursing the baby. She put Eldon in his crib next to the bed and placed the tray on Kathryn's lap. "Just think, if Dr. Nolte is pleased with you tomorrow you can stay up, Mama."

Kathryn sighed as she sat higher against her pillows. "I certainly hope so. I feel weaker than I did right after delivery. I think I need exercise."

"But you look much more rested." Elizabeth gave her mother a quick peck on the cheek.

Conversation around the supper table in the kitchen that night centered on the drought. "I didn't have enough water to finish the alfalfa today. Pressure just too low to flow to the end of the corrugations." Merrick shook his head and took another boiled potato.

"Guess everyone's plenty worried." Elizabeth recounted the conversation she overheard in the office that day. "Mr. Griswold didn't sound too worried, though."

Merrick ran a hand through his thick curly hair, which had recently started showing more gray streaks. "Odd. Griswold's crops never seem to get as dry as ours. I wonder what his allotment is."

"Should be the same as ours." Clarey held a thick chunk of ham on his fork. "It's all based on original usage from the creek, isn't it? And wasn't that land reclaimed about the same time as ours?"

Merrick nodded. "Pass the gravy there, will you, son?" He spooned thick ham gravy over his potato. "About the same time, and yes, water rights are assigned on the basis of the original appropriations to stay with that parcel of land. If he'd been willing to fiddle, however, he might have diverted some to his own land when his corporation started the Avalon Orchards. It wouldn't be right, but he'd likely get away with it."

"You should have bought into that, Dad," Boyd said. "They've done right well with their apples, haven't they?"

"I even heard they were going to plant a grape vineyard next," Alex said, then hastily grabbed for her glass of milk, having talked with her mouth full.

Elizabeth turned to her father. "What do you think about that, Dad? Surely they wouldn't try to use the grapes to make bootleg wine, would they?"

"What? With a county commissioner part owner?" Boyd said. "Juice for Communion. Surely that's all."

"Well, I know how we can get water to that lower alfalfa field, Pa." Clarey returned to the original topic. "Did you hear about Mrs. Olaphson, that lady farmer over Melba way?"

Apparently no one had, so he continued. "Fellow was telling the story at the feed mill the other day. Water didn't get to the end of her onion rows by Saturday evening when she was supposed to hand it on. When it didn't come on down the ditch her neighbor went over to see if she'd taken her dam out on time. She had all right, but Mrs. Olaphson was sitting in the ditch herself—with all her clothes off. 'Didn't know there was anything in the rules against a lady taking her Saturday night bath,' she said. While the water she was stopping flowed on down her corrugations."

The family enjoyed Clarey's story, but two days later Elizabeth found that water rights were no laughing matter. She first noticed a crowd around the newspaper office when she drove by on the way to the stable. When she walked back, she could hear angry shouts.

"I've got my rights!"

"I paid my water bill!"

"We don't need your meddling!"

"Rationing's just a way for the powerful to grab theirs first!"

Elizabeth stopped in her tracks as a stone thudded onto the wooden walk in front of her.

"You just try your fancy formulas—we'll get ours first —it's just first come, first served."

"You've no right to take our water away from us!"

This time a stone smashed against the side of the building.

Elizabeth stood there in confusion. What should she do? She was already late for work. Should she try to force her way through the mob? She eyed the heavy stick in the hand of the man in front of her.

"Elizabeth. Er—Miss Allen. Here, my dear."

Elizabeth looked around and located the harsh whisper calling her name from the shadowed side of the building.

Mr. Griswold was wiping the perspiration off his forehead with his apron.

"What is it? Why are they angry?" Elizabeth stepped around the building with him.

"It's my editorial in the paper that came out last evening. You haven't seen it yet."

She shook her head, and he put a paper into her hand. "It's the only sensible thing. If we don't have rain soon we'll have to ration the water."

Elizabeth nodded. She knew. Not enough snow in the mountains last winter. Reservoir at Arrowrock dangerously low.

"People who live to the east, closer to the canal, don't want rationing. They say they paid their bill and they should get what's theirs. But farms like your father's and mine, and the orchards—those farther down the line—wouldn't survive. Water'd be all gone by the time they used their share."

Elizabeth nodded again. It was a tough problem.

"But never mind now, my dear."

She wished he wouldn't put his hand on her arm.

"You go back home today. Stay there until this quiets down. We couldn't get any work done with all this going on. I'll come for you in a few days when things are back to normal."

All the way home, the angry, worried faces of the men and their harsh shouts rode with Elizabeth. What was right? Rationing seemed the fairest approach. Of course, as the protestors said, they would lose the money they'd already paid for their water, but wouldn't everyone lose an equal share? In hard times everyone had to pull together, sacrifice together. And wasn't this another problem that could be overcome with hard work?

She thought of the steep canyon road she had traveled a few weeks ago. Hauling water from the Snake River would be no more grueling now than it had been a generation earlier. Then, it had allowed the homesteaders to survive until irrigation arrived. Couldn't they do it again?

That evening she put her questions to her father. They sat on the wooden bench on the front porch because Elizabeth didn't want to worry her mother with news of the protest at the office or of talk about water rationing. Kathryn wasn't strong yet and needed all her energy for supervising her household.

Merrick read the editorial slowly, then took time to scan a couple of other articles before he crumpled the paper to his lap. "I hope it won't come to that. I don't like the idea of rationing any more than the next fellow."

"But what else is there to do?"

"Probably nothing. Trouble is, the protestors have some good points. Things like this never wind up being done fairly, because someone always figures out how to get more than his fair share."

"But that's cheating."

"What ever gave you the idea there weren't cheaters in the world, daughter?"

Elizabeth sighed and leaned against the rough screening of the porch. "I know—life isn't fair. But people should try to be."

"Certainly. That's the best we can do. But I sympathize with the protestors because they're seeing what we all know—no matter how fair a formula the commissioners try to work out, someone will find a way around it."

"So that's why they're mad at Griswold. As a county commissioner he could fiddle his own ration."

"Could." Merrick ran his hands over his lined face, then pointed to another article, a larger one but one that had drawn less attention because it dealt with issues farther from home. "I'll tell you, Elizabeth, this is what worries me more in the long run than the prospect of rationing."

Elizabeth took the paper and read the report of a speech Senator Borah had given in Boise the previous week. "You mean that pact they signed in Paris, Father?

What's wrong with it? Senator Borah thinks it's a great step forward."

Merrick shook his head. "Relying on the notion that you can make people and nations behave by getting them to sign pieces of paper is dangerous."

"But we have to try."

"Oh, yes, we have to try to get people to get along with each other. But people like Borah, who put their whole faith in it, worry me. I'm old enough to remember documents like this being signed before the Great War, and what did it get us?"

Elizabeth looked again at the article. "But if the U.S., Great Britain, Germany, Japan, and all those others signed a pact against war, maybe something can be accomplished. Mr. Griswold seems to think so. His reporting sounds very enthusiastic."

"Oh, yes, Griswold never leaves his readers in doubt as to his politics."

With a few days off work Elizabeth took time to catch up on some deep cleaning she saw the house needed, in spite of Kathryn's protests that such work could wait. Elizabeth liked the linoleum best when it was mopped and shiny with wax, even if her arms ached afterward with the effort of rubbing the paste wax to a high gloss after it had dried over the gray-swirled pattern of the floor covering.

Then the next day Aunt Nelly drove over in her elegant black Model T to bring them up to date on her family. Besides the prolific Vina, Lucy—who had been a nurse in the Great War—had married one of her patients and now lived in Portland. Davey, also married, farmed a few miles away.

As soon as Elizabeth had shared a cup of tea with them, Nelly shooed her off to take a break. "You work far too hard, young lady, take life far too seriously for one your age. You need to have more fun. Go spend some time giggling with your friends. It'll do you good. Don't hurry. I'll

41

stay with your mama until you get back." She picked up baby Eldon and cooed to him. "My goodness, what a sweetie. Did I tell you I spent three days with Alvina and her new one last week?"

Kathryn smiled and scooted herself more upright on the horsehair sofa where she rested. "Oh, how nice. How are she and Myron doing on their farm?"

"Right fine. Moving to that place in Nampa was a good move for them. Myron had it in his head he wanted to be a businessman, but he never really took to it. Or maybe business didn't take to him."

Elizabeth closed the door quietly and went out. It would be good to see her friends again. She hadn't seen anyone since that terrible graduation night. With the new baby to take care of and all, she hadn't even gone to Rudy's funeral.

"Going someplace?" Clarey came in just as she put her hat on. "I can give you a lift in the car. Have to get some stuff at the lumberyard. Those new pigs Dad bought may be good porkers, but they're sure a lot of work."

"Yes, I'm going to visit Celia. You can drop me at the Cottrells'."

"Oh, going to congratulate her, huh?"

"Congratulate her?"

"Haven't you heard? She and Walter got engaged. Right after Rudy's funeral, I guess. What's the good of working at a newspaper office if you don't get the news first?"

"Maybe they thought they would wait to put it in the paper," was all Elizabeth said. She was still wondering about the wisdom of Celia's decision when they drove up the elm-lined lane to Cottrells'.

Celia lived in the nicest house in the area. Her family had moved there from the Midwest. There, farmhouses were all two-story with wide, open porches across the front, so that was what they had built, in spite of the fact that all the other farms around Kuna had only small, one-story houses.

Elizabeth never failed to wonder what it would be like to live in a big house like Celia's with indoor plumbing and rugs covering the wooden floors. She rubbed her knees; having rugs sure would cut down on the waxing.

Celia met her knock with an impulsive hug. "Lizzy! Where have you been hiding yourself?" She grabbed Elizabeth's arm and pulled her into the house, then paused to whisper, "Glad you're here. Maybe you can help me cheer Mavis up."

Celia led the way upstairs to her bedroom, where Mavis sat huddled in the only chair, dabbing her red-rimmed eyes. Celia and Elizabeth flopped down on the quilt-covered brass bed.

Elizabeth didn't know what to say. Should she try to console Mavis or congratulate Celia? She was surprised at Mavis's tears. She knew, of course, that she had liked Rudy, had dated him several times, but she hadn't realized it was serious. She turned instead to Celia. "I heard—er, Clarey said I should congratulate you."

"I guess you should! Look at that!" Celia held out her left hand, where a small diamond sparkled on a gold band.

"Walter?"

"Of course Walter. Who else could afford a ring like that?"

"So you decided?"

"That awful thing happening to Rudy really helped me see sense. Life is so uncertain. Just like that—you can be having a really great time at a party, and then just be gone. So I decided right then and there that I was going to get the most out of life while I had the chance."

Elizabeth forced a smile at her friend, but she couldn't say anything. Should she try to talk sense to her? What *was* good sense? Her own reaction to Rudy's death had been to increase her belief that there was little security in money and good looks and that pleasure was too short-lived to place importance on it. But who was right? Mavis sniffed, and she turned to her.

"Mavis, I'm so sorry. I know you really liked Rudy . . ." She couldn't think of anything else to say, so she tried changing the subject. "What's everybody going to do this summer?"

Celia started chattering about plans for her wedding. She couldn't decide between blue or lavender dresses for her bridesmaids. She preferred blue, but her older sister, who would be matron of honor, looked her best in lavender.

"Why don't you use both?" Elizabeth asked almost offhandedly, then turned to Mavis. "And you?"

Mavis shook her head. A dark curl escaped from its marcelled wave and fell over her forehead. "I don't know. I just don't know."

Celia filled the silence that followed with happy chatter, and it seemed no time until Clarey was back for Elizabeth. To her surprise, Mavis wiped her eyes, lipsticked her rosebud mouth, and went downstairs with her. She even mustered a smile for Clarey.

Clarey produced a lot more than a smile. He pulled his hat off his head and held it over his heart. Elizabeth almost thought he was going to bow. "Mavis! What a nice surprise to see you here. I haven't seen you since—ah, er —for a long time. Er—I just saw Walter at the feed mill, Celia. He said you two are going to the grange social tomorrow."

He turned his hat brim around in his hands three times. Elizabeth couldn't believe the easygoing Clarey could be at such great discomfort with someone he'd gone to school with all his life. "How about going with me, Mavis?"

Elizabeth was amazed at the transformation that came over Mavis. She flipped the wayward ringlet back into place with a toss of her head, and the sparkle she had as she turned her brown eyes up at Clarey, who stood a full head taller than herself, gave no hint of the girl that had sat crying upstairs a few minutes earlier.

The next day, however, fears for the success of the potluck only slightly dampened the rejoicing over the sight of dark clouds hanging over the Owyhee Mountains. All day everyone looked westward with held breath as the clouds slowly covered the sun. How much rain did that heavy looking cloud hold? Would it drop it where it was so sorely needed? Or would it go on across, not stopping until it hit the Sawtooths behind Boise? Could this be the end of the drought?

By mid-afternoon the cloud had spit a few drops of rain on the dry ground and dusty crops, then rolled on eastward. By evening the sun was out again, leaving the air heavy with the scent of dampened dust.

Clarey hurried through his chores, then put on a white shirt and slicked his dark hair back before going to get Mavis. Elizabeth couldn't help thinking what a handsome couple they would make with Mavis's dark head coming barely to his shoulder and her round black eyes and rosy round mouth smiling up at him.

In spite of her brother's joy, though, Elizabeth worried that the dashing of everyone's hopes regarding a break in the drought would increase tensions over the water rationing issue. Oddly, however, it had the reverse effect. People seemed to reason that if a few dark clouds could blow by and drop a little rain, next time they might linger long enough to do some good.

4

The next morning Mr. Griswold's shiny black car rumbled into the Allens' yard, and he summoned Elizabeth to work with three sharp toots on his horn. With the slight easing of tension yesterday's sprinkle of rain had brought, Elizabeth expected her recall to the office, so was ready to pull her cloche over her waves and hurry to meet him with only a quick call to her mother and a wave to Alex, whose blond head was bent over baby Eldon.

In the few days of her absence the letters and paperwork had piled high on Griswold's desk. Elizabeth removed her hat and set about with vigor to bring order out of chaos. At noon she paused only briefly to eat the waxed-paper-wrapped sandwich she carried in her purse, then returned to her work with the goal of having all the work caught up by five o'clock.

She was on her last letter when a click of the gate in the railing that separated office from printing shop told her that her employer was behind her. "Miss Allen, would you take a look at this, please?"

She was puzzled by the tone of his voice. He sounded emphatic, but not angry, almost excited—a strange reaction to what must have been an error in her work. She swiveled her oak desk chair around and rose to look at the paper he held. She was never quite sure whether her heel caught on a foot of the chair's pedestal, pitching her forward into Mr. Griswold's arms, or whether he pulled her forward. Either way, there was no doubting the fact that she suddenly found herself locked in a firm embrace.

Cyrus Griswold was breathing heavily, and she could feel his heart pounding as he pressed against her while his lips came down hard on her mouth.

She struggled, but there was little she could do. A slight, strangled sound issued from her throat. She flailed her hands in the air, but her arms were pinned to her sides by his embrace. She felt herself being bent backwards over the now-cleared desktop.

She twisted and writhed, struggling for release. If she could knock the phone over would the operator send someone to investigate what was wrong on the line? Unlikely. A jangling noise sounded over her head. Had she knocked something over? Griswold's breath was hot, his skin sweaty. His mustache scratched her skin. She screamed again in her throat and tried to turn her head.

Then miraculously, she felt his weight lift. She opened her mouth to gasp for air, and a sob came out. Then she saw why Griswold had moved.

Her father, standing head and shoulders over the little newspaperman, held her attacker by both shoulders and pushed him against the file cabinet. "Don't you ever lay a finger on my daughter again!"

"Then talk to your daughter. She wanted it."

Before Elizabeth could protest her innocence her father's fist silenced Griswold's lie.

Merrick turned to her and gathered her into his arms. "Come, daughter, let's go home."

Only when she had taken two steps toward the door, still in the protection of her father's arm, did Elizabeth realize he had not entered the shop alone. A stooped, gentle-looking, gray-haired man stood just inside the door. Behind him a tall young man, his sleek blond hair parted smoothly in the middle, made a handsome entry in a three-piece brown suit.

"Oh." She drew back, her hands flying to her rumpled hair.

Merrick gave Griswold a cold stare. "I had thought to bring you an item of interest for the paper. Reverend Hamilton, formerly of the China Inland Mission, is holding services at our church. But the story obviously has no appeal to one of your interests." At the door he turned again. "Not within ten feet of her, Griswold, or I'll have the sheriff on you."

Griswold was still gripping the filing cabinet for support as he growled, "I'll get even, Allen. If one word gets to my wife you'll be the one to suffer. And don't you forget it."

The bell jangled again as the door slammed closed.

"Oh, thank you. Thank you," was all Elizabeth could think to say as she sank into the seat of her father's 1918 Ford.

"Just thankful we came in when we did." Merrick was still shaking too, although Elizabeth could see that he had his temper well under control.

Rev. Hamilton spoke from the back seat. "Another example of God's gracious timing. We saw so many of those in China. He always watches over His own. I'll be telling of some tonight. Always we learned to live by Romans 8:35, 'Who shall separate us from the love of Christ? Shall tribulation, or distress, or persecution, or famine, or nakedness, or peril, or sword?'" The missionary bobbed his gray head to emphasize each word and appeared to be winding himself up to deliver a sermon. "Like the time in Shanghai where Hudson Taylor—"

"That's all right, Father. You don't want to spoil it for tonight." It was the first time the young man had spoken. His voice was rich with an unusually clear diction that compelled attention even when he spoke gently to his father.

"Oh, forgive me, Miss Allen. I don't believe I've presented my son. If I may have the honor, Eliot Hudson Taylor Hamilton."

The missionary's old world manners charmed Elizabeth and helped soothe the hysteria she was fighting, but she shrank from the eyes of the young man. What must he think of her? Had he heard Griswold's blatant lie that she had invited his attentions? Did he believe it? If—*please, God*—he had entered too late to see anything, what must he think of her disheveled state? She acknowledged the introduction and was grateful, indeed, when the cozy, familiar sight of Aunt Nelly's house appeared before them. The guest speaker and his son were staying there, but Merrick had volunteered to meet them at the station because Uncle Isaiah was irrigating today, and what little water came to him must be carefully shepherded.

"You'll not be working for Griswold again" was the only additional comment her father made when they were alone in the car. She knew that without being told. She was sure she could never look at the man again. But what would she do without a job? Oh, there was no question of there being plenty of work to do—but how could she earn money for her college fund? Was this the end of everything? The missionary's words came back to her: Should tribulation, distress, famine separate her from the love of Christ? Surely her problems were small compared to those faced on a mission field, but even if they couldn't separate her from the love of Christ, she feared they might separate her from a college education.

No one could have been more surprised than Elizabeth when they pulled around behind the house, and a cry of delight broke from her lips. "Oh, they're cleaning the cistern!"

Memories of her childhood filled her mind as she ran to the edge of the deep cement-lined hole and watched Alex whirling in circles at the bottom to catch the tiny green frogs that had made the Allens' water supply their home.

"There's one on the wall above your head, Alex. Oh, don't let him jump in your hair!" she cried when her sister's grab was ill-timed. But one more quick snatch and the frog joined his brothers in the lidded bucket.

Clarey and Boyd approached the ladder with the long brushes they would use to scrub the cistern before the water wagon arrived to refill the well. The water would then be filtered through a small ditch lined with screen and charcoal before entering the pipes of their long-handled pump.

But as much as Elizabeth enjoyed laughing at Alex and the frogs and remembering her own turns at performing the frog-catching chore, always done by the youngest capable child, she could not long escape the nearer memory of what had happened to her today. She needed to talk to her mother.

Kathryn sat on the sofa in front of her beloved flowered wallpaper, nursing Eldon.

From habit, Elizabeth reached up to pull off her hat, then realized she was bareheaded—she must have left her cloche in the bottom drawer of her desk. With her purse. She would ask her father to retrieve them for her. Carefully controlling her desire to sob, Elizabeth told her mother about Griswold's forced caresses.

Kathryn inserted the tip of her finger into baby Eldon's mouth to break his suction, then switched him to the other side before she answered. "Have you told me all, Elizabeth?"

"Yes!" Elizabeth was shocked to think that there might have been anything more.

"Did he hurt you?"

Elizabeth shook her head, slowly realizing that, unpleasant as the experience had been, it could have been so much worse.

"There's water in the kitchen. Go take a good scoop of it—two scoops, even, and have a good wash. Then bring me my Bible."

Throughout her life Elizabeth had been impressed with her mother's common sense approach to life, her practical solutions to things that seemed insolvable. By the time she had scrubbed her hands and face and put on a fresh shirtwaist, she knew that this was another such time.

Kathryn had finished nursing Eldon and was rocking him, singing gently, when Elizabeth returned, Bible in hand. "Open it to Philippians. Chapter four, verse eight," Kathryn directed.

Elizabeth did as she was told.

"Read it."

"Finally, brethren, whatsoever things are true, whatsoever things are honest, whatsoever things are just, whatsoever things are pure, whatsoever things are lovely, whatsoever things are of good report; if there be any virtue, and if there be any praise, think on these things." Elizabeth, the Bible still open on her lap, looked at her mother.

"And by implication, that says that things that are impure, unlovely, lacking in virtue are things we're not supposed to think on. Elizabeth, if there's anything I've learned in life it's that there's a lot of evil in this world—and a lot of good. It's my theory that people just have to choose which they want to fill their mind with. God gives His children the privilege of living above the evil of the world. We are to pray for sinners and minister to the needy, but we can have our minds fixed on things that are lovely."

"Is that how you survived homesteading?"

Eldon squirmed, and Kathryn put the little bundle on her shoulder, patting it gently. "It's how I survive every day. I choose to look at the roses rather than the sagebrush."

Another part of Kathryn's philosophy, based on experience, was that hard work could help take your mind off the most traumatic experience, so she asked Elizabeth to go peel the potatoes and shred the coleslaw to accompany the chicken she was roasting for supper. "And make a batch of beaten biscuits," she added. "If you're feeling you'd like to hit that miserable man, you can take it out on the biscuits. As a matter of fact, I'll come help you."

Clarey hurried through supper without even allowing time for seconds. He was taking Mavis to hear the special speaker at church. As much as Elizabeth had liked the gentle missionary, however, she didn't feel sufficiently recovered from the day's experience to go out.

Nor did she sleep well that night.

The next morning Kathryn took one long look at the dark circles under her daughter's eyes and applied more of her practical medicine. "I've been thinking. What with the new baby and all, I haven't had time to put my new incubator to much use. Let's get it set up this afternoon. It can be your job, and the money from the chickens you raise can go in a special college savings." She took a heavy crockery pickle pot from a shelf and lifted the lid.

Elizabeth was amazed to see several dollars already in there. "Mother, how did you manage that?"

Kathryn shrugged. "Saved a bit here, a bit there. I was getting a good price for my eggs back last spring, even had some money left over after I bought the incubator."

"But, Mother, that was before I said anything about college."

Kathryn smiled. "You think I don't know my own daughter? It's my dream too, you know. I would have loved to go to college, but there was no question of it. I want you to go for both of us."

Elizabeth had never hugged her mother tighter.

That afternoon they set up the kerosene-heated incubator in a corner of the henhouse, filling it with clean straw to cushion the eggs, and began nesting all the freshly laid, fertilized eggs they could spare. This remarkable machine could hatch three dozen eggs at a time—several times as many as Kathryn's best Rhode Island Red broody hen could set on.

"Now the eggs have to be turned every day." Kathryn held a black wax pencil out to Elizabeth. "Mark an X on the side of each one. That way if you get interrupted in turning, you'll know where you are."

Long after Kathryn had gone back to the kitchen, Elizabeth stood gazing at the incubator. There was still hope. Her mother hadn't given up—Mother never gave up—so *she* wouldn't give up. She would carry on with her dreams.

She ran back across the barnyard to her little back porch bedroom. She pulled a box out from under her iron bed and flopped down on the cotton bedspread with a great creaking of the coiled springs underneath.

"Northwest Christian College, Seventeenth Annual Announcement, 1929-1930, Description of Courses," she read on the cover of the booklet in her hands. She turned the pages, stopping to read in detail wherever her eye caught something of interest: "NCC combines high scholastic attainments with deep spirituality. When, as sometimes happens, education militates against religion it means that either the education is unsound or the religion is based on false principles. NCC believes that it is possible to excel intellectually and at the same time be intensely spiritual and possess a deep passion for evangelism . . . "

Oh, how wonderful it would be to live on a campus where everyone believed in such high ideals. To study and work and pray with others toward such objectives! Life could hold nothing more exciting.

Turning eggs, however, was not an exciting job. Nor was slopping hogs—even such fine specimens as the black Poland China pigs with white bands around their necks that were Merrick's pride and joy that summer. Such tasks, along with baking bread and scrubbing laundry on the washboard, gave Elizabeth lots of time to think. With so much work at home she had little time for the picnics and socials that filled her former classmates' summer, although Clarey managed to make time for attending quite a few of them in Mavis's company.

Occasionally, though, after the day's work was done she would sit in the wooden rocking chair with the horsehair seat in the living room and wind up the old cracked Victrola that Merrick had brought home as a surprise for Kathryn years before. Marches by John Phillip Sousa, hymns, and Viennese waltzes completed the repertoire the cylinders offered. But they made a nice background for what had become her favorite reading—the college catalog.

"It is the policy of the institution to give to its students proper channels to express their social life and to guard against anything that would not be in keeping with the highest standards. Accordingly, it is expected that the young men will not visit young ladies in their rooms nor accompany them to and from services, about the campus or elsewhere . . . ."

She looked up as Clarey walked in.

"Are you still reading that old thing? I can't believe it! You should have come down to the creek with us. Franklin asked about you." Clarey went on to describe Millie's antics, to tell how Celia and Walter spent all evening out of sight, and to boast of the attention Mavis paid him.

Elizabeth was glad her brother had had a good time, but it all sounded so much like the night Rudy had drowned. Hadn't they learned anything? Had nothing changed? "Don't you want to look at this?" She held the catalog out to Clarey. "You should be deciding which classes you'll take."

He shrugged. "Oh, just required curriculum the first year, I expect." The tone of his voice indicated how boring he thought the prospect.

The next morning, however, an exciting change of routine presented itself in the comfortable round shape of Aunt Nelly. Elizabeth was just returning from the henhouse after turning a new batch of eggs—her first brood had successfully hatched themselves into charming, soft yellow balls that followed the hens around the barnyard, chirping and pecking as naturally as if the hens had set on them themselves. She looked up and smiled at the speed at which a stream of dust was approaching their house. Only Nelly took the rutted, dusty roads that fast, but then her Model T had isinglass curtains, which she could roll down to protect against the clouds of dust she raised.

Elizabeth walked toward her, smiling, as Nelly braked with a screech, then piled out of the car, pulling her straw hat off her still-shiny blond coronet and fanning the dust away. "Go get your mother, Elizabeth. I'll have no arguments today. You need a break. I have to go to Boise. And it's your mother's favorite treat. So that settles it."

Elizabeth was uncertain as to the details of the plan, but she knew better than to argue with Nelly when she was in one of her managing moods. "Alex can give the men their mid-day meal. My Vina did it when she was much younger. I'm taking you and Kathryn to the Idan-Ha for lunch," Nelly continued as they walked toward the house.

Kathryn didn't offer the slightest resistance, and it took her only a few minutes to instruct Alex as to which cold meats to cut and which jars of canned fruit to open. Then she packed a basket with the diapers, blankets, and other items she would need for taking a baby on such an adventure.

Merrick was in the south field, so they drove out there for Kathryn to tell her husband of their plans. He seemed happy for their treat and kissed all of them good-bye. But as he stood waving them away, Elizabeth noticed how tired her father's intensely blue eyes looked and how much grayer he was becoming. *It must be the water worries,* she thought.

The rare treat of a visit to the big city provided a glimpse into another world for Elizabeth. They drove past the mansard-roofed Delamar rooming house, just one of the many old mansions that were home to Boise's Basque population, so numerous that Boise was known as the Basque capital of America. Then past the polo field, center of Boise's social life, for Boise was also known as the polo capital of the Pacific Northwest. And then past the capitol and the statue, unveiled two years earlier, of Idaho's assassinated Governor Frank Steunenberg.

At their quiet luncheon of crisp seafood salads served on elegant china on white linen, Kathryn, with the softened look that always stole over her face when remembering the old days, recounted attending the trial of Steunenberg's assassin. ". . . long before I married Merrick. What happy years. Funny how one tends to forget the struggles and remember the good times."

As they pulled away from the curb later, one of the newly instituted city buses lumbered by, making Nelly swerve over the old, rutted streetcar tracks. She turned up Capitol Boulevard with the capitol and Governor Steunenberg behind them and the fine new, Spanish-style Union Pacific Railroad station at the top of the hill ahead of them.

Elizabeth exclaimed with delight as the chimes from the station's tower rang out.

They had actually started out of town when Nelly's hands flew from the steering wheel to slap her rosy cheeks. "Oh, my stars and garters! I almost forgot! What would Isaiah have said if I'd driven all the way into Boise and back and not gotten that cylinder for his tractor?"

They laughed so hard they woke baby Eldon, sleeping in his mother's arms.

But it became less than a laughing matter when the second machine shop they visited didn't have the part in the right size. They had to drive a considerable distance from the center of town out State Street to a farm implement dealer the previous one had recommended before they could find what Isaiah needed.

With a glow of success they turned toward home. Only then did they notice the black clouds building in the west. "Oh, look at that! Do you think we'll get rain? Wouldn't that be wonderful—rain and lunch at the Idan-Ha all in the same day!" Nelly sped up. "Pull those curtains down beside you, Kathryn, if that's too much wind on the baby."

They were nearing Meridian when the first drops fell. Elizabeth raised her curtain a few inches and stuck her hand out to feel the glorious drops. It was better than pearls falling from the sky. But she pulled her hand in with a jerk as a peal of thunder shook the car.

The rain came thicker and faster as the wind increased. By the time they had turned south on the Kuna-Meridian road, the dust had turned to thick mud that stuck to the tires, and Nelly had to reduce her speed even more because it was so hard to see through the water sloshing across the windshield. "It's a little frightening, isn't it?"

Kathryn clutched Eldon closer to her. "Cloudbursts are such a rarity in this country. I remember when I was a girl in Nebraska we used to have rains like this all the time."

"Do you think anyone had their second cutting of hay down yet?" Elizabeth asked, thinking that even something as much needed as rain could be a mixed blessing.

Nelly shook her head, though she didn't take her eyes from the road. "I don't think so. Alfalfa's been growing pretty slow with so little water. Now it'll jump up nice. End of July or first of August we should have a good crop. I think the good Lord timed it just right. He even waited until we had our shopping all done."

By the time they neared the Allen place, water was running across the rutted road in streams, sometimes up to the running boards of the car. They had just turned up the lane when Elizabeth remembered. "Oh, no! The chicks! They were all out in the yard pecking with the hens . . ." She stifled her dismay with a hand over her mouth.

Kathryn said nothing, just set her jaw firmly and moved to the front of her seat, as if to urge the car forward faster. As soon as it stopped she thrust Eldon into Nelly's arms. "Give him to Alex. I have to help Elizabeth."

Elizabeth was already dashing across the yard, oblivious of the water streaming off her head and shoulders and the mud splashing to her knees. Outside the barn she grabbed two buckets and rushed toward the henhouse.

The first sad cluster of chicks she found sheltering against the wall of the shed. She scooped three dripping yellow balls into her bucket and dashed on. Five bedraggled lumps of feathers had gathered around a hen under a wagon. Two more were half-floating, half-swimming over by the pigpen. She didn't stop to count as she scooped and dashed, but from the weight of her buckets and with the knowledge that her mother was working as fast as she, Elizabeth knew they must have most of them. Better to stop now and let the stragglers go while there was a flicker of life in some.

"Bring them in the kitchen!" Kathryn called and led the way.

They grabbed every dry towel and blanket in sight and spread them out on the floor in front of the wooden cookstove. The sad little lumps lay all anyhow, on their sides, backs, or necks as the women scooped them out of their buckets.

Elizabeth grabbed a towel and began rubbing a ball of limp feathers.

Kathryn held one in a cupped hand up to her cheek, a forefinger pressed gently against its throat. "I think I feel a heartbeat. Just a flutter. We have a chance. Keep drying." She moved the chick closer to the stove and picked up another one.

Elizabeth fought her own sense of desperation. If she worked too hard, squeezed too tightly, she could easily do more harm than good.

But in the end it didn't matter. The fifth chick she held to dry felt even limper and stiller than the others. She placed a finger on it as she had seen Kathryn do earlier. She felt nothing. As if she could will it to live she even shook it gently between her cupped hands. But there was no doubt. The lump in her hand was lifeless. She set it down with a sob. Then one she had already dried, one that had been sitting somewhat upright, suddenly toppled over. Within half an hour, all were dead.

"So we not only lost the chicks, we're also out of the profit we could have had from selling the eggs, plus the price of the chick mash we fed them." She tried not to sound bitter.

The waste of it all. The death spread out in front of her brought back the horror of Rudy's death. How could so many things drown in the desert? It didn't make any sense. Nothing made sense. She stumbled to her feet. She knew she should help her mother clean up the mess. The men would be in from the barn for supper soon. But she needed to be alone.

In the chill damp of the sleeping porch she rolled over on the protesting springs and looked again at the NCC announcement. Under Tuition and Fees: tuition, $50.00; dormitories and dining hall, $110.00. Both cash in advance per semester, a total of $160 per semester, and that didn't even count such incidentals as: registration fee, $1.00, library fee, $1.00, Glee Club fee, $1.00, laundry, $3.50. The list went on and on. Electric iron, $1.25—did that mean the socket for an iron, or did they actually furnish the implement? Wouldn't that be fun?—to have an electric iron!

She threw the catalog across the room. She would never know. The summer was two-thirds over, and the pickle pot contained less than twenty dollars—not even half of the first semester's tuition. And all the chicks were dead.

5

A week of rain, although much lighter than the disastrous cloudburst that announced its arrival, followed by a week of temperatures that were above normal even for the end of July, brought the promise of a bumper hay cutting to balance the very skimpy first cutting the earlier drought had caused. Kathryn, Elizabeth, and Alex worked every minute baking bread and pies and simmering soups to feed the haying crew.

There would be six extra hungry men to feed for the three-day operation. Jules Sperlin and his boys, Albert (who was Boyd's age) and Fred (a year younger but already bigger than Clarey and able to work harder), would hay with the Allens, then be repaid the following week by the Allen men helping bring in the Sperlin hay. The job would require the services of three itinerant hired men as well. And all would be ravenous.

Although Marie Sperlin, with Grace's help, would feed her men breakfast at home, the six eating at the Allens' would require pancakes, fried eggs, bacon, toast, hot and cold cereal, canned fruit, and quarts of coffee to start the day. Alex and Elizabeth would then scramble to get the water heated on the stove and the dishes washed and dried and back on the table, while Kathryn saw to roasting meats and peeling potatoes for dinner at noon. Then the whole process was to be repeated for supper at six, leaving time to do evening chores in the waning daylight.

Merrick had begun the process the week before, pulling the mower behind the tractor to cut the alfalfa, then gathering it into long rows with the side-delivery rake. After two days of curing in the field—the one time no one wanted rain—the rows were turned with another swath of the rake and, finally, shocked into pitchfork-sized bunches in preparation for the real work.

Elizabeth and Kathryn were up before sunrise Monday morning, up even before the men, because Kathryn always liked to have the first pot of coffee perked before Merrick arrived in the kitchen. Elizabeth slipped out with the excuse of turning her eggs before the day got too busy, but really desiring to be out of doors in the dewey freshness to enjoy the dawn chorus.

The many robins, sparrows, and wrens living in the cluster of locust trees that circled the pond at the foot of the pasture didn't let her down. It was a glorious morning.

"Going to be a scorcher. Can tell already."

Elizabeth jumped at the voice of one of the hired men who was walking toward the house from the barn where he and his companions had slept. Elizabeth agreed, then hurried on toward the henhouse. If the men were up already, Mother would need her to gather the eggs and get them fried.

By mid-morning the girls had the dishes done, ready for the next onslaught, and Kathryn was taking a break in the rocking chair while she nursed Eldon. "Alex, you start scraping those carrots. Elizabeth, it's time to take the drinks to the men."

"Sure, Mother." She gave her mother an extra-bright smile. Kathryn was tired, and this was only the morning of the first day. She needed to help keep her spirits up.

Elizabeth brought four gallon jugs from the bench on the porch and filled them. One with iced tea, another with lemonade, another with water, and one with her father's favorite—buttermilk.

"Don't forget to wear a sunbonnet," Kathryn called after her. "The sun will turn your skin to leather by the time you're thirty."

Elizabeth took her mother's old blue bonnet off the peg by the back door and tied it under her chin.

This morning they were working the field closest to the house, so she simply put the jugs and nine tin cups in the small wooden wagon they had all played with as children and pulled it rattling behind her. She stood at the top of the field, breathing deeply. She loved the smell of the warm sun on the mown hay. At the foot of the field Merrick turned a wide swath and started back toward her. She raised her arm to wave, and he saluted her back.

Most of their neighbors thought her father had been crazy when he bought that tractor ten years before—the first in the area. Real farming was done with real horses, they told him. But never worry, when the thing broke down they'd bring their teams over and help him out. But the next year Uncle Isaiah had bought a shiny new John Deere. Now a few others, including Jules Sperlin, were farming with modern equipment.

The tractor progressed slowly up the field, pulling the broad, flat, wooden slip behind it. Her brothers and the two Sperlin boys walked on each side, pitching shocks of hay onto the slip in accord with the directions of one of the hired men who was serving as tripper—the man in charge of loading and dumping the slip.

They had seen her signal, so Elizabeth turned to take her refreshments behind the barn where the hay was being stacked, knowing they would join her when the slip was loaded. She wiped a drip of perspiration from under the deep brim of her bonnet. She was glad she had heard the birds that morning, for none sang now; it was already too hot. There would be no more birdsong until evening. But bees buzzed along the banks of the irrigation ditch, and white and yellow sulfur butterflies flitted over the dandelions and clover.

Jules Sperlin waved to her from the top of the growing haystack where he was directing operations. He was her favorite neighbor, a giant of a man, yet always so gentle.

Just then the tractor arrived, and Elizabeth watched as the loaded slip was pulled into place beneath the tall poles of the derrick. The tripper hooked the slip's chains to the one extending from the long arm of the derrick. When the tripper nodded that all was secure, Carlo, the hired man who had spoken to her that morning, moved his team forward, and the slip swung into the air.

Elizabeth held her breath when the loaded platform swung high and hovered over their heads. At a shouted signal from Jules, the tripper pulled the rope, and the hay fell neatly onto the stack.

Now those workers could gather at Elizabeth's wagon while the others who had finished their drinks returned to the field with the second slip. Jules, given deference as the stacker, took his mug of iced tea first, then the second tripper, but Carlo hung back.

"What would you like? Lemonade? Buttermilk?" Elizabeth asked.

Carlo removed his straw hat and wiped his forehead, his white teeth gleaming in his tanned face. "Just a glass of water, little lady. How about you bring it to me?"

She didn't like the way his eyes followed her as she moved toward him with the tin cup. He took the water, then reached for her hand, but she jumped back sharply. "More iced tea, Jules?" She turned to the security of their old friend.

As soon as the jugs were empty she gathered her things into the wagon and turned toward the house at a rattling run. What was wrong with her? Franklin, Mr. Griswold, now a hired man—was she doing something wrong that men misinterpreted? Certainly such attentions were the last thing she wanted. She was certain she never flirted like Celia or Mavis. She wouldn't know how to go about it and knew she'd look ridiculous if she tried. So why did they think she wanted to be pawed?

Sweat poured down her face, and she was gasping by the time she got to the kitchen.

Kathryn looked her up and down. "Elizabeth! What's wrong? Is your father . . ?"

Elizabeth caught her breath, shaking her head. "No, no, everyone's fine. I—I—" Then she told her mother.

Alex came in carrying a chunk of cheese from the cellar. "Put that on the table and go check on Eldon," Kathryn directed. As soon as her youngest daughter was out of earshot she said, "No, my dear, it's no fault of yours. You always behave very circumspectly. I would certainly speak to you if you didn't. But you must face the fact that you are a very attractive young woman."

Elizabeth gasped in surprise.

"Very attractive," her mother repeated. "You just hold your head up and do the right thing. When the right man comes along you'll want him to hold your hand."

Elizabeth, still wondering how anyone could find her tall, broad-shouldered build and strong features attractive, winced. "Yes, and he won't want to."

"We'll worry about that when the time comes. Right now stir that potato soup, then you can cut those pies in quarters."

"How many shall I cut?"

Kathryn thought for a moment. "Better do five pies—most of the men will want two pieces."

By the morning of the third day only the assurance that the haying would finish that night gave Elizabeth the strength to drag herself out of bed. Even the birdsong floating in her open window did little to encourage her. How many years had her mother been doing this? How did she have the stamina to go on?

Elizabeth thought again of her determination to get an education. She loved the farm and the people on it, but she wanted a different sort of life. Her mother was wonderful, but Elizabeth, even with her capacity for hard work, wouldn't want to live her mother's life.

Indeed, Kathryn looked tired, her pale hair limper than usual as it escaped from the knot at the nape of her neck, but she spoke kindly to every man as she set the bowls of oatmeal and Wheatena on the table, then turned back to frying bacon. "Elizabeth, bring up some more butter from the cellar."

Elizabeth went, knowing her mother had sent her rather than Alex because Carlo had been staring at her again. It had been Alex's job to take drinks to the field ever since that first time. Although, at the sound of the fretting wail that greeted her emergence from the cellar, she wondered if perhaps she should offer to go again today because Eldon hadn't slept well during the night. Mother was sure to need more help in the house today.

The baby was asleep by midmorning, however, so Alex took the wagon, leaving Elizabeth with time to turn her eggs.

The mood of the men at dinner was not the happy one she thought it would be. She had expected to hear talk of what time they would finish and what a good job they had done and how soon they would start on the Sperlin place. Instead there was grumbling and rehashing of troubles.

Somehow one slipload had been off-balance and fell short of the stack, causing loss of time, hay, and tempers. It was uncertain whether the fault had been Carlo's, the tripper's, or Jules's as stacker, but it had heralded a series of small disasters: A harness strap on the team broke at about the same time a belt slipped on the tractor, bringing both areas of operation to a halt for repairs. Then Boyd had misjudged a pitch of hay, landed it on top of Albert, and they had stopped to scuffle, bringing out Merrick's rarely seen temper. The fact that it was at least five degrees hotter than the previous day was no help either.

"We must finish today." Carlo spoke as the senior hired man. "We have promised Mr. Young to hay his field tomorrow, then the Jayne place after that."

"We'll make it."

Elizabeth knew that when her father's eyes took on that level, steely-blue look he meant what he said.

But an hour later when Freddie Sperlin rushed in, grasping a bleeding forearm cut from elbow to wrist on the handle of a broken pitchfork, even Merrick's determination seemed inadequate.

Kathryn left her wooden spoon in the big crockery mixing bowl and wiped her hands on her apron. "Elizabeth, you clean that wound good, look out for any splinters, then bind it up and send him home—no, he's lost quite a bit of blood. He'd better rest here and go home with his pa. Then you finish my banana cake—and see that you don't overbake it. That's my best recipe. I don't want it spoiled." She reached for her sunbonnet.

"Mama! Where are you going?" Elizabeth gasped at what Kathryn appeared to be doing.

"They'll need another pitcher. I've been doing it all my life."

"No, Mother. I can pitch hay. You take care of things here."

Kathryn shook her head, the emphasis enlarged by the brim of her bonnet. "No, Elizabeth. I'll not have you in the fields with those hired men. I'll be back in to nurse Eldon, and Alex can walk back out with me with the afternoon refreshments. You'll have to see to supper on your own." The screen door banged before Elizabeth could protest.

It was a long, hot afternoon—as hot in the kitchen with a big pot of stew simmering on the stove as it was in the field.

When Kathryn returned with the men that evening Elizabeth and Alex had everything on the table just as she would expect, but Kathryn was too tired to eat. "Just bring me a glass of something cold to sip while I nurse the baby." She sank into the rocking chair as if she couldn't have taken another step.

Alex took a red-faced Eldon and a large glass of lemonade to her mother, then turned to help serve the men.

When the last pan was scrubbed, Elizabeth was so tired she thought she would sleep like the dead. But the poorly built porch, which was so cold in winter that her breath froze on the outside of her quilts, was now stifling, holding the heat of the day even as the desert around them cooled. And every time she started to drift off, Alex would turn beside her, rocking the bed and creaking the springs. Or Eldon would cry from her parents' bedroom—a sharp, piercing wail that reminded her of her mother's stories of coyotes howling outside their homestead shack in the old days.

It must have been about 3:00 A.M. when quiet fell over the house, and Elizabeth dropped into a deep sleep. It was so deep that nearly an hour later, when her mother's insistent whisper finally penetrated her consciousness, she realized that Kathryn had been shaking her shoulder for some time.

"Elizabeth, I'm so sorry to bother you, but—" a sob interrupted her whisper "—it's Eldon. Your father has gone for the doctor, but I need you to brew some peppermint tea while I work with him."

Elizabeth sat up with a jolt. "Eldon? But he isn't crying. That's why I was asleep."

Kathryn sobbed again. "He's barely breathing. I think it's his stomach—I must get back. Peppermint—strong— but not hot."

Alex sprawled over the bed when Elizabeth got out and padded barefoot across the wooden floor.

Merrick returned at sunrise with Dr. Nolte. Kathryn had been able to dribble only a few eyedropperfuls of the soothing tea into the tiny mouth of her infant son.

Elizabeth stood by, trying to pray, trying to support her mother, but finding that it took all her strength just to control her own tears as she watched her baby brother, too weak to cry, pull his knees to his cramping stomach as his face slowly turned gray-blue. She didn't need to see Dr. Nolte's sadly shaken head to know it was too late.

The funeral was two days later at the Kuna Cemetery beside Indian Creek. "Suffer the little children, and forbid them not to come unto me, for of such is the kingdom of heaven . . ."

Marie and Grace Sperlin sang "Jewels." "When He cometh, when He cometh to make up His jewels, all His jewels, precious jewels His loved and His own . . . ."

Elizabeth looked beyond the tiny mound and read the names on the tombstones. She had come here many times with her mother to bring spring flowers or to clear the weeds from graves of family and friends.

She knew the stories: Aunt Thelma, who had been Uncle Isaiah's first wife and died with her baby just before Kathryn and her papa arrived to homestead; Ned Brewington, Aunt Nelly's first husband, who died of rattlesnake bite; Adam Jayne, her own grandfather, who preferred preaching to ploughing and had reaped Merrick's soul just before his own death. The ragged little rows went on, most of them names Elizabeth connected with families who had pioneered in that area. Benji Young—first Kuna boy to die in the War. Kathryn had been his Sunday school teacher.

". . . Amen." She jerked to attention as Rev. Brown ended his prayer, then took a few steps back to let the others pass by first.

Nelly and Isaiah kissed Kathryn and shook hands warmly with Elizabeth, as did Jules and Marie behind them. Then Albert and Freddie, stiff with discomfort, mumbled their condolences without lifting their eyes from their shoes.

Next came a clutch of her school friends, expressing a quick, "Sorry your brother died." "It's so sad." "What a pity." Celia, holding to Walter's arm; Edith, whose soft brown eyes had tears in them; Millie, who couldn't move even at a funeral without shimmying; Franklin, who clutched her hand and held it too long, without saying anything; Mavis, in an unbecomingly tight skirt, who clung to Clarey and sobbed.

At last the family was alone. Elizabeth still held back. This was the part she always hated most. Alex and her brothers stepped bravely up to the grave and tossed in their handfuls of dirt. Then her parents. Elizabeth knew she must do it. She picked up a lumpy, gray-brown clod and tossed it toward the little box that held all that was left on earth of the pink, cooing, little person who had been her baby brother. She closed her eyes as the dirt fell, but she couldn't close her ears. She knew she would hear that thud for the rest of her life.

Boyd was the one who thought of stopping at the post office on the way home. It was good that he did, for the act brought comfort to him at least. He returned to the car with a brown paper parcel bearing a number of odd-looking stamps.

"From Scotland!" He brandished the package, then his pleasure faded. "Uncle Robbie must have sent something for the baby."

Boyd started to pull off the string, but Kathryn spoke from the front seat. "Since it comes from your father's cousin, you'd best let him open it."

"Yes, but I'm the one who writes to Ian all the time. They probably wouldn't have known about Eldon at all if I hadn't written."

"Perhaps it would have been just as well to spare them the sorrow," Elizabeth suggested. "Now we must write again."

"Go ahead and open it, laddie." Merrick rarely called his sons by the title he had been raised with. "I'm glad you thought to write to your cousin. I keep little enough touch with my family."

Boyd looked mollified and pulled the string from the parcel as Merrick drove on. It contained a silver feeding spoon engraved *Eldon Egan Allen* with a Scottish thistle on the end. The Egan had been chosen for his Scottish grandfather. In the circumstances Boyd muted his response, but it was clear he thought the object beautiful as he ran his finger over the silver thistle and stared long at the cover on the box—dark blue-green with the red line of the family plaid.

"Boyd, why don't you keep it?" Kathryn said softly. "You seem to have inherited the strongest dose of your father's Scottish blood."

Unfortunately, there was no such comfort for Alexandra. Eldon had, from the first, been her special charge—he had been more like her baby than her brother. Even though she was still a child herself, or perhaps because of her youth, she was disconsolate. She cried little but returned from the funeral with a cold, hard look in her blue eyes. "If that's what comes of having babies I'll never have one—never."

Nothing anyone said to her made the least difference as she set her square jaw, so much like her mother's.

That evening Elizabeth heard her mother playing the organ, a soft, plaintive melody she didn't recognize. When the song ended and no other followed, she went to look for her. She found her mother alone on the porch, holding her well-kept journal on her lap but not writing. Instead she was sitting very still, looking out across the desert.

"Mama?" Elizabeth ventured as she sat beside her on the bench. She seldom called her mother by her childhood term, but it came out now.

Kathryn sighed and picked up Elizabeth's hand, clutching it firmly in both of hers. "I was just thinking—so many deaths."

"I know, Mama. I thought of it at the cemetery today."

"Yes. And so many others. Some whose names I can't even recall. I know death is part of life. It happens every-

70

where, and we must carry on. But it seems the desert is such a harsh land. This is such a hard life. The dirt, the work, the heat. I've thought and thought about it. I'm sure my milk was bad. I worked too hard in the heat, then came right in and nursed him."

"No, Mama. He was sickly the night before. Remember how fussy he was? Surely Dr. Nolte didn't say it was bad milk?"

"No. He had a long name for it, which I suspect meant stomachache. But I'll always believe my milk was bad."

Elizabeth wanted to protest but could think of nothing to say, so they sat quietly for a time.

"But as I said" —Kathryn seemed to be coming out of a long dream— "we must go on. And that's what I wanted to say to you, Elizabeth." She clutched Elizabeth's hand even tighter and turned toward her. "You must go on. You must go to college. I want you to have a chance at a better life. I've been happy here with your father, but I want you to have a life that isn't so hard."

Elizabeth leaned over and kissed her mother's cheek. She could feel the dryness of her skin. She was thankful for her mother's words; it was what she wanted too. But all the encouragement in the world wouldn't put more money in the pickle pot.

6

Kathryn wouldn't even listen to Elizabeth's suggestion that she decline her bridesmaid's role in Celia's wedding on the grounds that it came so soon after Eldon's death.

"You need friends. You need happy times. We'll all go. Everyone will. The Cottrells and Potters have been leading citizens of this community for years."

Everyone, including the Griswolds, Elizabeth thought. This was far too small a community to be able to avoid one of its most prominent members. She would hold her head up and go ahead as her mother had always taught her to do—no matter how difficult the task she faced.

And Celia's wedding wasn't at all a difficult task. It was more like a party—like graduation night before the accident—where they were all school chums together, not yet across the threshold of adult responsibility. As matron of honor, Celia's older sister Arlette wore the lavender taffeta dress that best suited her blond hair. Elizabeth and Mavis wore matching blue gowns, fortunately supplied by the bride's parents. And the bride's gown was like nothing Elizabeth had ever seen. Long and elegant, of heavy bias-cut satin with its own train and long, pointed sleeves, it had been made in San Francisco and purchased through the most exclusive shop in Boise.

72

"Celia! You're beautiful! You look like a calla lily!" Elizabeth hugged her friend.

"Yes, Papa said he didn't mind how much anything cost. Wait till you see the cake! I ordered it from a Swedish bakery—it has icing made out of ground almonds!"

The ceremony was as perfect as Mrs. Cottrell's careful planning and Mr. Cottrell's pocketbook could make it. Even the intense heat of an August Sunday afternoon seemed to bother only Mavis. Elizabeth kept an eye on her companion bridesmaid in case a supporting arm should be needed.

I wonder if she feels the heat more with having put on weight, Elizabeth wondered. Probably eating to forget about Rudy. She smiled encouragingly at her friend, who swayed once but managed to stand steadily throughout the rather lengthy wedding sermon and three verses of "O Promise Me," sung by Grace Sperlin with Marie at the organ.

Elizabeth noticed, however, that Mavis seemed perfectly happy to lean on Clarey's arm throughout the reception at the grange hall. She also noticed that she needn't have worried about Mr. Griswold. Mrs. Griswold never let him out of her sight, except when she prodded him in the back with her fan to send him on his way to get her another glass of punch.

Afternoon was beginning to slip toward evening when Franklin, to whom Elizabeth had spoken only briefly before, managed to cut her away from the other guests— much like a sheepdog cutting a ewe from the herd, Elizabeth thought. She sidestepped only to find herself in a corner.

"Well, Franklin, when do you start classes at Link's?" she asked with desperate casualness.

"That's exactly what I want to talk to you about." He drained his cup with a quick gesture, sparing Elizabeth further fears of his punch landing in her lap. "I'd feel so much better—that is, I could be freer to concentrate on my studies—and you know how important these business classes are to my—er, our—er, any future success." He pulled a handkerchief from the pocket of his tan suit and mopped his forehead. "That is, if I knew for sure you were waiting for me . . ."

"What?" Could she possibly have heard him right?

"You've probably thought about this as much as I have. I mean, we've been such good friends for so many years. I would have talked to you about this graduation night, except—well, you know . . ."

Elizabeth nodded.

Unfortunately, he took that as encouragement to continue. "So, anyway . . ." He clutched fervently at her hand.

For a terrible moment Elizabeth thought he was going to drop to one knee right there in the grange hall with the wedding guests milling around.

"So will you?" He pumped her hand as if greeting her at the church door.

"Will I what?"

"Wait for me! Like I said. It's only a one-year course— nine months, really. We could get married next summer."

So that was it. As she had feared.

"Oh, but Franklin. I wouldn't be ready. I'm going to NCC for a full four years. And then I'll probably teach for a few years before I—er—do anything else."

"Oh."

"Yes. Sorry. Why don't you try Millie?" It wasn't fair to tease him like that, but she couldn't resist.

"Millie?" He looked over his shoulder just in time to see Millie's brightly lipsticked mouth break into laughter in response to a joke of Harold's. "Really, do you think she likes me?"

"I'm sure she likes you every bit as much as I do, Franklin."

"Well, gee whiz!" He adjusted the knot in his tie and ambled off to join Millie's group of admirers.

Elizabeth would have sunk into the nearest chair and allowed herself a fit of laughter, but a wave from Arlette told her it was time to help Celia change into the traveling suit she would wear to board the train for their California honeymoon. Celia must be in a hurry. Elizabeth noted that the bride had already removed her long veil.

A few minutes later Arlette clapped her hands. "Oh, Celia, you look smashing in red. Walter'll have to fight off every man on that train just to get the seat beside you." The bride's sister set a little red hat on Celia's blond curls as a finishing touch.

Elizabeth, busy folding the elegant wedding gown in leaves of tissue paper, looked up. "Perfect, Celia. You look absolutely stunning. Everything today has been perfect. Where's your veil? Shall I put it in here with the dress?"

"No, Mavis has it. But where's my perfume? She borrowed that too."

Elizabeth wanted to ask where Mavis was, but Walter's knock at the door sent Celia's attendants scurrying for her purse, handkerchief, and traveling case.

Mavis and the Lily of the Valley scent weren't at the train station. Neither was Clarey, Elizabeth noted, as she saw Harold and Whitmore standing at the edge of the platform without the third groomsman.

Then the train puffed up to the station, and the newlyweds boarded their Pullman car. A few minutes later, to the cheers of friends and family, the train let out a glory of steam, and the bridal pair were on their way.

It was not until late that evening, after Elizabeth had shared the story of Franklin's proposal with her mother, that Elizabeth asked herself some serious questions.

What was she *really* going to do? The sale of her last batch of chickens, carefully plucked and dressed with frills of paper around their legs—because Kathryn advised her that Mr. Martin liked them that way (enough to pay a few cents more)—had added several dollars to the pot. And there would be one more lot to take to Martin's Meat Market at the end of the month. But even if they all flourished and she got top price for them, there was no way three dozen more chickens could make up the deficit she needed for even a semester of college. It seemed futile to go for only one semester when she had no hope of raising money for the second.

The words she had spoken so bravely to Franklin that afternoon now returned to mock her. And equally foolish echoes followed: Her "I will wear it to college" when she was presented the Senior Sweater, and all that stuff about high hopes and assurance of success she had said in her commencement speech. What would she do? Spend the rest of her life right here on the farm raising chickens?

Maybe she should have accepted Franklin, she thought, not for the first time. It would be something to do with the rest of her life. And without an education there were few other options. She certainly didn't want to return to any kind of office work.

A slamming door and the sound of excited voices and giggles in the living room brought her to her feet. Who could be coming in at this hour? It couldn't be Nelly and Isaiah. The voices were too high-pitched. Elizabeth straightened her hair and slipped her shoes back on.

An amazing sight met her. Mavis, still in her blue taffeta bridesmaid dress, and with Celia's long tulle veil flowing from a band of wax orange blossoms on her head, stood in the center of the room with both arms around Clarey's waist, making excited little squeals in reply to everyone's questions.

At last it became clear. That was why Celia had taken off her veil at the reception—to loan it to her eloping friend. Clarey had borrowed a car, and they had driven to the justice of the peace in Nampa.

"I've had the marriage license for weeks." Clarey's voice was full of pride.

"But what will you do?" Elizabeth was always the practical one.

Clarey shrugged. "I'll do what I've always done. I'll farm."

"Since I don't have any brothers, Daddy'll be awfully happy to have help. And Mama says we can live with them." Mavis ended with an excited little gasp.

Mavis's father would no doubt be happy for help, Elizabeth thought. He was notoriously lazy, and their place the most rundown in the area.

"You mean your parents know?" Kathryn asked.

"Just Mama. I had to tell her, of course."

"Of course." Kathryn nodded weakly, overcome by the suddenness of her firstborn's behavior. Then she went forward with open arms to embrace them both. "Welcome to the family, my dear." She kissed Mavis, who returned her hug with fervor.

Alex showed her first animation since Eldon's death. She clapped her hands with delight at having a bride in the family—a new sister. Boyd eyed his big brother with awe. Merrick was the only one who seemed to show disappointment. He suddenly looked even tireder and grayer than he had at the height of the drought worries. Elizabeth knew her father had had high ambitions for his oldest son.

Suddenly Elizabeth's mouth fell open, and her eyes got wide. Ambitions for Clarey, money for college—she was afraid to ask, but she had to know. "Does this mean that you won't be going to college? That you won't need the money?"

Clarey looked at her, blinking his eyes. He had obviously not given the matter a thought. "No. I won't be going to college. Do you still have that bee in your bonnet?"

Elizabeth thought she would pass out from holding her breath while he got around to answering her. Finally he said, "Well, maybe we could have some of the money as a wedding present—it sure would help in getting started. We'll be wanting to build a house of our own one of these days. But you're certainly welcome to the education."

Elizabeth let her breath out in such a rush then that she almost did pass out.

7

From the moment Elizabeth, clutching her two Gladstone bags, stepped onto the broad, green campus of the tiny Christian college south of Nampa, she felt at home. Of course, she had seen the school many times when she had gone to Nampa on errands with her parents, but this was her first time to be a part of the place that had held central focus in her dreams for so long.

There had been much discussion over how she would get to school. Should her father take her? Should the whole family go? Should she take the train? In the end, necessity decided it. The third cutting of hay coincided with the opening of school, and although much lighter than the second had been, it still required the work of the whole family. So it was Aunt Nelly who let Elizabeth out on Holly Street in front of the campus, and, after one of her copious hugs, went on to do some shopping before spending the rest of her day with Vina.

I'm here! Thank You, Lord! Elizabeth smiled and breathed deeply of the crisp autumn air. The trees in the park across from the campus were beginning to turn gold. She could imagine what fun it would be to crunch through the fallen leaves in a month or so.

"Hello, are you new?" A lovely, smiling voice made Elizabeth jump.

"Oh. Yes, I am. I was just admiring the trees. It's great here, isn't it?"

"Yes, it's nice enough, I guess. A little barren, but you'll get used to it. I did." The voice was still lovely, but not enthusiastic.

"Barren? All those trees? And green grass?" Elizabeth didn't want to be rude, but where could this girl have come from to think *this* barren?

"Well, I'm from Portland, so all this brown is rather—well—rather brown."

"Oh." Elizabeth could think of nothing else to say.

"But anyway, hi. I'm Ilona Watkins, a sophomore."

Elizabeth was amazed to see that Ilona was taller than herself. She had always been the tallest girl in her class, and until the last couple of years, when the boys spurted ahead, she had been taller than most of the boys as well. But Ilona was so graceful—tall, yet fine boned with narrow shoulders, slender wrists and ankles.

"Oh, yes." Elizabeth set down a suitcase so she could offer her hand. "Sorry. I'm Elizabeth Allen." Elizabeth noticed as they shook hands that Ilona had the longest, slimmest fingers she had ever seen.

Ilona looked at the suitcases. "Want me to show you to the dorm?" Elizabeth nodded and started to speak, but Ilona laughed and went on. "Not that it's much of a trick to find it on this campus." She pointed. "Administration building right in front of us. Hadley Hall, womens' dormitory, to your right. Gideon Hall, men's dorm, to the left. The Club behind the ad building."

Elizabeth thought the large, two-story, white-sided buildings were lovely. But she feared appearing gauche by saying so to this sophisticated girl from the big city, so she merely nodded.

Ilona picked up a case and set out at a long-legged pace toward Hadley Hall.

Again Elizabeth noted the girl's long, slim fingers as they gripped her battered case. "Do you play the piano?"

Ilona laughed. It seemed that everything about her was musical. "Yes. How did you know? I'm in the school of music. What do you want to study?"

Elizabeth felt that studying to be a schoolteacher sounded very mundane, but all she could do was tell the truth. In a few minutes their steps rang hollowly across the broad, wooden porch of the girls' dorm, and Ilona opened the glass door.

A stout woman with steel-rimmed glasses, her dark hair pinned severely into a tight bun, met them at the door. "Mrs. Wenschler, this is Elizabeth." Ilona's voice seemed to register a lower scale in the presence of Authority. "Mrs. Wenschler is dean of women," she added to Elizabeth.

Mrs. Wenschler peered skeptically at Elizabeth, then gave a curt nod, and finally a welcoming smile, as if she had decided that the new girl had committed no infraction of the rules—yet. "Yes. Elizabeth Allen, isn't it? I received your forms. Welcome."

"Thank you, Mrs. Wenschler."

The dean of women checked her clipboard. "Yes, it's just as I thought. Good thing you girls have met. You're to be roommates." Both girls emitted surprised and not displeased ohs, and the dean continued. "Here is a copy of our handbook. Please note the rules carefully. Ilona, you may show Elizabeth to your room."

"Yes, Mrs. Wenschler."

"Thank you, Mrs. Wenschler."

The girls managed to keep from bursting into laughter until they were safely up the stairs and down the hall.

Elizabeth hoped their room would be on the front of the building. She could think of nothing more delightful than looking out over the trees of Kurtz Park. But Ilona led her to the back of the U-shaped building and opened the door into a room that looked out on an alfalfa field. *Well, at least I'll feel at home,* Elizabeth thought. And when Ilona showed her to the bathroom just down the hall, she could barely restrain herself from exclaiming over the indoor plumbing and hot and cold running water—and they weren't the ones to be doing the running.

"You've loads of time to unpack." Ilona flopped down on her bed, already made up with a red and gold woven bedspread with heavy gold fringe around the bottom. "Dinner at five o'clock in The Club."

Elizabeth blinked in surprise, then realized—oh, yes, here dinner was the *evening* meal. There was so much to get used to.

The Club was the only single-story building on campus. Its arched roof-line gave it a vaguely Spanish look, which Elizabeth thought very appealing. Since about half of the 120 students lived on campus and ate at The Club, it was a busy place when Elizabeth and Ilona arrived there just after five.

"Hi, Alice, this is Elizabeth." Ilona explained that Alice lived across the hall from them in Hadley. Elizabeth was sure she'd like Alice. She reminded her so much of Edith. But she couldn't let her thoughts linger, as Ilona pointed and waved to students all around the room: "The tiny one with platinum hair is Velda, Alice's roomy. Oh, and there's Bernard, Alice's brother—they're from North Dakota. He's nice, but too serious, going to be a preacher. The snitchy-looking one is Gladys Marquist—be careful what you say around her. Oh, here comes Roger. I think he's dreamy, but he's going with a girl who lives off-campus. And up there at front, that's Lawrence Smith—Lawrence of Arabia, we call him—because he has such a far-off look in his gorgeous eyes. Magnificent, isn't he?" She paused, then rushed on. "See the thin one over there? Ross. He's never still for a minute. And—"

"Wait a minute! I can't remember all that. I'm Elizabeth. You're Ilona. This is Alice. That's all I can handle at once."

"Sorry, I do tend to get carried away. But it is so good to see everybody again!" Ilona led the way to a long wooden table, and the three of them found seats. Velda—whom

Elizabeth did remember was Alice's roommate and therefore lived across the hall from her room—joined them.

Alice started to say something in her soft voice, when a fellow with sleek brown hair and wearing an argyle sweater vest and bow tie stood at the front of the room and tapped a spoon on a glass for attention. "Hi." He gave an awkward little side to side wave with his fingers spread out. Everyone laughed and called out, "Hi."

"For anyone who doesn't know," he continued, "I'm Charles Stoddard, ASB president for this year, so you're going to have to put up with me quite a bit." Again his audience laughed. "I just wanted to say welcome back to you returnees and welcome here to the freshmen. I thought about asking the freshmen to stand up and pray in unison, but that seemed kind of mean at our first meal here." About twenty-five heads nodded agreement, while the non-freshmen called out that it sounded like a good idea.

"Seriously, though, I am going to call on a freshman to lead us in prayer. Eliot Hamilton comes from a missionary family like I do, so I know he won't mind being put on the spot. Right, Eliot?"

Elizabeth gasped, and her hands flew to smooth her hair. Eliot looked as manicured perfect as the first time she had seen him. It was silly of her to worry, though. He would never remember her anyway.

After the prayer, bowls of mashed potatoes, gravy, and green beans, and platters of fried chicken were carried from the kitchen by students and passed around the tables. Chatter about what everyone had done that summer and plans for the coming school year, who had come back and who had had to drop out and work, or who got married, carried them through the meal.

At the end of the meal Charles Stoddard explained the campus tradition of having "family worship" after dinner each night. He gave a short meditation, then asked that all stand and sing "Now the Day Is Over."

". . . night is drawing nigh. Shadows of the evening steal across the sky." Ilona's clear soprano led out at their table, and Elizabeth followed. She had been here such a short time, and already she had a small sense that they were family.

"You have a beautiful voice," Elizabeth told her roommate when the song ended.

"Thanks. So do you. Second soprano? You should join the Glee Club. We meet Tuesdays and Thursdays before dinner in the chapel." Ilona picked up her dishes and moved in her graceful way toward the kitchen, greeting friends on every side as she went.

Elizabeth observed the busy, noisy room for a few moments, then turned to pick up her own dishes.

Surely it was a spot of gravy on the floor. She was nervous—her first night with everything so new—but she wasn't so nervous she couldn't walk. It had to be gravy. Nothing else could explain why one second she was walking toward the kitchen and the next she was sprawled face down across a table. No, she hadn't really focused on the fact that the tables sat at angles, so that each extended a bit farther into the aisle than the one before it, but surely she couldn't have just walked into it.

"Gravy on the floor," she declared to the owner of the hands helping her right herself. Then she blinked and gasped. "Oh—you." And as the appalling fact hit home she repeated, "It's you." She was painfully conscious of the fact that whether or not there had been gravy on the floor, there was now gravy down the front of her flowered dress.

"Miss Allen, isn't it? You seem to have a fondness for stretching across tables."

Nothing in the entire world that Eliot Hamilton could have chosen to say could have embarrassed her more. Elizabeth felt the hot blood rising to her face as she remembered the day last summer in Griswold's office. She had hoped Eliot hadn't seen. Now she knew he had.

"Sorry if I embarrassed you." For a moment he looked truly sorry—maybe even more embarrassed than she was—then he turned and began gathering her scattered cutlery. "I thought I recognized you earlier, so I came over to say hello."

Elizabeth still didn't answer.

"Er—guess I chose a bad moment. Er—I'll just take these to the kitchen for you, shall I?" He picked up her plate and water glass. "Can I do anything else for you?"

Gravy or no gravy on her blouse, she forced herself to stand straight. "You've done enough. Thank you."

Again a look of confusion, almost hurt, flickered in his eyes before it was covered by a flash of humor. He gave a mocking bow and walked away.

Elizabeth watched the back of his smooth blond head. Why did she have to make matters so much worse by being stiff and tongue-tied? Even if it was his fault. She could have thought of something to say if she hadn't caught the sparkle of amusement in his brown eyes. *Oh, dear Lord. Don't let him tell. Please.* If people started laughing at her or, worse, got the idea she was loose, there would be nowhere to hide on such a small campus. And she knew that no matter how she might try, there would be little hope of avoiding Mr. Eliot Hudson Taylor Hamilton.

For the next few days, however, although she saw Eliot at meals, chapel, and in classes, she was not obliged to have any individual contact with him. Indeed, campus rules that forbade young men to accompany young women about the campus suited her just fine. She did see more social interaction between classes and after meals than she suspected Dean Wenschler would have approved, but Elizabeth found it easy to avoid such contact as she became increasingly busier and busier.

Glee Club and women's volleyball on top of her schedule of general psychology, English 1, history, science, and biblical literature, plus the daily routine of meals, chapel, and study hours, kept her more than busy. But it was a new kind of busyness, far removed from the physical labor of farm life, and she loved it. Even Dean Wenschler's rules, which everyone complained about heartily, didn't bother Elizabeth.

Then, at the end of the second week, chapel was replaced by class meetings.

As freshman class sponsor, Mrs. Bauchman, the education professor, explained that their chief business that day would be to elect class officers. "The main duties of your officers will be to plan the class social you will have each semester, and preside at these monthly class meetings. Try to select officers with spiritual qualities you can look to for leadership."

Then each class member briefly introduced himself, including giving his name, where he was from, and his intended major. From that they went straight to the nominating and voting process.

When the dust had cleared, Elizabeth was amazed to find that Eliot Hamilton had been elected class president, and she secretary. At least she knew then that the story of her struggle with Griswold hadn't gone around the men's dorm, or she would never have been elected. That pleased her, although the thought of working so closely with Eliot didn't.

It was easy to see that Eliot would do well majoring in oratory and expression. He assumed easy control of the remainder of the meeting. "OK, let's have some suggestions for our class social. We only get one a semester, so let's make it good. I think it should be fairly soon. That will help us get to know one another. Any ideas?"

Suggestions flew. Weiner roast. Hayride. Sing-a-long. Hike and picnic.

"Whoa." The new president held up his hand. "Is my secretary taking notes?"

Elizabeth had not brought her books into chapel with her, so she didn't even have a piece of paper. She scrambled around and borrowed while the class watched and grinned. At last she was organized. She held her head high. "Ready."

"Why don't you come down here where you can hear better?" Eliot indicated a small table beside the speaker's platform.

"I can hear fine from here." She bent over her paper and began listing the suggestions already made.

In the end they decided on a hayride to be held in October. "Will you check on a date for us?" Eliot delegated to his secretary. "We can't have a social during fall revival, and we can't come too close to exams. You work out what seems best and report back."

"Yes, sir." Those around her laughed at her reply accompanied by a smart salute. She would have liked to ask him if his mother ever taught him to say please.

8

Elizabeth soon found that the class president and other members were willing supporters, cheering on her progress and encouraging her to do more, but they were not particularly willing workers. Of course, Eliot was busy on the debate team and in Christian Workers' Band. Elizabeth found her own busyness increasing, as she too was drawn into the work of CWB, helping on Sunday evenings at the North Side Mission, which a local pastor had opened to take the gospel to those living in huts on the far side of the railroad tracks.

She had turned down two of Eliot's invitations to go with him. But when Ilona asked her to join a women's quartet to sing for the Sunday evening service that would follow the serving of soup, Elizabeth couldn't say no. And when she saw the gleam that sprang to hungry eyes as she handed around steaming bowls of chicken vegetable soup, she was glad she hadn't refused.

Then Eliot introduced their quartet, and the girls took off their aprons to sing, "Let the lower lights be burning! Send a gleam across the wave! Some poor fainting, struggling seaman you may rescue, you may save." They were a long way from the sea, but Elizabeth thought the song an appropriate choice.

It seemed even more appropriate when Eliot spoke. He talked about Jesus rescuing Peter from the waves and calming the storm on the Sea of Galilee, and how He could save one from life's difficulties.

He illustrated it with the story of a man with sores on his legs, whom his mother had nursed in China. Too poor to buy bandages, the man had put paper on his sores—when one layer soaked through he added another. "The stench was unbelievable when my mother peeled off the layers and dressed the leg in clean bandages. As she did so, changing the bandages every day, she talked to him of God's love. He showed little response and then went away.

"We didn't hear from him for several weeks. Then one day a woman appeared at the compound and told us she was his wife. Their whole family had become Christian and wanted the missionaries to come take down their idols." He went on to apply the illustration to his listeners' lives.

Elizabeth was amazed that anyone with his smooth good looks and carefree ways knew so much about life's hardships.

After the service the whole team, Eliot and Roger, Elizabeth, Ilona, Alice, and Elsie crowded into the car Eliot had borrowed and journeyed back across town. Somehow Elizabeth ended up sitting by Eliot. She began a tentative conversation. "That was a good sermon."

"Thanks."

He wasn't helping her much.

Then he added, "Your song was good too."

"Thanks."

After another pause she asked, "Are you going to be a preacher?"

He gave a curt nod. "Missionary." It was amazing that anyone who was so fluent in front of a crowd could be so inarticulate. "Roger's going to be a preacher." He nodded toward the back seat where Roger sat with tiny Elsie Tyson on his lap and Alice and Ilona on each side.

With that Elizabeth left the conversing to those in the back seat while she wondered about the man beside her. What was wrong with him? It was as if she had insulted him by complimenting his sermon—and opened an indelicate subject when she asked if he was going to preach. Missionary, he said. Like his parents. Seemed natural enough —yet she had met no one on campus who seemed less suited to such a calling.

She blinked at her own thought. Why in the world would she say that? He was perfect for it: from a missionary family, a fluent speaker, accustomed to preaching and praying in public, already involved in mission work . . .

Still, there was something about him—must be attitude, she decided. He was probably rebelling. Knew he was called to the mission field but didn't want to go. That would explain what always struck her as his too-nonchalant attitude, his willingness to laugh at the rules. *Definitely rebellion,* she decided. *Probably wants to make a lot of money and have fun instead of taking the gospel to the heathen. And yet—* She looked sideways at his fine features.

When they parked in the sanded space between Gideon Hall and The Club, Eliot delayed her while the others moved ahead. "Elizabeth, may I take you to prayer meeting Wednesday?"

She was so surprised she wasn't sure which shocked her more, the fact that he asked her or the impropriety of the suggestion.

"You know men aren't allowed to go with women to church!" *See,* she thought, *a missionary candidate shouldn't be out to break the rules.*

He grinned in the way that she had heard so many girls in the dorm giggle over, and threw both hands into the air. "Heaven forbid! I merely meant that, if you are going to prayer meeting, and I'm going to prayer meeting, we might just happen to choose seats that aren't too far apart —like right next to each other, for example."

Elizabeth frowned. "Isn't that breaking the rules in spirit? I don't think that would be right."

He shook his head and grinned again. His manner wasn't really mocking, but . . . "As you wish. Perhaps I'll be permitted to sit by you on the hayride, then? We'll have social privileges for the party, you know." Without waiting for her to answer he went on. "I take it everything is ready? I suppose I should have called another committee meeting, but there's been so little time."

"Everything's ready," she assured him with a toss of her head.

"Good. Knew I could count on you." He turned toward the girls' dorm. "We'd better hurry. The others are ahead of us."

They caught up with the rest of the team on the porch of Hadley Hall. There was no time to say good night, for Dean Wenschler opened the door. "Good night, gentlemen." She closed the door on her own last word.

"Ladies." The dim light from the single bulb overhead glinted off the steel rims of her glasses. "You were not going about unchaperoned in the company of gentlemen, surely?"

Ilona stepped forward. "Oh, no, dean. We've been holding the service at the North Side Mission." When the dean seemed to require something more, she added hastily, "It was most rewarding work."

"Very well. To your rooms then. You have just half an hour until lights out." They were halfway up the first flight of stairs when she added, "Oh, Miss Allen. There is a message for you."

Sickness in the family was all Elizabeth could think of as she backed down the stairs. Mother? Alex? Suddenly she missed them terribly. But when she looked at the note Dean Wenschler gave her she discovered quite another problem.

The farmer who had promised them a wagon and team for the hayride found he was going to need it, as he didn't have all his corn in yet. And the hayride was in five days. It would spoil everything if they had to postpone it. The scheduling for the last week in October had been perfect since it made the social a Halloween party as well—many people even had costumes planned.

She was still worrying about the problem after lights out as she tried to pray for her family and friends at home. "Help Mother and Alex be comforted." She knew they mourned for baby Eldon. "And help Boyd settle down." The last note from her mother had told of her worries about the seventeen-year-old's restlessness. "And strengthen Father." Whenever she saw him in her mind she recalled how tired he always looked last summer. "And help Clarey and Mavis—keep her well and make the baby strong." Kathryn's last letter had revealed that Elizabeth was to become an aunt next spring.

It was when she went on to pray for Aunt Nelly and her family that Elizabeth had an answer to her problem—Alvina and Myron, farming out Twelfth Avenue Road just beyond the college, would have a haywagon. If only she could get a message to him, she was sure Myron would help her.

After chapel the next morning she caught up with Eliot. She explained the problem. "Do you think you could borrow a car again and drive out to make the arrangements? I'll send a letter of introduction."

"No need to do that. Father and I stayed with the Jaynes when he spoke in Kuna last summer, remember?"

"Oh. Yes." She still blushed at the memory.

"Mrs. Jayne's daughter Vina was there then. I think she'll remember me. But just to make sure, why don't you come along? What time is your last class over?"

"Oh. No, I couldn't." Would this man never stop making improper suggestions? But she didn't want to sound like a prude—again. "I—uh—have volleyball practice. And our quartet practice. And loads of studying."

"OK, OK." He held up his hand. "I get the picture. You don't want to go. I'll get Roger to go with me."

She turned to hurry to class, took two steps, still looking at the books in her arms, and walked right into the broad form of Dean Wenschler. "Miss Allen! Must I be forever reminding you that social interaction between men and women is not conducive to the proper spiritual and academic climate of our college?'

"Yes, Dean Wenschler." She had thought of trying to explain that it was business, but Elizabeth knew explanations would be hopeless, and the bell had already rung for class. Miss Benson's English class was the highlight of her day. She hated being late.

Friday evening, thirty-five of the forty freshman, and five chaperones, clambered aboard Myron Sperlin's hay wagon and set off at a slow clip-clop toward Lake Lowell on their pre-Halloween social. Roger, wearing a big red-and-white polka-dot bow tie, sat on the highest pile of straw with his girlfriend, Dora Marie, beside him and plunked out songs on his ukelele.

Elizabeth, who had put a bandana around her head and hung fruit jar rings from her ears in suggestion of a gypsy, sat between Gladys, dressed as a farmer in straw hat and overalls, and tiny Elsie Tyson, who had put a pink bow in her hair and painted red circles on her cheeks as a doll. They leaned back in the clean-smelling straw and sang "Home on the Range" and then "Red River Valley" with the relaxed abandon that only a hayride could induce.

Until they came to the second verse of "Red River Valley," and Elizabeth remembered that the last time she had sung that song had been graduation night. *Oh, Lord, please don't let anything go wrong tonight. Keep us safe.*

It seemed that her prayer was answered. It was a beautiful night. They sat long around the roaring bonfire at the lake, roasting marshmallows and weiners on willow sticks. Once again she was surprised at Eliot's depth when he brought the devotional. She smiled at what a dashing pirate he made, even though the costume seemed an unlikely choice for him. Had she given it any thought, she would have more expected him to wrap himself in a bedsheet and go as a Roman senator—or Greek god. Caesar or Zeus. She was sure he saw himself much more in that light than that of Black Pete.

On the return trip, when the stars were shining clearly overhead and everyone was softly singing choruses ("Give me oil in my lamp, keep me burning, burning, burning . . . ."), Elizabeth turned at a rustle in the straw beside her and discovered that Elsie had been replaced by a tall, blond pirate.

"You did a great job planning this, Madame Secretary."

"It has been fun, hasn't it? I think the class feels much closer now. We know each other in a new way."

"That's what I think." With another slight rustle she felt him clasp her hand under the straw.

She looked around wildly to see if any of the chaperones were watching. None were. And the handclasp did feel nice and warm in the sharp evening air.

"Good thing we had this tonight. It'll be too cold by November."

She hadn't meant it as an invitation, but she didn't protest when he inched slightly closer. It was unlikely anyone would notice in the dark. And she was so comfortable.

Elizabeth spent the next two days jumping every time she came in sight of the dean of women but began to relax by Monday. Wednesday morning she was confident enough to return Eliot's smile as they went into chapel. It was a good thing, because that seemed like the last time anyone smiled for a long time.

As soon as they had sung "Hallelujah, Amen," the college hymn, President Gilchrist rose in an usually somber manner and began speaking in funereal tones.

Elizabeth looked at the other faculty members on the platform. Professor Rutland, the debate coach. Mrs. Benson, her English teacher. Miss Ferney, head of the music department. They looked tight-lipped and pale. What was wrong? Had someone died?

"And so, according to newscasts on the radio this morning, as some of you may have heard. . . "

Everyone looked around blankly. Apparently no one had heard anything.

Dr. Gilchrist cleared his throat emphatically. "And as announced in this morning's paper—" he held up a newspaper "—let me read to you." He adjusted his glasses and the newspaper. "'Market Collapses,' the headline says. 'Confusion reigned on Wall Street yesterday, a day many are calling Black Tuesday, as hysterical selling washed away billons of dollars, threatening disaster to the economy of the entire nation.'"

He read an article headlined "Merchant's Suicide Laid to Stock Losses" and another speculating on massive bank failures.

Elizabeth tried to understand. It sounded terrible, but she found it hard to relate to such happenings. What did this mean to her—to the people around her? Wall Street was thousands of miles away. She didn't know any millionaires. Would the little bank on the corner in Kuna close? She doubted that her father had much money in there, but would it be gone if he did?

She turned at the sound of soft sniffling behind her and was startled to see Ilona in tears. Then she remembered. Ilona's father was a banker. She reached across the back of her seat to squeeze her roommate's hand. But the gesture was never completed, because Dr. Gilchrist was asking the entire student body to stand and move to the front of the chapel. They would spend the rest of the hour on their knees praying for their nation.

9

Confusion reigned in the coming weeks. Reports of market rallies and further plummets alternated every day. John D. Rockefeller led New York bankers in buying large quantities of stocks to support the market. President Hoover declared that America's business basis was sound. Economists stated that stock prices had stabilized and that the outlook was favorable. Yet banks continued to close, stock prices continued to fall, and people continued to lose their jobs.

Two weeks later Elizabeth went to help with the service at the North Side Mission. "Will we be overwhelmed?" she asked Ilona. "From everything we read it seems most of the nation must be homeless and hungry. What if the mission can't handle it all?"

Ilona didn't answer, but her round blue eyes seemed wider than ever. The girls held hands as they stepped across the threshold of the mission.

Inside the door Elizabeth stopped to look, then gave a sigh of relief. It was the same chilly, dingy room filled with unwashed bodies that she had been ministering to for months. Perhaps a few more bodies than before, but there was no sense of panic here, no fear that the soup pots would run empty.

95

Elizabeth learned the reason as she ladled soup into empty bowls. "We had our bank closures here years ago when the farm prices fell," an old woman with a black scarf over her head said. "I know—my son was just starting out as a banker then. Now he works for the railroad somewhere. I hear from him at Christmas."

"What's all the excitement about this here depression?" The man behind her tugged at the suspenders holding up his baggy pants, then held out his soup bowl. "We've been in a depression for ten years, and nobody ever paid us no mind. Now it's catching up with New York and Chicago, and they're going crazy."

The difference seemed to be the sense of fear the news brought to the quiet campus. It was as if a terrible storm were raging on the other side of the mountains, and any day now it could blow over the top to embroil them.

Ilona's fears struck closest to Elizabeth. She came in from class one day to find her usually vivacious roommate sitting on her bed staring blankly at the wall, a crumpled letter by her side. "Ilona, what is it? Has your father's bank . . ?"

"No, not yet." Ilona gave herself a shake. "It's really just the tone of Mother's letter. It would be better if she'd *say* she's worried, instead of sounding so depressed and so desperately brave. With three younger brothers and two sisters at home—I just don't see how I can come back after Christmas. Oh, Elizabeth, I've always been so lucky—everything we needed was just there. I never thought that someday it might be gone. That old woman at the mission—her son was a banker—I can't get her out of my mind. I don't know if I could carry on."

Elizabeth put her arm around her friend's slim shoulders. "Of course you could. You'll have strength for whatever you have to face. God has promised." Elizabeth knew she needed that reminder as much as Ilona did.

In spite of the brave face everyone tried to maintain, however, a great cloud hung over the campus the week before Christmas vacation. Though it wasn't the end of the semester, most professors were giving exams or requiring that final projects be turned in.

But the questions uppermost in all minds were not those asked on examination papers. Everyone was preoccupied with guesses as to what the future would hold. What would things be like when they got home for Christmas? Would they be able to return to school? Would their friends be able to come back? Would the college be able to continue to operate?

Elizabeth felt confident of being able to complete the semester—that had been paid in advance—but what of second semester? Part of the money had rightly gone to Clarey and Mavis. And now that they were to have a baby, perhaps they would need more. Suddenly everything seemed upside down. The richest students, such as Ilona, had the most to fear. The poor ones, such as Edna and Alice, who already had jobs to help pay their tuition, seemed the least worried. Elizabeth was thankful that, although she might have to drop out of school, at least she didn't have to worry about her family going hungry. There would always be milk, eggs, and vegetables on the farm.

Lunch in The Club on the last day before vacation was a tearful event. Charles led the students in singing several carols, but not "Joy to the World" because no one felt joyful. Then he asked Eliot to pray for everyone's safe travel and a blessed time with their families. Friends bade each other farewell, trying to put a smile on calls of "Merry Christmas."

Elizabeth hugged Ilona, knowing she might never see her again. She even smiled at Gladys. Her petty spying seemed so irrelevant in the face of larger troubles.

"Merry Christmas, Eliot."

He turned at her greeting, and it was like a light bulb coming on in the room. Why had she never before seen the kindness in his smile—so like the one that had attracted her to his gentle father last summer?

97

"Elizabeth." With no thought of demerits on either side, he took her hand. "Will you be able to come back?"

His concern seemed so genuine she caught her breath. In the past weeks she had seen some classmates become more frivolous in the face of disaster, and others more closed, less generous, but the effect on Eliot had been beneficial. He had lost his air of superficial casualness and unconcern. Now she could imagine that the person he seemed to be when he preached or prayed was the real Eliot, not the person who skated smoothly through life and was amused by her discomfort.

"Th-thank you," she stammered. "I'll be back. At least to finish the semester. And you?"

He shook his head. "I don't know. I had a job lined up working for a lawyer over vacation. Now—? Retired missionaries just live on faith and their memories, you know." Then he smiled again. "But I don't want to lose touch. If I can't come back, may I write to you?"

Her hesitancy had nothing to do with fear of demerits, but Eliot said, "I don't think there's any rule against it. I could have my sister address the envelope if there is."

Elizabeth laughed. "No, I'm sure even the Wenschler hasn't made a rule against receiving mail. Please write. If you can't come back, that is. But do come back—the debate team needs you."

She often remembered his parting laughter during the next two weeks at home.

And she had been right in thinking that little would be changed on the farm. Her first night home there was a party at the grange hall. The whole community sang carols to Marie's piano playing. Aunt Nelly proudly displayed her newest grandchild, a bouncing nine months old now. Isaiah, seeming suddenly old, sat quietly in the corner.

Although Elizabeth tried to avoid Mr. Griswold, there was no escaping his loud voice that carried so well in the small, wooden hall whenever there was a lull in the singing. "Absolutely nothing to worry about. This correction in the market's the healthiest thing that could have happened to the country. Too much buying on margin. Should be more like me—cash on the head, I always say. Did you see that new Packard I just bought? Every penny cash."

Elizabeth turned to greet Celia with a hug. "Oh, I was afraid you hadn't come! I've been looking for you all evening. How are you? What a beautiful new dress! How's Walter?"

Celia laughed and returned her embrace, then set about at a fast chatter telling Elizabeth how wonderful their honeymoon had been, how much fun she was having buying furniture for her new house, about the old Rudolph Valentino movie Walter had taken her to in Boise, about her new jazz records. But Elizabeth noticed her friend had very little to say about her new husband.

The surprise of the evening was Franklin and Millie. Franklin, just home from business school, had managed to get Millie to quit doing the Charleston long enough to slip an engagement ring on her finger. Elizabeth congratulated them both with a perfectly straight face. No one would ever know of her role in playing Cupid.

Another surprise was how much older Boyd and Alexandra seemed to be. Elizabeth had been away only four months, and yet it seemed that the experience of now being the oldest children at home had produced a markedly maturing effect on them.

Alex had taken over almost all the duties Elizabeth had performed around the house. "Except the chickens," she said. "How did you ever have the patience to raise so many this summer?" And, although Boyd declared he hated farming, he was a reliable worker, much more successful with repairing a broken tractor than nursing a sick cow, but a sturdy help to Merrick.

"And Mother." Elizabeth felt awkward embracing her mother so frequently, and yet she felt she couldn't get enough of her. Now that she was home with her family again she realized how much she had missed them. "I simply didn't have time to get homesick. But, oh, it's so *good* to see you!" Even the lack of electricity, running water, and indoor plumbing seemed almost welcoming—until she woke up her first morning home with her breath frozen on her quilt.

"Oh, Alex, I'd forgotten how cold it can get!" She snuggled deeper in her covers for a few minutes before rushing to the kitchen to dress by the stove.

"Why weren't Clarey and Mavis at the party last night?" she asked her mother when they were doing up the breakfast dishes.

"I wondered about that too," Kathryn answered. "Perhaps Mavis wasn't feeling well. The baby is making her awfully tired."

"Is Clarey excited about it?"

Kathryn started to give a noncommittal answer, but Elizabeth rushed on. "Just think—you'll be a grandmother! You look far too young!" She looked at her mother. It was true. Her mother was forty-four, but still looked like she was in her thirties. Amazing for one who had always worked so hard. "Do you realize you look more like my sister than my mother?" Elizabeth meant it, but it was a two-pronged comment, for she knew she herself had always looked old for her age.

Kathryn laughed. "Oh, my dear. Thank you. Most of the time I feel fifty. I guess it's just good bones and taking care to keep my skin protected from the sun—as I keep reminding my daughters. And good health. I do thank the Lord for health and strength."

That reminded Elizabeth of something else she wanted to ask her mother. "And how's Daddy? He's grayer than when I left."

Kathryn sighed. "He's fine, really. But he works so hard. I think he's always tired. And now the worries about the bank loan."

"Is the bank here in danger of closing?"

100

"I don't think so, but they are sure to get stricter about payments now with everything so uncertain, and farm prices are likely to fall even lower."

Elizabeth could think of nothing to say about that, so she returned to their earlier topic. "When is Mavis—er—" she fumbled for a delicate way to put it "er—when is the blessed event?"

Kathryn shrugged. "Spring. They'll be over for Christmas Eve. You'll see her then."

Elizabeth spent a happy day helping her mother bake pies and cookies for the celebration. By the time Merrick and Boyd came in from the barn that evening the whole house smelled of mincemeat and cinnamon.

After supper Kathryn even sat down at her little-used pump organ and played "Silent Night" in the glow of the parlor stove and the coal oil lamps. Merrick led out in his strong tenor. Elizabeth smiled, she loved to hear her father sing, but he did it so rarely.

Later, in the chill of the sleeping porch, the radiance of the evening followed even if the warmth didn't. She snuggled up to Alexandra. It was so good to be home, but she missed Clarey. They had never shared any unusual closeness as twins sometimes did, but she loved and cared for her generous, cheerful brother. She hoped he was happy. And her father with his pressures and worries—slowly her thoughts became prayers.

Dear God, help them all. Thank You for such a good family. Please take care of them. Then, just as when at college she had prayed for those at home, now she prayed for those she had known at school. For Ilona that her father's bank wouldn't fail and she would be able to return. For Alice and Bernard, who had been unable to make the trip home to North Dakota for Christmas, that they wouldn't be too homesick. Even for Gladys, who must be very unhappy to be so hard to get along with.

Especially she found herself praying for Eliot Hamilton as she saw in memory his kind, open smile, so different from the facade he usually wore. Now that she had seen that it was a facade, she prayed that he would come to accept the mission call he was so obviously fighting. *Let him find peace, Lord. Please.*

Then Christmas came with a blur of memories—of licking gingerbread off her fingers and exchanging small presents around a Christmas tree hung with tinsel and colored-paper chains. Mavis was as cheerful as always, although her face was thinner while the rest of her looked enormous. "Does Dr. Nolte think you're going to have twins?" Elizabeth asked Clarey.

Clarey looked at his wife and smiled in his slow way. "No. Hasn't said anything about it."

"Well, it's no wonder Mavis has been tired. Take good care of her, big brother." She squeezed his hand, knowing that Clarey would always take good care of those in his charge.

Then with another round of hugs from her family, Elizabeth found herself back at school. As she had feared, Ilona was unable to return. Elizabeth knew she would never forget the elegant girl who had been her first friend on campus. Ilona, with her grace and charm, seemed to represent everything Elizabeth wished she could be. But she had no idea how much she would miss Ilona until Dean Wenschler knocked on her door and presented her new roommate—Gladys Marquist.

"The Wenschler knows who needs close watching," Alice and Velda teased when Elizabeth fled to their room across the hall to tell them.

Elizabeth tried to take the uncomfortable situation in good grace. "Well, I prayed for Gladys. Maybe God wants me to do some personal missionary work on her personality." The thought gave her a brief glimpse into what Eliot's struggle over a call might be like. Then she added with a giggle, "The trouble is, Gladys considers me a mission field."

But the thought helped bring into focus a vague feeling she had held in check for some time. She wanted to help Eliot—not just pick up the pieces and make him look good as class president, not just sing when he held a service at the mission but really help him accept his call. She would continue to pray for him, encourage him, and look for an opportunity to talk to him—in spite of the demerits Gladys's observations threatened.

But in the rush of final exams and registering for a new semester such goals had to be put aside, as well as concerns over national economic problems. That wasn't difficult because other than small worries and small economies, the great stock market crash that had so overshadowed all other news for the past months still seemed to be a long way off.

Panic rumors of instant poverty, of government collapse, and of the school's closing were forgotten in the everyday schedule of college life. The steam heat in the dorm rooms was reduced to a minimum when the price of coal rose, and Elizabeth was more thankful than ever for her heavy black Senior Sweater, which she wore everywhere, including to bed. And one morning when she found her tin of tooth powder empty and had no pennies in her purse to purchase a new one, she gladly adopted Gladys's economy of brushing her teeth with baking soda. Life went on.

Then suddenly the depression came much closer home. Aware of the students' financial difficulties, the college was lenient about second semester fees, waiving the requirement that all be paid in advance and allowing monthly installments. But the college had bills to pay too. Students who got too far behind couldn't be allowed to continue. And at the end of February Elizabeth realized she couldn't make her monthly installment.

Her first thought was to get a job. She went to Mrs. Nylander at The Club. She could serve tables and wash dishes like Alice and her friends. But there were no vacancies. Knowing the students' need, Mrs. Nylander had hired to capacity, taking on students to work for their meals.

Overcoming her aversion to her experience last summer, she next went to the campus print shop. At least she had experience to offer. But they had no openings to offer her. What next? She knew heavy janitorial jobs such as caring for the steam heating system were given only to men. With little hope she went to the academic dean to inquire about being a student assistant. It was just as well that her hopes weren't high because, although Dean Cuthbert was kind and encouraging, she explained that such positions were held only by juniors and seniors.

Kicking her feet in the mounds of snow at the edge of the path, Elizabeth made her way back to the dorm.

"What's the matter?" Gladys looked up from her book as Elizabeth flopped down on her creaky bed.

She sighed. "The usual. Money. Bill due next week, and I can't find a job."

Gladys' mouth fell open. "You? I thought you were so rich. Everyone says your father owns a big farm."

"And a big bank debt," Elizabeth added. Then she laughed, thinking how she had struggled over money. *"Rich?* How could anyone think that?"

"Well, you dress so beautifully, and you never seem to worry about extra things like the Glee Club fee, and you're so—so—I don't know—it's just the way you carry yourself, I guess."

Elizabeth was too amazed to answer. Yes, she did have a few nice dresses because her mother was such a skilled seamstress. And she supposed she did have good posture—her mother again—how many times had she told her to stand up straight? But it was the remark about fees that brought a new understanding.

"Gladys, is that why you didn't try out for Glee Club?"

Gladys didn't look up from her book.

"Listen, if I can get the money, I'll pay your fee. I think you'd really enjoy it."

"No thanks. You're too busy to notice, but I work in town every afternoon at the Electric Bakery. No time for rehearsals."

Elizabeth let it drop. If a miracle didn't happen she'd have to quit more than Glee Club. She would have to quit school. But Gladys had given her an idea—she could apply for an off-campus job, even if it would mean giving up most of her activities.

And then the miracle happened. The next day Elizabeth was sitting in her room, alternately studying and worrying about her unpaid bill, when she heard a light, familiar voice call her name.

"Elizabeth!" It couldn't be. That sounded like Alex. "Elizabeth!"

She went to the top of the stairs and peered down. "Mother! Alex!" She raced down the stairs. "How wonderful! Whatever are you doing here?"

"We brought your payment. And Mama let me miss school to do it!" Alex clapped her hands.

"My payment?"

Kathryn nodded. "I knew you were short, but I didn't know what to do about it, so I wrote to Dr. Gilchrist with a suggestion. He wrote back that the college would be glad to accept barter for tuition, so Alex and I fired up the incubator again."

"Oh, Mother." Elizabeth hugged her. "You mean you've come to pay my tuition in *chickens?*"

"A monthly installment." She nodded.

Elizabeth put her hands to her face. She wasn't sure whether she was laughing or crying. "Oh, I've been so worried, and here you two were, turning eggs and plucking chickens all this time."

"Turning eggs is an awful bore." Alex made a face.

"Yes, I seem to remember you mentioned that. But thank you, thank you." Elizabeth hugged her sister.

"Oh," Alex cried, "and we've got more news—Mavis had her baby!"

Elizabeth was suddenly solemn. "Already? Is it all right?" She looked at her mother's furrowed forehead. "What is it? Two months early—more?"

"No, no," Kathryn assured her. "He's fine—doesn't look at all premature. Small, but healthy. It's just strange—with Clarey and Mavis both being so dark you'd think . . . Still, nothing cuter than a red-headed grandchild. Boyd's thrilled—he's sure it's pure Scottish blood, although I remember your father's people as being mostly dark—black Scots, he called his father. His sister had red hair, took her coloring from their mother, he said."

Elizabeth nodded. "Just so they're happy." But still she wondered. They had been gone a long time alone the night of the picnic.

"I think they're happy." Kathryn was quiet for a moment, then, with a little shake, said, "Come on—let's go pay your bill."

Each of them hauled a crate of well-plucked chickens from the back of the Model T and carried it across campus in a procession, right into the business office. A little bookkeeper with deeply marcelled waves looked at them in alarm and fled to find her superior.

Mr. Jenns peered at them first through his steel-rimmed glasses, then over the top of the thick lenses, and finally removed his spectacles and cleaned them. At last Kathryn was assured that the chickens would be valued at the current market price and full credit applied to Elizabeth's bill. Kathryn promised that such monthly payments would be made regularly.

For the rest of the semester, whenever fried chicken, chicken soup, or chicken and noodles were served in The Club—and they frequently were—Elizabeth smiled, knowing of the loving care that had gone into raising those birds.

10

"Eliot, we really need to talk." Elizabeth stopped by his table at The Club after dumping her own used dishes and cutlery.

He looked up from an intense discussion with Larry, blinked as if he didn't recognize her, then grinned in the overly familiar way that never failed to irritate her and yet made her catch her breath at the same time. "Yes. Right. Anytime you say. Go to prayer meeting with me tonight?"

"Eliot, you know that's not allowed. Look, Campus Day is coming up fast. Freshmen have to clean the ad building—that means organizing teams for washing windows, scrubbing floors, dusting. We'll need rags, brooms, mops . . ." When she saw Eliot's eyes stray back to the newspaper clipping he'd been arguing over with Larry she gave up.

This semester she had been busier than ever as the NCC choir and orchestra added to their schedule a weekly Sunday broadcast from the college church by direct wire to the studio of KIDO in Boise. It was thrilling to be involved in such a project—sending gospel music to hundreds, maybe thousands, of homes over the seeming magic of radio waves.

But the added activity had left even less opportunity to talk with Eliot. As important as it was that they get the class organized for the annual spring cleaning day, that was the mere surface of what she wanted to talk to him about. Ever since she had determined to pray for him and seek a chance to discuss his spiritual conflict with him, her concern had increased and her opportunities decreased.

This time it did seem that Eliot had a good excuse. He was part of the four-man team that would soon be competing for the Southern Idaho Intercollegiate Debate Championships. One of Idaho's congressmen, Representative French, had given the college a bound set of the *Congressional Record* for use by the Forensic Society, and it seemed that the team was bent on memorizing the whole set.

Elizabeth was amazed. She had never seen the rather slaphappy Eliot show so much dedication. Anyone sitting within two tables of the debaters at any meal in The Club could hear them arguing among themselves on the topic "Resolved: That the nations of the world should adopt a plan of complete disarmament except such forces as are needed for police purposes."

As Elizabeth listened to their discussions she recalled her father's thoughts on the subject, especially when Ross quoted Senator Borah, giving the cause of isolationism added emphasis with thuds of his fist on the table. One of those sudden, brief waves of longing for home that Elizabeth had discovered could come over her without warning made her lay down her buttered roll and offer a silent prayer for her family—and for her nation.

Campus Day dawned tingling clear. A brisk breeze had done its part by sweeping the sky clear of clouds. Across the campus students raked, mowed, trimmed, and called to one another out the open windows they were washing.

Elizabeth had assigned herself to head the task she assumed would be the least popular but with which she was most familiar—scrubbing floors. She had given Gladys what she thought the easiest—dusting. Eliot was to do what he did best—supervise.

Elizabeth had just poured out a nice pool of soapy water and was swishing it around with her brush when Eliot approached her. She sat back, leaning into the corner, and looked up at him.

"Ha, got you cornered." He grinned and knelt down beside her. "I've been wanting to talk to you for ages."

Her heart leaped. She'd been wanting to talk to him too—although this seemed like a strange place.

They were interrupted by Gladys hurrying around the corner brandishing a dust rag. "I'm not going on with this, Elizabeth. You gave me the worst job. The dust makes me snee—" A violent sneeze caught her. At the same moment she stepped onto the soapy water.

Only Eliot's lightning reflexes prevented disaster. He sprang up and caught Gladys before she could crash onto the cement floor.

She looked at him with startled eyes. "Oh! Oh, Eliot. Thank you." Then she remembered herself and primly shook herself free of his grasp. "Holding women in the ad building!" She stalked off, apparently not realizing she had knocked the bucket of water all over Elizabeth.

Elizabeth threw her brush into the soggy mess, leaned back, and laughed. "Do you suppose she'll report herself?" She choked, wiping her eyes with the back of her hand.

"Talk about a crisis of conscience." Eliot shook his head. "And to think I thought I had tough decisions to make."

Elizabeth sobered immediately. She wanted to ask him more. But then Lawrence Smith strode around the corner.

"Hamilton. Listen to this. What do you say to Borah's argument that—"

"Watch out for the water!" Elizabeth cried.

Lawrence stopped, glared at the puddle of water around him in his level-eyed way, and continued as if it weren't there. "Borah says—"

Eliot took his colleague by the elbow and led him down the hall. "Aren't you supposed to be raking the lawn?" They disappeared up the stairs.

Even though she was soaked, Elizabeth returned to her scrubbing, but her heart wasn't in it. She wanted to talk to Eliot. She had been concerned for him for months, and this was her first opening to say anything. She hoped it wouldn't be her last.

It proved to be the last for some time. The following week Glee Club began preparing for their spring concert with added rehearsals every evening, and that weekend the debate team went to the College of Idaho in Caldwell for the most important tournament of the year.

At Sunday noon dinner in The Club, Professor Rutland, the debate coach, presented a shiny, brass loving cup to the team, who had returned victorious—state intercollegiate champions. "And as two members of the team, Mr. Hamilton and Mr. Arabia—" the room broke up with laughter, and Coach Rutland grinned "—forgive me, Lawrence, but that suits you so much better than the Smith you were born with. Anyway, since these two men are only freshmen, we can look forward to a great deal more glory coming to NCC from our debaters."

Elizabeth joined in the enthusiastic applause.

The presentation would normally have been made in chapel, but Monday was the beginning of Spring Revival with a special missionary speaker, Lottie Richardson, an NCC graduate, who would be returning to Africa in May. Accordingly, all secular activities such as debate were put in the background to make more time for twice daily services, special prayer meetings, and personal devotions.

The first morning in chapel the members of the Foreign Missionary Band all sat on the platform, and FMB president Howard Schwartz, whose parents were presently serving in Swaziland, welcomed Miss Richardson. Elizabeth noticed that Eliot sat in the back row of the group, his features immobile.

Lottie Richardson was a stirring speaker, holding her overflow audience on the edge of their seats. The service was open to the public, and the walls were lined with people who couldn't find a seat but were happy not to be left standing in the halls behind the auditorium as many others were. It seemed everyone in the room held his breath as Miss Richardson recounted story after story of the overt evil the missionaries encountered as they battled the demon powers of the witch doctors, and of the miracles God never failed to perform.

Elizabeth could feel the excitement of challenges such as missionaries faced: working to your utmost to help people, fighting the forces of evil, bringing light to the darkest corners of the earth where men and women had never heard the gospel. What a thrill Eliot must be feeling—looking forward to having part in all that. Surely this was just what he needed to help him yield to his call with enthusiasm. Elizabeth smiled at the thought and looked up, seeking his eyes on the back row of the platform. But the look on his face was hard, shuttered.

On Friday, Miss Richardson painted another graphic picture of her work: accounts of conversions amid gruesome tortures and tribulations. She spared none of the hardships of her work, played down anything that could smack of glamour, and at the end asked all who would be willing to answer such a call, should the Lord place one on their hearts, to come forward to pray. The response was immediate. There was scarcely an occupied seat in the auditorium as everyone surged forward.

Elizabeth, herself moving to the front, caught just a glimpse of Eliot. He had been one of the first to respond. He must have left his seat even before Miss Richardson finished speaking. *Thank You, Lord!* She joined the fervent prayers, praises, and snatches of choruses that filled the auditorium. The time came and went for the next classes to start, and still the students prayed, some leaving, others —who had left—returning to pray.

At last Dr. Gilchrist, after repeated attempts, managed to call the assembly to order for a testimony time.

Howard Schwartz told how he had left Africa determined never to return. He had seen what his parents had suffered. He had no intention of living a life like that. For three years he had sturdily resisted God's call, telling himself it wasn't God, just a natural feeling that he should follow in his family tradition. But this fall, the stock market crash had shown him graphically how valueless earthly treasures were. On October 29 he had surrendered wholeheartedly to God and never had he been happier.

Howard's testimony set off another time of praise and prayer, and Dr. Gilchrist abandoned his attempt to conduct an ordered service.

Elizabeth was too thrilled even to pray. Surely those words were exactly what Eliot needed to hear. Surely that was his story too. She looked for him. The spot he had occupied earlier was empty. Had he gone out? She turned around. Perhaps he had gone off to pray by himself in a quieter atmosphere.

Then she saw him. Sitting as if frozen in the back of the auditorium. His eyes were hard, his mouth drawn in a bitter line. She went to him. "Eliot?"

He blinked but didn't answer. It seemed he feared losing his steely control if he unbent the very least.

"Eliot, I'm praying for you."

She thought he was going to remain silent, but at last he said, "Don't bother. God doesn't hear my prayers. Why should He hear ones you pray for me?"

She laid a hand on his arm. She didn't care how many demerits they gave her. "Eliot, don't fight it. You heard what Howard said. You can be as happy as he is."

"I would be if God wanted me."

She couldn't have heard right. "Wanted you for what?"

"Anything. Always I've wanted to follow in my father's footsteps. I never resisted like Howard. Nothing in the world ever seemed so wonderful as being a missionary to

112

China—just like Hudson Taylor. How many times did I hear that when I was growing up!"

The bitterness in his eyes gradually softened with nostalgia as he told her about the mission compound where he had spent his growing up years: the hospital, church, Bible school, and homes built of handmade bricks all surrounded by a nine-foot wall, standing serene among trees planted by earlier missionaries.

"The language is so difficult they say the devil invented it to keep the Chinese from hearing the gospel. But I grew up speaking it—and still God doesn't want me to preach in it."

"But I don't understand. I thought you were fighting a call."

He shook his head. "I was begging God for one. But no more. I'm through begging."

She thought for a moment. "But isn't the desire you just described—isn't that a call? Maybe you have one and don't know it."

"I thought so for a long time. Hoped so. But there's a difference. You heard Howard—no matter how little he wanted it, he knew he had one. I'm just the opposite. When I think of the future, of what I want to do, there's no light on it. I have no sense of God's blessing. There's no sense of His guiding when I pray or read the Bible. Obviously He doesn't want me."

"Now that's nonsense. How long has this been going on?"

"At least two years, I guess. Ever since I've been saying I wanted to be a missionary."

"Did you ever think it might be Satan tempting you?"

"I don't know. I just know God isn't speaking to me. I'm not good enough."

"Now that is too much." The common sense example Kathryn had always set for her daughter took over. "You're just sitting here feeling sorry for yourself. You can't expect God to bless such self-centeredness. When you were on the mission field and things went bad—would you sit around and mope there?"

"So what do you suggest I do?" He still sounded down in the dumps, but Elizabeth thought she could detect the glimmer of a twinkle in his brown eyes.

"Same thing my mother always told me to do when things were tough—get up and get to work. If you can't work on what you *want* to do, work on what you *have* to do. I assume you have classes to study for and forensics to work on? Go get busy."

The fervent prayer still rising from the front of the chapel covered his low chuckle. "What a tonic you are, Elizabeth Allen. Has anybody tried to recruit you for the debate team yet?"

11

If Elizabeth's medicine didn't solve Eliot's problem, at least it spurred him to more work, which included taking on file clerk and errand boy duties for Ted Kirkland, Nampa's leading lawyer. His having done similar work during vacations at home in Spokane helped him land this plum job even when work was so scarce.

Elizabeth rejoiced in her friend's good fortune and began wondering what she would be able to find for a summer job. But first there were all the end of the year activities, including the Glee Club concert. The last payment of chickens was due, so the whole family, including Aunt Nelly, drove in on a warm Friday evening in May.

The girls had made blue satin drapes to wear over dark dresses and had put their pennies and nickels together to buy a white carnation with blue ribbons for Miss Ferney.

The conductor welcomed the audience. "And we hope that the pleasant harmony of this evening will be a perfect ending to a year that has been full of turmoil and triumphs."

Elizabeth wasn't certain how much absolute success the year had held. It seemed that most of the questions the year had raised still lingered, but the fact that so many of them had simply held on to the end was a triumph in itself.

She looked at her mother sitting proudly between Merrick and Aunt Nelly. It seemed impossible that the last time she had sung like this was a year ago—before Eldon had been born and died, before Rudy had drowned, before Celia had married, or Clarey and Mavis married and had little Tommy, before the stock market crashed, before she had met Eliot. How could so much happen in just one year? What would happen in the next year? In the next three, if she could finish her degree?

Already they were at their final number, "The Tales of the Vienna Woods." At Miss Ferney's direction the girls linked arms and swayed back and forth in alternating rows. "Away, away, with your dreams come away, away . . ." Elizabeth thought it was the most beautiful song she had ever sung.

Kathryn had wonderful news for her after the concert. "Mrs. Oldham came over Monday."

Elizabeth was so removed from her Kuna school days that it took her a moment to realize her mother was talking about the wife of the school superintendent—the one who had awarded her the Senior Sweater.

She nodded, and Kathryn continued. "Mr. Oldham has been awarded a scholarship to study at the College of Idaho for the summer, and his wife wants to take some art classes. They want you to go with them and take care of their children. It won't pay much, but—"

Alex interrupted her. "But we'll raise chickens for you."

"Oh, Alex, thank you! It's a wonderful offer." Then Elizabeth paused. "But that would mean I'd be away from home all summer."

"Better not turn down a job offer."

She turned at the voice. "Eliot! Were you eavesdropping?"

He grinned. "No. I just came over to thank Mrs. Jayne again for her hospitality last summer."

Aunt Nelly recognized him immediately and hugged him soundly.

Then Eliot went on. "Seriously, I'm going to be staying on in Nampa. Mr. Kirkland's offered me a room in his basement, and jobs in Spokane are scarce as eyebrows on chickens, so I can't refuse."

"Well, then—" Nelly hugged them both "—now we won't be all that far apart. We'll just get together whenever we can, and thank the good Lord for His blessings."

And that's what Elizabeth did. She especially tried to remember to thank Him when the three Oldham children, Chip (age eight), Clarissa (six), and Molly (three), were in one of their rowdy moods, which seemed to be most of the time. The Oldhams had borrowed a two-bedroom trailer from Mrs. Oldham's sister to live in for the summer. The children shared a bed. Elizabeth slept on the couch. There was little room to play indoors, but Elizabeth took the children to the park every day.

"Chip, come down out of that tree right now!" Molly squirmed in her arms as Elizabeth repeated her command for the third time. "Chip, your parents will be back from the library any minute, and I have to get supper started."

Reluctantly the eight-year-old slid down the trunk, removing only a small patch of skin from his leg. But it was a sufficient amount to keep him howling all the way back to the trailer as Elizabeth dragged the tired, dirty children the three blocks. The work was far easier physically than if she had been on the farm, but at times like this she would have traded it all for a nice field of corn to hoe.

Then she reminded herself of how lucky she was to have a job and how good Mr. Oldham's recommendation would look on her résumé when it came time to find a teaching job, although that day seemed far in the distance.

It was late August before Aunt Nelly's prediction that they would all get together that summer came true. In spite of the depression and reports of drought and dustbowl in parts of the country, crops in the Boise Valley were bountiful and would be celebrated as usual at Nampa's annual harvest festival and rodeo. Each community around Nampa had nominated a girl to be festival queen, and Grace Sperlin was Kuna's nominee. It seemed the entire community had turned out to cheer her in the three-mile parade that opened the festivities.

The Oldhams brought Elizabeth and their children in from Caldwell, and they joined the Sperlins, Jaynes, and Allens at their chosen viewing spot on the lawn of the Dewey Palace Hotel.

Just before the parade began, Nelly came up with a big grin on her face. "Didn't I tell you we'd all be together? See who I found." She patted Eliot on the back. "Now you youngsters go find a good viewing spot down front. I'm gong to stand on that nice shady veranda. I've heard tell it'll take this parade a full hour to pass any one spot, so I have no intention of standing here in the sun."

Regardless of the heat, the viewers drew forward when the band boomed its announcement of the start of the parade. Twenty-two princesses from all over the valley rode by in greenery-draped open cars, waving and smiling.

"There she is!" "Hi, Grace!" The cheers were loud for Kuna's favorite daughter. Elizabeth thought she had never seen a prettier girl than Grace, sitting up on the back of the little roadster in a white dress with a sparkly tiara in her blond curls. And one glance at Eliot standing beside her told Elizabeth that he never had either.

Banner-draped cars, local officials, music groups, costumed school children, floats sponsored by merchants displaying their wares and farmers their produce rolled by. Elizabeth's favorite was the float with a six-foot-diameter Bermuda onion fashioned of paper with a sign proclaiming, "Nampa onions, the best in the world."

Following close on the heels of the parade was the arrival of the bicycle marathon race from the state capitol in Boise. A local boy won by finishing the twenty-some mile course in one hour and three minutes. Then everyone moved toward the refreshment stands set up on the lawn of the Dewey Palace and enjoyed lemonade and the antics of a local businessman dressed up as the mythical Chief Nampah.

There Grace joined her friends. Flushed and glowing from the parade, she looked even prettier than before as she received everyone's congratulations—and an introduction to Eliot by Aunt Nelly.

"You're all coming to the pageant, aren't you?" Grace asked, and Nelly assured her they all were, although Elizabeth wasn't sure how long the Oldhams intended to stay.

She needn't have worried, however. No one missed the pageant, "The Kingdom of Plenty," staged in the Majestic Theatre that evening. As the centerpiece of the show, the princesses, all in pastel dresses, sang the theme song written especially for the pageant to the accompaniment of a thirty-five-piece violin orchestra.

And when Grace Sperlin, looking like a fairy queen, stepped forward to sing the solo part, Elizabeth saw the look in Eliot's eyes. She caught her breath at the pain in her throat. She had never known jealousy before. She had perhaps been mildly envious—really, more curious as to what it would be like to be in another's place—when she had seen Celia's affluent lifestyle or Millie's popularity, but she had never before experienced actual jealousy. It was an ugly, dark-brown feeling. She didn't want to have anything to do with feelings like that.

But almost as quickly as the feeling came, it was followed by another, even more alarming. If she was jealous of how Eliot looked at another girl, she must care a great deal for him. All year he had alternately embarrassed her, irritated her, and aroused her concern. It had never entered her mind she could love him. That was such a strong word—surely she didn't mean *love*. She looked at the handsome face in the semidarkness beside her, and her heart lurched. Whatever the exact word was, she certainly cared deeply.

She felt dizzy. She would have liked to leave right then, to get alone and think all this through, but there was no place to go. So she sat stiff and still, letting the pageant flow around her until it was time to leave and she could go back to Caldwell with the Oldhams to put their three very excited children to bed.

The next day they all returned to the ceremony in Lakeview Park, where the Festival Queen was chosen by lot. Elizabeth was never sure whether she was sorry for Grace or sorry for her own relief when the girl from Meridian drew the winning number and had the wreath of flowers placed on her head. Elizabeth only knew that she hated herself for the smallness in her that would deny queenship to a lifelong friend.

Yet when Eliot offered his arm to Grace to escort her around the elaborate booths of grange displays, showing the finest flowers, fruit, and vegetables in the valley, she was glad that she could flee with the excuse of taking the Oldham children to the carnival.

Elizabeth thought her secret was safe, but five days later when she returned home for a brief stay before going back to college, Kathryn invited her to sit a spell on the porch, then told her straight out that she had seen and understood.

"But how could you?" Elizabeth was amazed.

"Because I felt exactly the same way once. They say history repeats itself. It's sure true in this case. I've never told anybody—haven't thought of it myself for years—but I once thought your father was in love with Marie."

"Father? In love with Grace's mother?"

"Yes—long before he was your father, or Marie a mother, of course." Recalling, her eyes took on a faraway look, and a small smile played around her mouth. "I had invited Marie to come out to Idaho to live with me after my papa died. She came all the way from Nebraska. She was a

120

wonderful companion, but I had failed to consider how beautiful and talented she was, how eclipsed I felt next to her—especially when Merrick smiled at her."

"What did you do?"

"I perked up and paid more attention to him. I always tended to be a bit too independent for my own good." She grinned. "Like you, my dear."

"Mmm," was all Elizabeth said.

"And I carried on. It sounds almost too simple to bother mentioning, but I've found that much of life comes to that. Determine what's right, and carry on—with your head up, if you can. Sometimes that's the hardest part. So many times when we came to the desert I just wanted to go put my head under the pillow, but I didn't—not very often, anyway."

Elizabeth looked beyond their own small lawn with a few faded roses still clinging to the fence, on out toward the desert where the sagebrush bloomed its sickly yellow flower, then on to the purple mountains beyond. She nodded slowly.

"Yes. Carry on. Just carry on."

12

And carry on she did. They all did. As Kathryn had said, it was all they could do. For the depression that had at first seemed so far away now drew closer. Most of those who started college together as freshmen were still there three years later at the end of Elizabeth's junior year, plus several who had been upperclassmen and had dropped out to work for a while, then came back. They were a small group, but close, drawn together by shared goals, shared spiritual values, and shared adversity.

Elizabeth found work at Samaritan Hospital just across the street from NCC, facing the leafy green park. Since the nursing school, founded ten years before by Dr. Thomas Mangum as a training school for nurses and medical missionaries, operated year-round, Elizabeth could live in the nurses' quarters while working in every capacity from file clerk to cook's assistant to cleaning woman.

She continued to work there a few hours a week during her junior year. That meant giving up volleyball and basketball, but she was able to continue with Glee Club, which was more important to her. As always, she kept her grades up. She never lost sight of her ultimate goal to be a teacher.

In the spring of their junior year, money couldn't be found to publish a yearbook. But the seniors proudly received their diplomas to the strains of the college hymn, "Hallelujah! Amen!" —then went out to seek jobs in the worst year yet of the depression. And Elizabeth and Eliot became seniors.

That summer the biggest bank in Nampa closed one week before the harvest festival, carrying the festival board's deposits with it. The immediate response of the board was to cancel the festival, but determined businessmen, who had themselves learned the secret of carrying on, pledged the money to back the event and held the most successful festival and rodeo ever.

But the festival wasn't the only organization with its savings in Central Bank. NCC lost $400 in the closure. Dr. Gilchrist immediately launched an economy program and fund-raising campaign. "I am determined to keep Northwest Christian's doors open," he announced in chapel to applause and cheers from students and faculty. "Our dedicated faculty has agreed to continue working for reduced salaries, and the college has offered them housing in the dormitories. We know you students will make them welcome."

Elizabeth clapped along with the others. Any restriction on dorm life that might result from such a plan would be far better than closing the school. Besides, she'd been living in the same building with the Wenschler for more than three years now. Nothing could be more restrictive than that. The president's next announcement, however, caused her more concern.

"In order to reduce the strain on our heating system caused by allowing the ad building to cool over the weekends and then firing the boilers for Monday mornings, classes will be held on Saturdays as well."

Elizabeth caught her breath. What about her work at the hospital? And Eliot's for Mr. Kirkland? She understood what Dr. Gilchrist was saying about shortening the school year so that students would have more time to earn money in the summer, but they had to get through this year first.

123

Dr. Gilchrist was concerned that they get through it without freezing. "Even with these measures," he continued, "the need is great. Our heating system must be repaired, as well as the roofs on the women's dorm and the ad building." He went on to outline the fund-raising plan he was launching.

The college and community shared Dr. Gilchrist's determination that Northwest Christian's doors should remain open, but the question as to whether or not those doors would open onto heated rooms was a growing concern as the funds trickled in slowly, then seemed to dry up.

"What we need is something to really spark the campaign. Something to bring prestige to the college so people all around the state will support it," Eliot, again class president, explained to the twenty-three members of the senior class at their first meeting of the year. "NCC is *our* college. It's given a lot to us. Now it's our turn to give something to it."

Elizabeth, again class secretary—it seemed some things never changed—waited to take notes. There were many heartfelt speeches about how much NCC meant to each student, much expression of the opinion that, indeed, they must do *something* and that anything they did should have double value because it would show the community how much the students cared—it wasn't just the administration's college. But there were few concrete suggestions.

Finally Alice ventured to propose that the class sponsor a musical evening for the public. Tall, square-built Enoch Gertsen suggested a Buy-a-Shingle program to finance the new roofs. Someone else offered the idea of going door-to-door with flyers. Elizabeth duly noted the ideas, but her mind wandered.

She was always amazed that time could flow so quickly—that she could be starting her final year in college. Through all the struggles they were all still here, their heads crammed with knowledge, their lives enriched by friendship, their spirits broadened by experiencing God's power. Yet—Elizabeth looked around and wondered how much they had really changed.

Roger and Dora had broken up last year, and Roger now seemed to be sweet on Alice; Bernard and Velda had announced their engagement last spring; her better understanding of Gladys had led to an eased atmosphere in the dorm, and they continued to be roommates. But no matter how much such happenings engaged the emotions, they were still externals—they didn't change the real people inside.

Gladys still ran to the Wenschler to report infractions of the rules. Alice still saw only the best in everything. Lawrence was still flamboyant. Elizabeth knew she still felt the same insecurities, had the same desire to teach, felt the same drivenness to work hard. And her caring for Eliot hadn't changed over the past two years since she'd recognized it. The only change was its deepened intensity.

She looked at him now, feeling the little lurch of her heart that the sight of his tall frame with the light falling on his smooth, gold hair never failed to produce. And as always, the quickened sense of her own love for him made her think of God's love for him and called forth the prayer that was never far from her heart: *Dear God, speak to him. Show him Your way. Thank You that he's searching, but help him find.*

She looked at the paper in front of her and realized she had scribbled notes even as her mind had been elsewhere. "Charge a fee for the social hour after church," she had written in response to someone's suggestion. This was now stirring a lot of negative debate since that was the one time of the week dating—double dating, that is—was freely permitted.

"How about organizing an excursion to Arrowrock Dam?" someone called out from the back. The highest dam in the world, just a few miles above Boise, was the most popular attraction the area offered and had captivated visitors from France, Korea, and elsewhere around the world.

Elizabeth's pencil flew in an attempt to keep track of the discussion. Everyone wanted to go, but no one could afford it. It was a well-known formula that the trip required the proceeds of eight hours' field labor for a bachelor and sixteen hours to take a date. It was obvious such a venture would hardly be a money-maker for the college.

Elizabeth looked at their class president. His clear blue eyes and classic features presented the unruffled face he usually showed the world, but Elizabeth could sense his growing frustration. As his mouth tightened she held her breath, hoping he wouldn't give way to one of his explosions over seemingly small matters, which she had witnessed lately. Although he always quickly covered up such lapses with his old carefree facade, they hurt Elizabeth deeply because she knew their real source was his spiritual struggle, and she felt so helpless.

Now his eyes narrowed, and he struck the podium in front of him. "Such stupid—"

Elizabeth jumped to her feet and touched his arm. "Larry seems to have a suggestion." She pointed to Lawrence's upraised hand, then gave Eliot's arm a tiny squeeze before sitting down.

The old Eliot's mask slipped into place as he grinned at Elizabeth, then nodded to Larry.

"How about an exhibition debate?"

Lawrence's suggestion sent Elizabeth back to her note-taking.

"I got a letter from the president of the Stanford team. They're offering a return on the exhibition we did last year when we were in California for the Western States Conference. It's going to be in Salt Lake this year, so they could come up here."

"Would a debate draw as big a crowd as a musical evening?" Bernard asked. "I know they're really popular, but—"

"I think this one might," Lawrence interrupted him. "Here—" he ruffled through some papers and pulled out a letter "—let me read: 'One of our finest debators this year is Will Rogers, Jr., oldest son of the humorist. Bill is not only an exceptionally clever and entertaining chap, being more or less a chip off the old block, but he is also a good debator. In fact, he was on a team that won a major tournament last month.' Well, that's probably enough, but you get the idea." Lawrence sat down.

Eliot looked nervous. "I don't know, Larry. We need an event to raise the prestige of the college. What if we lost?"

But his doubts were overruled by his classmates. "Yes! That's it!" "You've got it, Lawrence!" "We'll get the governor and the mayor and a senator or something to judge!" "Think what it'll do for the college!"

"I'll get to Professor Rutland right away." Lawrence declared it decided without a vote.

"Er, well—I guess we've decided to sponsor a debate." Eliot resumed control of the meeting, and the class laughed. "So I guess we better get organized. Bernard— you be in charge of arrangements, the room, ushers, things like that. Enoch—programs. Elizabeth—the reception afterwards, refreshments, stuff like that." He went on to appoint an advertising chairman and others, but Elizabeth sat shaking her head. That was something else that hadn't changed—he still hadn't learned to say please.

As the date Stanford proposed for the debate was two months away, they had plenty of time to prepare, but Elizabeth set straight to work. She arranged with Mrs. Nylander for use of The Club and her willingness to supervise the making of coffee and punch.

"But you'll have to provide all the fixings, you know." The cook shook her head—her hair and face as white as her dress. "I just don't know what we're going to do for food. I've got about a week's supply of flour and noodles. I know we're supposed to keep on trusting, but sometimes I

127

feel like the widow of Zarephath. Every day I make my last cake, then the next morning there's enough oil and flour to make one more—but that's all. Oh, dearie me—" she laughed with a shaking of her rotund, aproned tummy "—how I go on. Don't you worry about a thing I've said."

Elizabeth started to thank the cook, but her narration wasn't over. "Do you know a group of businessmen heard we were serving dinners here for ten cents apiece? They didn't believe it could be done—at least not with healthy food. So I said, 'Bring your dimes and come on out for dinner.' I served them a right good meal that cost seven cents apiece to prepare." She clapped her hands over her stomach and laughed at her own triumph. "Smell that?"

Elizabeth nodded. It smelled wonderful.

"I got a fine big soup bone for twelve cents—just you see what a good dinner we have tonight."

As promised, dinner was delicious. But Elizabeth could understand the problem. Many students, like herself, had managed to get some kind of job for the summer; therefore, their first few payments would be made in cash, rather than the barter that would come when the money ran out. Accordingly, the school had used the money to pay taxes and salaries, not to buy supplies.

The conversation at the table that night seemed focused on the economic situation. "Well, everyone says prosperity's just around the corner." Alice was always the hopeful one.

"Yes," her brother agreed, "but they don't say which corner. Everytime I look around a corner all I see is an ash can overflowing with unpaid bills." Bernard looked around. "I don't know—sometimes I worry about being here. I mean, maybe I should do my part to end the depression by earning some money and putting it into circulation."

Roger disagreed. "That sounds like a lack of confidence. What this country needs, besides faith in God, is a revival of confidence in Americanism and the fundamental laws of democracy."

Lawrence put down his soup spoon. "Bern, if you quit now, what happens to your preparation for the ministry? You're pledged to seek first the kingdom of God. If God calls you, you mustn't descend to deflections from the main line."

Bernard shrugged. "Yes, yes, I know. But what is seeking first the kingdom of God? How can I feed people spiritually when they're starving physically?"

Elizabeth was wondering how this talk about a call was affecting Eliot, who seemed to be concentrating intently on his soup.

Alice interjected her bright optimism again. "Well, I guess if there's anything good about this depression it's that it teaches us to rely on God for all our needs."

At last Eliot looked up. "Depression. I just wish those bigwigs in Washington who keep telling us we shouldn't use the word—because 'if we think there isn't any, there isn't'—had my bills to pay." And as so often lately, Elizabeth heard the note of harshness in his voice.

But Lawrence took up the idea with vigor. "I think they may be right. What we need is less 'hard time' talk and more 'hard work and timely thinking.' Now what I say is—"

Eliot pushed his chair back from the table with a loud scraping noise. "Save it for the debate case, Larry—that's what needs hard work. I'll see you in my room in ten minutes." He strode from the room.

"Yes, sir. No problem." Lawrence saluted his partner's departing back, then shook his head. "I think this debate's really getting to him."

"What's your topic this year?" Velda asked.

Lawrence stuck his left hand in an imaginary vest and held up his right for emphasis. "Resolved: That the powers of the president of the United States should be substantially increased as a settled policy." He cleared his throat and bowed as his classmates clapped. "We shall take the negative."

Discussion continued around the table, but Elizabeth's mind went to her responsibility for the event. She wanted to have everything organized perfectly. If representatives of Stanford University, the governor of Idaho, mayor of Nampa—whoever they had for judges—were coming to a reception in her charge she wanted it to be memorable. First thing she needed was a good committee.

"Alice, you're an applied arts major—will you help with the reception? You could do the decorations."

"Oh, I'd love to. We're just learning how to make block-printed scarves—we could do those for the tables, and make parchment shades for the lamps—paint them all real bright so no one will notice the water stains on the ceiling."

"Great! That's just what I had in mind. Thanks, Alice."

On her way out she saw Gladys. Even though they were roommates it seemed they had very little time to talk between Elizabeth's activities and studies and Gladys's work schedule. But Elizabeth still felt Gladys needed to be more involved in campus life.

"Gladys, let's walk back to the dorm together. I've been wanting to talk to you. You know I'm in charge of the reception for this debate thing—do you suppose you could help me on the refreshments committee?"

Gladys seemed to consider for a minute, almost glad to have been asked, then turned toward the dorm in a brisk pace. "Sorry. I wouldn't have time."

Elizabeth let her go and walked on slowly. Sometimes she wondered why she tried. Her best efforts to help people never seemed to do any good.

But all those thoughts fled when she opened the door of the dorm and saw a familiar figure seated on the brown, slip-covered chair in the Hadley Hall parlor. "Aunt Nelly! What a wonderful surprise! What are you doing here?"

Nelly pushed her rotund form from the chair and engulfed Elizabeth in a hug. "I expect I'm meddling, that's what, but I did think you should know—even if your mama didn't want me to tell you."

Elizabeth's smile faded. She held Nelly at arms' length by the shoulders. "What should I know? Is mama sick? Is it the mortgage? Did the bank foreclose?"

Nelly led her to the sofa and sat beside her. "No, Kathryn isn't sick—your papa is. And the bank hasn't foreclosed—not yet, but—"

"Oh, Nelly! Tell me what's wrong. Should I go home?"

"No. That's exactly why your mama didn't want anyone to tell you. She didn't want to upset your studies."

"But Papa—how bad is he?"

"Dr. Nolte says it's just fatigue and worry. Your daddy is getting along in years—not as old as I am, but he's several years older than your mama, you know."

Elizabeth nodded. Yes, she knew, but Father was always so strong and vital. Even with his graying hair it was impossible to think of him as an old man. "Is it his heart or something?"

Nelly shook her head. "I don't think so. He just needs to rest—and quit worrying—as if that were possible these days."

Then Elizabeth thought of something else. "Oh, but it's harvest time. There must be ten acres of corn to pick—more—and I can't remember how many acres of potatoes he planted. Boyd and Alex can't possibly dig all those . . ." She started to her feet, but Nelly pushed her back down.

"No use worrying about that. There won't be much harvest."

"No harvest? What do you mean? The plants looked fine when I left."

"Oh, lots of potatoes, big, healthy ones. But it's no use digging them. They aren't worth the price of the sacks to haul them to the market. The corn's worth a little, but onions are the same as potatoes. Isaiah says anyone who wants 'em can come dig his—carry off all they can use."

"But that doesn't make any sense. People are starving to death—it says so in all the papers."

"That's why Isaiah says they can have his onions. But it costs too much in transportation and labor to get them to the cities where they're really needed."

Elizabeth shut her eyes in an attempt to block out all the troubles around her—her family, the college, the whole country—what was going to become of them all? Was there any use struggling on? This was one of the times she couldn't obey her mother's injunction to hold her head high. She thanked Nelly for coming and went to her room with slumped shoulders and dragging feet.

Gladys was already asleep. Elizabeth tipped the shade on her lamp to keep the light out of Gladys's eyes and looked at the books she needed to study for tomorrow's classes: methods, principles of education, Bible . . .

Bible seemed the only one worthwhile in these circumstances. When she opened it, a card she used for a bookmark fell out. It was the verse she felt God had given to her when this whole economic disaster started, the one Eliot's father had quoted to her that long ago day when they met under such embarrassing circumstances. "Who shall separate us from the love of Christ? shall tribulation, or distress, or persecution, or famine . . ."

She smiled at how much worse things were now than when she had first found that promise. Then her father had been well, potatoes sold for only a few cents a sack, but they did sell. She didn't have Eliot's or Gladys's or anyone else's trouble to worry about. And yet, look at all she had accomplished in that time, in spite of the fact that economic conditions had gotten steadily worse. Then she had thought going to college was a hopeless dream—and here she was, on her last year. Eliot and the others, though they presented problems, were blessings too.

She looked long at the card. Then she realized that the promise wasn't for help in distress and famine; the promise was Christ. Christ and His love didn't change, no matter what else did. She could always count on Him.

She bowed her head to pray but instead, found herself concentrating on the small pool of golden light her lamp made in the dark room. Just as Christ was always there with a light for her life—no matter how dark all else was.

She knew what to do.

13

The next morning she looked around The Club at breakfast. Eliot wasn't there, but Lawrence was. She'd tell him her plan.

"Mrs. Nylander said her cupboards are bare, and the onions and potatoes are just there in the ground, waiting to be dug. If we explain to Dean Cuthbert, I bet she'd even excuse a day or two of school. We could dig enough to keep the school going all year, plus bring back some for the North Side Mission—and take some to the Hooverville too."

Lawrence held up his hand. "Whoa, why not the whole population of Nampa while we're at it?"

"Don't laugh, Larry. I'm serious."

"I know you are, and I think it's a great idea. Really I do. Your ideas are always great, Elizabeth."

She blinked at the intensity in his voice but went on. "And while we're there, it would only take one extra day to harvest the corn so my father can make his bank payment. Just taking that worry off his shoulders would make him feel so much better."

Lawrence nodded. "Sounds really good. Great, even. We'd have to arrange transportation and something to haul the produce in—a wagon or something."

"If we can get the kids out there, I'm sure we can use one of our wagons. Oh, thank you, Lawrence!" She squeezed his arm right there at the breakfast table, then saw the look her roommate was giving her. "Never mind marking that down, Gladys. I'm on my way to see the dean anyway."

She knew Dean Cuthbert wouldn't worry much about her exhibition of unchecked enthusiasm when she had a plan to feed the entire school. They might get a little tired of potato soup before the year was out, but it was nutritious.

The academic dean agreed to suspend three days of classes for the harvest project and recommended that the Christian Workers Band give special emphasis to gathering produce for the destitute. With the weekend included, that would give them five days—more than enough time for the harvest—well, four really, because they wouldn't work on Sunday. And that would be a special treat for Elizabeth because she would stay at home for that time. The only person who didn't seem delighted with the plan was Eliot.

"That's fine. You go have a nice field day." His arm swept those still sitting around the tables in The Club. "But Lawrence and I will stay here and work on our case."

"We'll what?" Lawrence spun around to face his colleague. "Who elected you emperor? There's three weeks left until the debate, and I for one promised Elizabeth I'd help on her project. I have no intention of going back on my word."

Eliot's features tightened dangerously. "I may not be emperor, but I'm the manager of this team, and I insist."

"And I refuse." Lawrence walked out of the dining hall.

Their angry argument became the talk of the campus. It appeared that the logic and showmanship of the Stanford team wouldn't be required to defeat the NCC team—the warring members would do that themselves.

But the harvest scheme was a great success. Nearly one hundred college students descended on the Allen and

Jayne farms armed with shovels, trowels, and sharp sticks. Those students—almost a third of them—who had been raised on farms took charge of groups, instructing their city-bred classmates in the back-breaking art of potato digging, while others came behind gathering them into baskets or boxes, which they dumped into borrowed wagons. The sun shone on them, and they sang as they worked—hymns, folks songs, popular tunes.

Merrick, fretting at his enforced rest, walked through his fields with Kathryn on his arm, both with the biggest smiles they'd had on their faces for many months, if not years.

The students departed at dusk with aching backs, grubby hands and faces, and shouts that they'd be back tomorrow. Elizabeth waved them off with a special word to Lawrence. She knew he still had the job of supervising the unloading of the wagons when they got back to the campus.

Then she turned to her family in the blessed quietness that followed the departure. "Oh, Mother, Daddy, Boyd, Alex, it's so good to be here with you! I want to hear all about everything. It seems like years since we've really talked." With arms linked they turned toward the house. "Oh, I'm so hungry! What's for dinner, Mother?"

Kathryn threw up her hands. "Oh, my. You'll never guess. Potato soup!" And they laughed all the way across the yard.

After dinner, when they sat around the table in the gentle light of the coal oil lamp, sipping cups of coffee, Elizabeth was reminded that in spite of her big plan to help her family there were few laughing matters here.

One piece of good news, however, was that Nelly's oldest son, Davey, had been appointed to fill a vacancy on the school board. "It should make getting a job easier for you when the time comes—having a friend at city hall, so to speak," Kathryn said.

Elizabeth shook her head. "That seems like another world, but it's really only a few months away. I hope my credentials will be good enough to speak for themselves— but it's always good to have friends."

Then the talk turned to the crops.

"We may get enough for the corn to pay the bank and our taxes. This time. I can't thank you enough, Elizabeth. This whole project of yours has been a great tonic." Merrick said the words, but she saw the worried look return to his eyes when the mortgage was mentioned.

Kathryn responded to the tired note in his voice. "What Dr. Nolte would have to say to me I can't imagine. Letting you galavant all over the south forty today, then sit up all night talking. Come with me, husband." She stood and started toward the bedroom.

Merrick frowned. "I'm quite capable of putting myself to bed. Not an invalid yet, no matter what that sawbones says."

"I'll be very happy to have you put yourself to bed," Kathryn replied. "I only intended to give you your tonic— which you never manage to take by yourself without spilling."

While they were out of the room Elizabeth turned to Boyd. "And how are you? Do you like farming any better?"

"Any better than what? Grave digging? That's what it seems like to me. Digging my own grave here."

"Can't you do anything else?"

"What would you suggest? And who would help the folks if I did?"

"What about Clarey? I know he's busy helping Mavis's dad, but now that Father is ill, you'd think he could get home some."

Boyd scratched his head. "Yeah. Funny thing. Her folks act like they own him just because they're giving them and that kid of theirs a home." Then he broke into a grin. "Got to admit, though, that little Tommy's about the cutest thing I've ever seen. Likes me, too. I take him with me on the tractor when they visit."

"But what would you like to do if you could, Boyd?"

"Wouldn't be raising cattle, that's for sure. Dad gave me a scrub calf that was born late last spring. Said I could raise him for my own and keep the money."

Elizabeth nodded. "The steer you coddled all summer? I saw it a couple of times."

"Right. Bullard. Well, it wasn't anything I especially enjoyed, but I sure did my best—fed him by hand, best feed I could get. Took him to the auction last week. You know how much I was offered?"

Elizabeth waited.

"Fifteen cents. That's it—top price. Fifteen cents."

"Did you take it?"

Boyd shrugged. "Had to. Couldn't afford to feed him through the winter, and he wasn't ready to butcher yet."

Elizabeth felt so sorry. It seemed hopeless. She didn't know what to say.

But surprisingly, Boyd sprang to his feet with a burst of energy. "But let me show you something! Ian sent me this." He pulled a magazine from a pile in the corner. "Look at these airplanes they're making in Europe." He turned a few pages. "Here, this one—she's French. Isn't she a beauty!"

Elizabeth almost expected him to start making engine sounds like a child with a toy. She was glad that at least her brother had something to dream about.

Kathryn came back, and Boyd got up to leave. Elizabeth was amazed to note how tall he had grown to be at nineteen. Alex wandered off to bed, too, leaving Kathryn and Elizabeth alone.

Elizabeth poured fresh cups of coffee. "How is Dad—really?" she asked.

Kathryn sat beside her. "Really just worn out, I think. The worry is worse than the work."

Elizabeth nodded. "If only I could help. Sometimes I feel so guilty—spending money on college when I could use it to pay off the bank."

"No! Don't you even think such a thing." Kathryn slapped her hand on the table so hard it made the lamp waver. Then she grinned. "Besides, the bank doesn't accept barter. Alex and I got the incubator set up again. You've got a payment due next month, and I expect some chicken gravy will taste pretty good on all those potatoes they dug today."

"But, Mother, why is the bank riding us so hard? They didn't at first when the stock market crashed, and that was when so many banks were worried about closing. I know things have gotten tighter, but I still don't understand . . ."

Kathryn took a sip of her coffee. "There've been some changes at the bank. Cyrus Griswold was elected chairman of the board of directors last spring."

"Oh, no." Suddenly she understood. "He threatened Father the day he rescued me. He said—I don't remember exactly—but something about getting him. But that's awful! It's all my fault."

Kathryn gripped Elizabeth so hard she thought her mother was going to shake her. "Don't you ever say that. Don't you ever think that. Griswold is an evil man. You are not responsible for the evil in the world." And then with her usual turn to common sense, she ushered her daughter to the sink where they washed the dishes.

Elizabeth tried to follow her mother's commands, and the next day when the harvesting crew returned and she joined them with shouted greetings, it seemed like an easy world in which to forget evil. Especially when a group of them sat in the shade of a tall row of corn to eat the sandwiches Mrs. Nylander had sent for their lunch, and Eliot joined them.

"I'm glad you came today!" she said.

He shrugged. "I remembered the story of The Little Red Hen. Had to do my share of work. I'm sure to want to eat my share of food this winter."

They were just finishing eating when a cloud of dust announced the approach of a large car from the west. Elizabeth caught her breath. She remembered that flashy green Packard. No one else in the area could afford such a vehicle. She turned away, waiting for it to go on.

But it didn't go on. Instead the driver braked and got out. Several fellows went over to admire the elegant machine. "Any of you know where Elizabeth Allen is?" the driver asked.

Elizabeth had managed to avoid Mr. Griswold for three years. But he was just as repugnant as she remembered him. When Bernard pointed her out she had no option but to stand there while everyone watched him approach her with his hand extended. Fortunately she was holding several lunch sacks, so had an excuse not to offer hers.

"So sorry your family has fallen on hard times, my dear."

She controlled her urge to shiver.

"But then, these are hard times for us all. I'd like to do what I can, though. So I came to tell you that your old job is open anytime you want it. If you feel like you should drop out of school for a while to help your family I could offer you a good salary, since you're experienced."

Elizabeth heard Alice give a little squeal. It undoubtedly sounded like a wonderful offer to anyone who didn't know the truth. "If you really want to help my family, Mr. Griswold, you'll extend their mortgage."

He smiled. If it weren't for the reality of the situation Elizabeth would have burst out laughing. She almost expected him to curl his mustache and snatch at her with a cry of "Aha, my proud beauty!" Then Eliot would flex his muscles and rescue her just before Griswold drove off with her in his powerful car.

But it was no laughing matter, and his answer was deadly serious. "Oh, but you know I can't do that—I have my investors' interests to look out for."

Then from behind her, Eliot did step forward. "Cyrus Griswold. You wouldn't remember, but we have met before—in your newspaper office when Mr. Allen took my father in for an interview."

Griswold did remember. He gave a hard stare at the hand Eliot offered him, then turned and strode to his car. "Think it over, Miss Allen." He slammed the door and roared off, covering them with dust.

"Don't worry about him. It'll be all right, Elizabeth." Eliot's quick squeeze of her hand stayed with her through a long afternoon of corn picking.

But on the last night before she would return to school with the harvesters, Elizabeth was still thinking of Griswold. What if she did accept his offer? She was a big girl now, not the silly teenager he had hired almost four years ago. She would look out for herself. Wasn't she selfish to refuse him?

The implication was clear—not only would there be a good salary, but the pressure would be taken off her family if she accepted the job. And she was a good secretary. She tried to ignore the niggling at the back of her mind that told her, yes, she could keep Griswold at a distance, but if she did the benefits of the job might not be forthcoming. Her mother would be so upset. She toyed with the idea of accepting the job and not letting her mother know—but that was ridiculous.

A knock at the door interrupted her confused thoughts.

"Celia!" She ran to hug her friend. "Celia, you're as beautiful as ever. And that dress! You look great!" She pulled her visitor into the parlor. "I heard you were living in Boise. How's life in the big city?"

To her surprise tears rolled down Celia's creamy pink cheeks. She dashed at them with her hands. "Oh, rats! I didn't want to do that. I wanted to come here and tell you how happy I am and all about my new dresses and our fancy house, but I never could lie to you, Lizzy."

"What's wrong? Tell me."

Celia did. About how the first time Walter stepped out on her was on their honeymoon. About how much she wanted to have a baby, but how Walter just yelled at her and stormed out whenever she mentioned it. About how she had absolutely everything money could buy. And how absolutely miserable she was.

Elizabeth listened to her friend, made her a cup of tea, and finally prayed for her.

When she left, Celia kissed her. "I do feel better now. Thank you so much. There wasn't anyone I could tell. Daddy would kill Walter if he knew."

"What are you going to do?"

"Do?" She gave a high, forced giggle. "Oh, I think I'll join a musical society. Boise is very musical, you know, and I haven't played my violin for ages. I'm sure that will make me feel better."

Elizabeth suggested she find a church.

"Yes, I might do that. A lot of the big churches have musical groups. That's a good idea, Lizzy. You always did have the best ideas." She hugged her again.

That wasn't quite what Elizabeth meant, but it seemed it would have to do for now, because Celia was at the door. She paused, her hand on the knob. "Just one thing, Liz."

"Yes."

"My advice is—don't ever do anything just for money."

Then Celia was gone in her fancy little roadster. But Elizabeth knew the advice would stay with her for a long time. Advice she had given Celia once, but now needed to hear herself.

14

Then the whole campus focused on the most important event of the year—on what could be the most important event of many years if the debate were to accomplish all everyone at NCC hoped it would for the survival of the college. No one dared ask what if it failed.

"How are the decorations for the reception coming?" Elizabeth asked Alice at dinner the Monday before the big day.

"Oh, wooly. Miss Leisman is giving our whole class credit for working on it. I designed the table spreads myself with big purple iris. You'll love it."

Before Elizabeth could reply, Eliot's voice rose from the other end of the table. "Larry, you're not following me. Now look, if they say there are eighteen million people on relief and that the federal government can control the economy by ending laissez faire excesses of the Wall Street barons, it'll be a great support for their contention that the president needs more power to promote deficit spending to prime the pump."

Lawrence pushed his bowl aside. "Of course I follow that. I just don't think it's a very strong argument. All we have to do is say that greater regulation of the economy can be done without a change in presidential powers. We won't—"

"You're missing the whole point," Eliot interrupted. "They're sure to argue that democracy needs not simply an administrator—it needs a leader . . ." He dropped his head in his hands. "Ooh, I've got a headache."

A waitress leaned over the table to fill his water glass. "Hi, fellas, we're sure rootin' for you."

Eliot looked up with a forced smile. "Hi, Edna. Thanks."

"Yeah, everybody in my wing at Hadley is so excited. We know you'll do great." She moved on down the table filling glasses.

Eliot rubbed his forehead and pointed a finger at Lawrence. "Now, let me try once more—"

"Congratulations, men!" A freshman carrying his bowl of potato soup stopped by the table. "I'll say it early because I know you'll do us proud."

"Thanks, Bill. Thanks a lot." The debaters answered in unison and, to the relief of the rest of the table, turned their attention to their food.

The respite lasted almost long enough to eat half of one of Mrs. Nylander's excellent rolls before a blast of cold November air announced the entrance of a latecomer.

"Ross!" Elizabeth greeted the tall, thin young man in spectacles. "We haven't seen you for ages!"

"Just had to come back to see you now that my alma mater's so famous."

"Famous?"

Ross unfolded the *Herald-Leader* he carried under his arm. "Haven't you seen the evening paper? Look: 'Capacity Crowd Expected to Hear Will Rogers, Jr.'" He read the headline.

Everyone but Eliot and Lawrence seemed thrilled as Ross cleared his throat and read in a voice that reached the whole room, "Representing an extensive pilgrimage and the most complete forensic coverage of the United States yet attempted by an intercollegiate debating team, Stanford's Transcontinental Debate tour this autumn carried Cardinal orators from the Pacific to the Atlantic and from Montreal to the Mexican border. They met the cream of the country's collegiate crop in some three-score debates with fifty leading American universities, including: Notre Dame, Princeton, Columbia, Duke, Harvard, Vassar, Yale . . .' Isn't that great! We're really up there with the big time, huh?"

All those around Elizabeth applauded, but she was worried about Eliot. Surely he wasn't getting sick. He really didn't look good.

Ross continued. "'Highlight of the four weeks of intensive study prior to commencing the tour was the interview granted the teams by none other than President Herbert Hoover with whom the debators thoroughly discussed the New Deal.' Isn't that great?"

"Depends whose side you're on." Eliot's mutter was barely audible, but Elizabeth caught it.

Ross did too. "Hey, this is terrific publicity for you."

"Undoubtedly what Nero told the Christians before they entered the Coliseum," Lawrence said.

"No, wait a minute." Ross was determined. "Don't you see how good this will make you look when you win?"

Ross moved on to greet old friends at another table.

Eliot got up to bus his dishes. "Meet you in my room in fifteen minutes. OK, Larry?"

Larry nodded.

"Eliot," Elizabeth held out a hand to stop him as he passed her chair. "I'm praying for you."

He just nodded, but Elizabeth felt warmed by the softness she saw come into his eyes.

The next morning in chapel she was glad she had prayed but felt she should have prayed harder. After the opening hymn Dr. Gilchrist invited the debate coach to make an announcement. "I feel it's only fair to warn you ahead that what Professor Rutland has to tell you is rather disappointing, but never fear, we shall carry on."

Elizabeth held her breath. Disappointing? More economic problems? Someone sick? Eliot—she spun around

145

to check his seat in the row behind her. He didn't look too well, but he was there. What then? The debate canceled?

Professor Rutland adjusted his bow tie. "Yesterday I received this note from the manager of the Stanford debate team." He held up a paper lined in cardinal red. "'Our team has asked me to express their appreciation for your warm invitation and to tell you they are looking forward to meeting you.'"

Elizabeth relaxed. It wasn't canceled.

"'I must apologize, however, for an error which is entirely my own as manager of the team. I confused the dates, and Bill Rogers confirmed for November 12 instead of November 21. Unfortunately, he was confirmed for a chess tournament for the later date. Our team is in agreement that the only thing we have against Rogers is that he plays chess.'"

Groans of disappointment from the audience drowned out the assurances of Stanford's providing a first class team for the exhibition.

She turned to commiserate with Eliot, but strangely the disappointing prospects of a smaller audience and losing their star celebrity seemed to invigorate him.

He jumped to his feet. "All right, then! We'll just have to be good enough to make it up to the audience—right, Northwesterners?"

The student body jumped to their feet, cheering.

When Professor Rutland again gained control he continued. "That's the spirit! This will be a night we'll all be proud of. And remember, Rogers wasn't our only celebrity. I have some good news to announce as well. The chief justice of the State Supreme Court, the secretary of state, the attorney general, the superintendent of public instruction, and the superintendent of Boise schools have all agreed to be here to serve as officials for the event."

Another round of applause and cheers followed, none louder than Elizabeth's. With spirit like that they *could* win. She looked at the moisture blotches in the ceiling. They had to.

The enthusiasm of the morning carried over to the next afternoon when Elizabeth's committee of six girls met in The Club to bake cookies for the reception.

"I wish we had more raisins to put in these oatmeal bars," Edna said.

"Oh, pour boiling water over them first and let them plump up—that way they'll seem like more." Elizabeth recalled one of her mother's favorite tricks.

"I thought we were going to make two batches of cinnamon drops." A sophomore who had volunteered to help shook the last few sticky white grains out of a sack. "There's barely enough sugar for one batch."

"Oh," Elizabeth cried. "Don't use all the sugar. We have to have some to offer them with their coffee."

Little Elsie Tyson stood on tiptoe to check the sugar-bowls in the cupboard. "It's OK. There's some in the bowls —if nobody uses any before then."

"Do you think we should lock it up?"

"Oh, no, just tell everyone. They'll do anything to make this a success."

Elizabeth was still doubtful. "Even drink their coffee black?"

The three trays of baked cookies smelled wonderful but looked pitifully meager when she thought of how many people would be attending the reception.

"You don't suppose we could offer them some potato soup to sort of round it out, do you?"

Edna laughed with the others and held out a pan of dough. "Well, here's the oatmeal bars. The plumped raisins look great. They'll help."

"Thank you so much, everybody." Elizabeth smiled at her committee of willing workers. "It'll take these bars longer to bake. I'll stay with them. I know you all have studying to do, so you don't need to wait."

Elsie offered to wait with her, but Elizabeth assured her she was fine, she'd just read her methods assignment while they baked. So Edna and Velda dried the last bowl and, checking the clock on the wall, Elizabeth sat down to read.

She was only on the second page, however, when Alice came in. "Ooh, it smells good in here. Mmm, I love cinnamon. Here." She held out a small white envelope. "I just picked up my mail, so thought I'd bring this to you. Mmm, those do look good."

Elizabeth slapped her fingers. "No, you don't—we don't have enough as it is."

Alice left with a giggle.

Elizabeth glanced at the clock, then sat down to read the note from her mother.

"My dear, we miss you, but are all well—your father seems perkier now with the cooler weather."

The note went on to tell how little Tommy was growing and talking and of how Kathryn was looking forward to Thanksgiving. She had saved the bad news for the second page.

"I am so sorry to tell you this, as I hate to worry you. I know your second quarter payment is past due, but the heater on the incubator broke two weeks ago. Boyd fixed it without even having to buy a new part, and we've set a new batch of eggs, but I don't know what you should tell the business office about this payment. Sorry to trouble you with bad news. We must keep trusting.

Love,
Mother"

An acrid smell brought Elizabeth to her feet. "Oh, no. The cookies!" She yanked the oven door open with a hot pad. Smoke billowed out. She pulled the two pans of blackened oatmeal bars out of the oven, opened the window to let the smoke out, and sat down to cry. What in the world would they do? There weren't enough even with the ones she'd ruined. And there were no ingredients to make more. The debate was day after tomorrow. She started to pull her apron over her head, then stopped.

What had her mother said about not burying her head under a pillow? She got up, scraped the mess out of Mrs. Nylander's pans and set them to soak. She'd come back and scrub them clean later. The centers weren't entirely inedible; she'd take them back to the dorm. Maybe someone could snack on the disastrous crumble. At least they could pick out the raisins.

She found Gladys huddled under a blanket, trying to work at her desk. "Oh, Gladys . . ." Elizabeth was too upset to worry over whether her roommate would sneer at her. She just poured all her troubles out. "And with everyone trying to do extra good because Will Rogers, Jr., isn't coming, I have to go and ruin the reception!"

Gladys nodded and dropped her head in her arm curled over her desk.

Suddenly Elizabeth looked at her roommate. Really looked at her. "Gladys, you look awful. Are you sick? You've been losing weight."

Gladys shook her head. "No, I'm just tired." She pulled the blanket closer around her shoulders.

"Are you hungry? The middles are edible." She held out her platter of burned mess.

To her surprise Gladys ate ravenously, knocking off only the blackest of the burned edges. Then Elizabeth realized she hadn't seen her roommate in The Club for several days. "Gladys, when's the last time you ate?"

"Yesterday. They let me have stale stuff at the bakery, but I don't work on Wednesdays."

"No, I mean a real meal—at The Club."

Gladys shrugged. "I'm out of money."

"Oh, Gladys, why didn't you say something?" Elizabeth put her arms around her. "Everybody's out of money, but we could do something—arrange credit, maybe."

Gladys shook her head. "I don't know. I'm just so tired, it didn't seem worth the effort. If I don't get this Bible paper in tomorrow it won't matter anyway. I'll flunk out."

Elizabeth looked at the scribbled research paper Gladys was half covering with her arm. "You've got it done. All it needs is recopying."

The room was silent for a moment. "Gladys, I'm so sorry I haven't been a better roommate." She staunchly ignored any arguments her mind offered that Gladys's own attitudes and rebuffs were to blame. "You go to bed."

Gladys offered no resistance as Elizabeth rolled her onto the narrow bunk and added a cover from her own bed as well.

"Velda's an assistant in the commercial department. She can let me use a typewriter. I may make a few errors, but I can type this for you."

Gladys was sound asleep when Elizabeth returned with the typed paper and a steaming bowl of chicken vegetable stew from The Club. Gladys ate it, muttered her thanks, then turned over and went back to sleep.

The next morning at breakfast, with less than thirty-six hours left before the debate, NCC's star performers were hard at work over their oatmeal. Larry waved a sheet of foolscap. "Do you want to use the argument that Winston Churchill is warning of the necessity to be prepared for possible war in Europe, and if the president has too much power he could take the power to declare war out of the hands of Congress?"

Eliot considered. "No, we used that last month at C of I and lost that round."

Lawrence swallowed his unsugared oatmeal and nodded. "Yeah, I know. But we need a foreign policy argument."

"OK, let's say that the president should continue to seek the advice and consent of Congress in the conduct of foreign affairs—that we'll have more influence, power, and prestige if our allies know Congress is behind the president—" He interrupted himself with a shiver. "Is it cold in here, or do I have the flu? I'm chilling."

Suddenly everyone noticed what they'd ignored in their rapt following of the debate arguments. The room was like ice.

Bernard bent over the register against the wall and turned the black knob. "Nothing." He shook his head. "I've got it wide open. Nothing's coming out."

When Roger came in no one noticed the outside air he brought with him. "Hi. Bad news, folks."

"Roger, you've got black all over your face." Alice grinned at him.

"Yeah, I know. Been down in the boiler room with Shank." Everyone nodded. The head janitor was a favorite figure on campus. "The system's kaput. He's calling American Heating, but we'll have to keep our coats on today. At least it'll save fuel—the coal bin's almost empty."

Dean Cuthbert dismissed classes for the day and advised as many students as had off-campus friends to go to their homes. The remainder would gather in the kitchen where the stove would provide warmth.

By evening the system was fired up again and working —sort of. Roger, who had spent four years working for Shank, explained to those grouped around the stove. "Trouble is, there's a loss of pressure somewhere. The coal we have burns too slow to keep it up to maximum. If we had softer coal or something that burned brighter—of course, they'll get it all fixed sooner or later, but I'm afraid it'll be too late for our Stanford guests."

Elizabeth glanced at the clock on the wall. Less than twenty-four hours. "Well, what do you think?" she asked. "Shall we all wear our coats and tell them it's the style here, or tough it out in sweaters and tell them they're just cold because they're used to the California climate?"

Eliot grinned at her from the corner where he and Lawrence continued their preparation. "I'm for toughing it out, but will they believe us when we turn blue?"

The laughter eased tensions, and Bernard stood. "Well, it's probably about warm enough to go back to our rooms now. Let's close with prayer."

Elizabeth felt herself relaxing as their class chaplain asked for the Lord's blessing on the coming day, for His guidance and wisdom for their debaters, and even for the success of the reception. *Just don't let them be very hungry, Lord,* she added silently.

When everyone looked up, she knew what she wanted to do. "Let's sing 'Hallelujah, Amen!'" she said.

And they did. "They passed thro' toils and trials and though the strife was long, they share the victor's conquest, and sing the victor's song." That was true of those who had gone before them, and she was determined that it would be equally true of them—that students who sang that song fifty years later would be able to look back on their striving and appropriate strength to go on and build for the future.

15

The morning of the big day, Elizabeth woke with a prayer for Eliot on her lips. For almost four years now he had been struggling with the question of what he should do with his life. Perhaps somehow in the course of this contest the Lord could speak to him in a new way. Perhaps he would see, as he represented this Christian college, that the Lord did want him as a representative on the foreign field. Perhaps what Eliot had all along thought was a lack of call was really the Lord's telling him to wait a little longer, prepare a little harder. Perhaps the answer would come now. Perhaps.

Elizabeth let up the window shade and woke Gladys with a cry of delight. "Oh, just look! The Lord decorated the campus!"

A smooth, pristine blanket of snow lay over everything, covering dirt, sagebrush, and brown weeds, while just a pale sparkle of sun glinted an occasional diamond from a bush.

"I'll bet they don't have anything more beautiful than this at Stanford!" And in her delight she hugged Gladys, something she hadn't done in three years of living together but had done twice in the past two days. "How are you feeling? Come on, I'll share my breakfast with you—there's always loads of toast—not always butter or jelly, but plenty of toast."

It was almost enough to make her forget her worries over the skimpy refreshments. Maybe they could offer toast? It would be better than nothing. And it would be warm. She put on an extra sweater against the chill the faulty heating system failed to counteract.

She grinned when she heard the familiar discussion from the other end of the breakfast table.

"Now they'll say that strengthening the powers of the presidency can overcome the depression because the president can bring in the brightest economists and planners and thereby prevent future disasters, but we'll say . . ."

She wondered what anyone would talk about when the debate was over.

After lunch she and Alice, wearing their coats, were setting up The Club for the reception when a clatter of iron wagon wheels on the gravel road outside took her attention.

"Whoa, Rosie!" That voice sounded familiar.

Grabbing her knit hat, Elizabeth ran outdoors.

"Boyd! What are you doing? Don't tell me you drove the wagon all the way to Nampa in the snow?"

"Sure, Rosie doesn't mind a little snow." He jumped off the spring seat and hugged her. "I wanted to hear the debate—not everyday you get an opportunity to see Will Roger's son—and Mom needed to get your tuition payment to you anyway."

"Er . . ." Should she tell him about Will Rogers or ask her question first? Curiosity won. "Tuition? She said the chickens wouldn't be ready for a couple of months yet."

"Won't be. Just hatching now. Did she tell you I fixed the incubator?" He flipped the canvas cover off the bed of the wagon. "Brought fuel instead."

Elizabeth gaped. "Sagebrush? We're paying my school bill in sagebrush?"

"Why not? Don't you need fuel?"

She clapped her ungloved hands, and not just because they were cold. "We certainly do—we need fuel that burns fast and hot—this is exactly what we need! Come on, let's find Shank!"

She grabbed his hand and started to pull him toward the building when she almost bumped into Gladys. "Oh, hi, Gladys, this is my brother, Boyd."

"Hi." Gladys looked uncertain what to say in front of a guest.

"Can we do something for you?" Elizabeth asked.

"Well, I wondered if I could borrow your galoshes. I need to get to work, and . . ."

Elizabeth had a pretty good idea that the cardboard Gladys had put in her shoes was soaking through in the snow. "Of course you can. But wait a minute." She stopped Gladys who had turned toward the dorm. "I have a better idea. Why doesn't Boyd drive you down?"

Gladys started to protest, but Boyd insisted that it would be no problem for him or for Rosie, and they would have plenty of time to unload the wood when he got back.

"I'll get Shank and Roger while you're gone. And you can pick Gladys up afterwards too, so she'll be back in time for the debate."

Gladys started to protest again, and suddenly Elizabeth saw the situation. "Oh, Gladys. Don't be such a legalist. Rosie O'Day can be your chaperone."

To her surprise Gladys laughed. "Sorry. I know everyone hated me for reporting on the rules. It's just that I—I—"

"Oh, never mind." Elizabeth shoved her toward the wagon. "Hurry up or you'll be late to work."

When Boyd returned, the business office manager was ready with a receipt, and Shank was ready to stoke up his boiler. "We'll have this so toasty they'll think they're still in California!"

"But you said there's still a problem in the system?" Boyd asked. "I just happen to have a few tools with me."

Elizabeth smiled. He never went anywhere without his tools.

"Maybe I could take a look at it for you."

"Just don't get it too hot," Elizabeth called to their departing backs. "We don't want the dignitaries removing their coats on the platform."

She turned toward the administration building and saw that already Holly street was choked with traffic. Sleek black cars from Boise were angling for parking spots next to farm carts from Melba and Meridian. She watched in amazement as a tractor pulled up with six people on it. All jumped down, brushed off their Sunday-go-to-meeting clothes, and walked toward the auditorium.

With a gasp of panic Elizabeth wondered whether Bernard and Enoch were ready for this. She knew the programs had been printed, fortunately not until after they knew of the change in the team members, but were the ushers in place to distribute them? Surely no one could have guessed that the audience would start arriving mid-afternoon. Then she saw four men running toward the ad building from Gideon Hall, and she knew the matter was in hand. If only she could be as confident about the reception.

But there was no time left to worry. She had to change clothes, rehearse, and get in place herself, for the first item on the program was the Glee Club singing "Lead On, O King Eternal," accompanied by the orchestra.

Three hours later, Elizabeth held her head up and sang in her fullest voice to a packed auditorium, hoping those standing in the halls outside would be able to hear as well.

"Thro' days of preparation Thy grace has made us strong; and now, O King Eternal, we lift our battle song." Then the college band played a number chosen especially for the debate night, "I Am Resolved."

From her seat down front Elizabeth watched the debaters march in to their seats and smiled as she saw that Eliot was singing under his breath, "We are resolved . . ."

Opening formalities seemed to take forever as dignitaries from around the valley welcomed an audience of more than eight hundred.

But Elizabeth looked around anxiously as she heard an undertone of harsh mutterings. "What do you mean, he isn't here?" "It said in the paper . . ." "Huh? No Rogers?"

Perhaps the sentiment of those in the audience who hadn't seen the late announcements in the paper reached the speaker, because the secretary of state held out both arms. "And I believe that only one thing could have produced such interest in the citizens of our fair Boise Valley—you are here not for a social event, not here to be entertained, but you have come here tonight to hear a serious discussion of an important national issue that will affect the lives of each one of us."

Elizabeth smiled as she saw formerly frowning faces nod in agreement with the speaker. She let her breath out slowly. Another crisis averted.

The secretary then introduced the teams: Jack Fairlane, a pre-law major, and Rowland Amsbury, an economics major, also preparing for a career in law.

They looked so polished, Elizabeth thought. So sophisticated, so good. She knew how hard Eliot and Lawrence had worked, but could anything stand up to the experience of a transcontinental tour, debating against the best schools in the country, being prepped by Herbert Hoover himself? She breathed a prayer that she intended to be for both team members and the college as well, but just came out, *Help Eliot, please.*

The introduction of the judges was next: a justice of the Supreme Court of Idaho; the attorney general for the state of Idaho; and the superintendent of the Boise schools. Finally a hush fell over the auditorium, and the debate started.

Stanford's Jack Fairlane was the first speaker. Elizabeth noted that many in the audience took out pencils and notepads as he announced the resolution, defined the terms, and presented what the affirmative team saw as the major reason America needed a policy to strengthen the presidency.

The smooth, dark-haired Fairlane in his expensive looking suit exuded self-confidence. Surprisingly, though, he didn't approach his speech with strong logic or high-powered oratory, but instead opened in a rather folksy manner.

"My colleague and I are mighty happy to be here, and we appreciate your warm welcome. We've done a lot of traveling this year, and it seems we've been on all kinds of highways—gravel, paved, dirt—but I must say that yours are unique—it's the first time we've encountered a highway covered by jackrabbits."

The audience laughed appreciatively. Elizabeth could see that any animosity their rural audience might have felt toward these city slickers was easing. She could almost hear an Idaho twang in Fairlane's voice as he continued, "Rollie and I know you were all disappointed that Bill Rogers couldn't be here and all you got was just us instead, but we did our best to make it up to you by bringin' along some of the things Bill's famous daddy has had to say about our political situation, and we believe this is real appropriate to what we see as a crying need for change in national policy."

He went on for the remainder of his time quoting Will Rogers on the personal strength of Franklin Roosevelt, who had just been elected president, and the changes he would make in this country—changes that he argued should be established as settled policy.

Lawrence was next. He spoke well, his piercing eyes and energy that had won him the nickname Lawrence of Arabia held the audience. Elizabeth began to feel more and more confident of success as he argued the lack of need for a policy change to accomplish new goals as a nation.

The second Stanford speaker took his place and again relied on Will Rogers as his main source. "Now our friend

Will Rogers has probably had more experience with presidents than any person alive, having been a personal friend of every one of 'em from Teddy Roosevelt to Franklin Roosevelt, so he has some reason to know what he's talking about when he says, 'Now Mr. Hoover didn't get results, because he asked Congress to do something. That's where he made a mistake. Mr. Roosevelt, he'll just send a thing up there every morning and say, "Here's your menu, you guys, sign it!"' Now that's the kind of policy we need if Roosevelt's New Deal is to become a Real Deal for all Americans."

The speaker then went on to outline a recovery plan for the United States based on Roosevelt's ideas of national work programs and declaring that such could only be achieved by adopting a policy increasing presidential powers.

Elizabeth felt herself being swayed by the speaker's arguments. He was good. What could Eliot possibly say to counter such popular thought? But one look at Eliot as he gathered his papers and strode to the podium returned her confidence.

He was undaunted by the speaker's prestige and power because he had prepared well and he knew his own mind. The case was in good hands. He had so much ability, such intelligence and dedication. He was magnificent. Why didn't God call him? Surely God had created this man of such high caliber for His own purposes. She had at least a glimpse of the frustration Eliot had felt for so long. *God, aren't You listening? Don't You care?*

Then Eliot began his summary, and she realized she had missed most of his speech. "Yes, we agree that Will Rogers has probably known more presidents than any other living person. And do you know what he said? He said, 'We have lived under more than thirty Presidents. They couldn't have all been great. In fact if we told the truth about 'em, maybe some of 'em was pretty punk. But we drug along in spite of 'em.' Now, do we really want to establish a policy that will place all that power in the hands of a punk president as well as a good one?

"Let me remind you that the power to be wise and sensitive and good is also the power to be foolish, insensitive, and evil. Is this the kind of power we wish to place in the hands of one person at the head of our nation?"

Elizabeth was so intent on Eliot's words that she almost forgot to clap as he sat down.

The teams were then given two minutes to prepare for their rebuttal. The room buzzed as everyone expressed his opinion on the debate so far. On the platform each team turned through piles of papers on their tables and, heads together, conferred on the all-important final statements.

For the final moments of the debate, usually the most telling ones in the minds of the judges, the speaking order was reversed, allowing the affirmative team, who carried the burden of proof, the last speech.

That meant that Eliot took the podium again. Elizabeth knew that she was overrating Eliot's speech when she placed him beside the great orators of history, and yet to her what he said carried such power.

"William Gladstone once called the Constitution of the United States with its checks and balance system the greatest document ever struck off by the mind of man. It is precisely this system of checks and balances that such a policy as proposed by the affirmative would destroy. In adopting the resolution before you, we would lose all that our founding fathers fought for. Therefore I call for your concurrence with the negative. Thank you."

Applause thundered, but Elizabeth sat spellbound. *Yes, Lord. Thank You. Help him. Please.* Her heart was too full to be coherent.

Rowland Amsbury did the best he could for Stanford, but the judges chose two-to-one for the Northwest Christian team.

After that the evening was somewhat of a blur to Elizabeth. Somewhere in the midst of the cheering she realized she should be at The Club seeing that the coffee was perking and that the cookies were set out to the best advantage possible.

The blast of cold air somewhat cleared her head as she raced across the campus. Applause from the auditorium rang across the snow along with the golden lights from the windows. If only the quality of her refreshments could have held up to the quality of NCC's debaters.

She opened the door onto the dining hall and stood spellbound. She couldn't believe it. Alice's hand-designed tablecovers, glowing in the jewel-like light of the shaded lamps, looked like works of rare art. But even more amazing was what was on those covers. Cakes, pies, fancy sweet rolls, trays of chocolate-iced sugar cookies sat beside those her committee had baked.

"It's a miracle," she gasped. She could think of no other explanation.

A sound of running feet crunching in the snow made her turn. Gladys and Boyd ran toward her. "Surprise!"

"We wanted to get here first to see your face!" "What do you think of that?"

"I—I—well, I guess I know how Cinderella felt. How is it possible?"

"Well, don't tell anyone, but most of them are a teensy bit stale." Gladys giggled. "What the Electric Bakery calls day-old is usually more like three days old, but everyone's so excited over the debate I don't think they'll notice."

"You mean you got all this for free?"

"Well, not quite." Boyd stepped forward. "Unless you count the fact that sagebrush is free. Seems NCC isn't the only place running low on fuel, and for all they call it the Electric Bakery, they still heat with coal—and sagebrush— as soon as I can get back in with a nice big load for them."

"Oh, I never thought I'd call sagebrush beautiful. And you two—you're wonderful!" Elizabeth gave them such a big hug that they all knocked their heads together, then pulled apart laughing as their guests arrived to be served.

The excitement of the moment even extended to the Wenschler. Elizabeth had never before seen her wear anything so frivolous as the maroon velvet rose she had pinned to the lapel of her navy blue dress, and her cheeks were flushed almost as deep a red. "I think, my dears, that we just might extend dorm hours a little tonight, don't you? Gladys, I know I can rely on you to tell everyone." Gladys had her mouth open to agree, when the dean of women added the most amazing concession of all, "And social privileges for everyone."

She turned to greet the state superintendent of public instruction, glowing with the pleasure of having done an extraordinarily good deed, and leaving two of her young charges open-mouthed behind her.

Long after the last guest departed, satisfactorily stuffed with the elegant refreshments over which the Stanford debaters, the attorney general, and the Supreme Court justice had all been glowingly complimentary, Elizabeth was making use of her late dorm hours by washing dishes. But there was nothing in the world she would have rather been doing—because Eliot was helping her.

It was good to have something to do with her hands, because her attempts at conversation made little sense. She jumped from talking about the debate, the food, back to the debate, then the decorations, the debate, the prestige they had surely won, the debate . . .

Finally, with the last cup dried, she collapsed on a wooden chair and flung her towel on the floor. "Oh, Eliot, I forgot to tell you the most important thing of all. I prayed and prayed for you all evening, and I think I really understand for the first time how you feel about a call. It's just incomprehensible to me that He hasn't shown you—"

Eliot dropped to a chair beside hers. "Oh, but He has! I've been waiting to tell you—just tonight He did. That is, I expect He told me a long time ago, but tonight I quit demanding long enough to listen to Him. And He was there with the answer, just like He's been all along."

"What! Tell me. Is it China? Do you see your way clear?"

"No. That was the problem all the time. I was telling God what He wanted me to do—and I was all wrong. Elizabeth, He doesn't want me to go to China. He wants me to be a lawyer! I couldn't believe it when I realized that. It was when Condie was introducing the Stanford fellows—both going to be lawyers.

"For a moment the room seemed quiet, like when you've been praying and praying, and then you let go and listen to Him—and—well, I guess that's all. No voice from heaven, no blinding light. I just suddenly *knew.* And I said, 'Thank You, Lord,' and I had this great sense of peace—like nothing I've known ever since I started saying I was going to be a missionary." He paused and shook his head.

"That's it. It was like all the water had been dammed up—for years—and suddenly it started flowing. And then it was over, and I was back concentrating on the debate. The whole thing didn't take nearly as long as it's taken me to tell you, and yet my whole life is changed."

Somewhere in the midst of Eliot's tangled narrative he had taken both her hands, and now they clung to each other, both gasping for breath in the ecstasy of the moment. Elizabeth was the first to realize the impropriety. As she looked at their locked hands Eliot released her and drew back.

He ran his fingers through his hair, rumpling its sleekness before he went on more slowly. "Later I said, no, it isn't possible. That's not right. But even while I was saying it, I *knew.* I just knew that was the answer. Oh, Elizabeth, it's so *obvious.* How could it have taken me so long to see it?"

"That's wonderful. That's just wonderful. You're right, it does seem obvious now—you're so good at debate, you love logic and history and government—all those things I suppose a lawyer needs to know. So what will you do now? After graduation, I mean?"

"Well—I don't know. I hadn't thought. Law school, I guess."

Elizabeth nodded and smiled and repeated how happy she was for him, then he walked her slowly across campus where all the lights in Hadley Hall welcomed them. And because he was so happy and the night had been such a success, Elizabeth didn't mention how expensive law school would be.

16

Even final exams and the beginning of the new semester went almost unnoticed as new economic disasters hit the nation at the beginning of 1933. By February almost every bank in the country was closed. Industrial production was barely half of what it had been in 1929. More than thirteen million people were unemployed. And the Allen family was just one of millions of farm families in desperate straits.

On March 4 Franklin Roosevelt took the oath of office as president of the United States. "This great nation will endure as it has endured, will revive and will prosper," he said in his inaugural address. "The only thing we have to fear is fear itself." Then he set to work to enact the most sweeping peacetime legislative program in America's history.

On the NCC campus, as everywhere else, little was talked about but the National Recovery Administration and the alphabet soup of organizations it set in motion.

Students hurrying to classes, as seniors began the last semester of their college career, matched their steps to the sound of hammers pounding new shingles into the roof of the administration building—a direct result of the success of the debate. In spite of the hard times, public support had been generous to the school that represented the whole community so well.

Elizabeth, with visions of having her own students next year, worked harder than ever. Everything was fine except her school law class. She wanted to teach children, not wrestle with the intricacies of the Idaho Code, school administration, and the complexities of apportionment. At least she knew a future lawyer who understood such things and was willing to help explain their mysteries to her.

She hurried into The Club one day and saw him sitting at his usual table. "Eliot, the tax code doesn't make any sense to me. Can you—" She interrupted herself with a small scream and flung out her arms. "Ilona! I thought I'd never see you again. Are you back?"

"I'm back." The tall blond left her chair by Eliot to embrace Elizabeth. "I got a job in a grocery store almost as soon as I went home, but it hardly paid anything, and I had to give the money to the family until Daddy got a job. When he did, I could start saving to come back to college. And here I am."

"And right in time too. The Glee Club's starting on its music for the graduation concert. You can try out for a solo —Miss Ferney will be thrilled."

Elizabeth sat across the table from Eliot and Ilona but couldn't find a chance to ask help on her assignment, so she turned to Lawrence.

Winter days turned into spring weeks, and Elizabeth began her practice teaching. She was so enmeshed with the technicalities of lesson plans, grade books, and unit projects that she hardly felt like a college student. All she did was eat and sleep on campus. The rest of the time, at least mentally, she was with her class of fourth graders at Lakeview School.

So it came as a shock when Lawrence asked her to sit with him on the drive to McCall for senior sneak.

"Senior sneak? Already? But I haven't heard a word— have there been any meetings? I'm class secretary—"

Lawrence laughed. "Welcome to planet Earth. You were teaching when we had our last three class meetings. Ilona took notes."

"Ilona? But she must only be a sophomore—second semester sophomore, maybe if she got credit for the semester she left early . . ."

Lawrence nodded. "I think she did. But we voted her an honorary senior so she could go on the sneak with us, since we sort of all started out together. Anyway, a lot of people got their schedules messed up when they ran out of money, and—"

"Larry, stop making excuses. She's a lovely person, great fun. I'm delighted she can go on the sneak with us."

"Even if she's coming as Eliot's special friend?"

"Oh."

"I was pretty sure you'd been too busy to notice what's been happening. Then I heard Alice tell Roger yesterday that none of the girls wants to tell you. They've had social privileges three times this month."

"Oh."

"Elizabeth, I know you've always been really good friends. And I guess everybody just sort of took it for granted—even when you doubled with other people and all—but, well, I don't know what to say. I just thought you should know."

"Oh." She stood there feeling the world turn around her, fighting the blackness that threatened to overwhelm her. Then she squeezed his arm. "Thanks, Larry. You're a good friend. A really good friend. I'd like to sit with you. But you know what, I don't even know when it is. What's the plan?"

"Meet at the fish hatchery anytime before sunrise Friday."

"Before sunrise?"

"Sure, got to get the jump on the juniors—ever hear the story of the three little pigs? When we're all there and are sure there are no spies, we drive to Starkey's Plunge.

167

There's a lodge there—I think Velda's uncle knows the owner. Anyway, he's letting us use it."

"Free? Wow!"

"Leaves more in the treasury for food—there's talk of steak. And bring your bathing suit—it's a natural hot spring pool."

She nodded and smiled from habit. Eliot and Ilona? To be fair, she had to admit what a smashing couple they made—both sleek blonds, aristocratic features, gifted. If that was the way it was to be, she would have to get used to it. But for the moment, she had to do something or she'd explode. Thank goodness she was through with teaching and classes for the day. Lesson plans would just have to wait. She needed to do something physical. If only someone were out playing volleyball—they'd see a few slams now if she were on that court. But the sandlot beside the club was empty. Instead she simply began walking.

She walked fast out into the country, head up, shoulders back, arms swinging, forcing herself to stride ever faster. Think about walking, nothing else. At last she was able to slow her stride and concentrate on the beauty of the countryside around her. Evening shadows stretched across green pastures touched gold by the lowering sun. Purple and yellow wildflowers bloomed among the weeds at the side of the road. Black and white Holstein cows dotted the landscape.

Slowly the peace of the world around her combined with her own fatigue to slow her to a gentle amble. Then she realized where she was. This was Vina and Myron's place. She might as well go in and say hello.

When she walked up the tree-lined lane she recognized the familiar black Ford parked there with its isinglass curtains rolled down to protect the driver from the dusty roads. "Aunt Nelly, how good to see you!"

Nelly's engulfing hug was the best medicine Elizabeth's aching heart could have had.

"Well now, what a treat. Come in, come in. Vina'll be right pleased to see you." She drew her inside the comfortable farmhouse ringing with the voices of Vina's energetic brood.

Vina, bustling about in a flowered apron, had grown as plump as her mother, but her hair, worn in a fashionable bob, was a brighter gold. She hurried her children off to bed while Nelly poured Elizabeth a mug of coffee. It was all so—so homey.

Elizabeth could imagine herself ten years old again, looking forward to catching little green frogs in the cistern and swinging on the tire swing on the derrick in a world far removed from studying, teaching, and heartache.

They chatted comfortably until she said, "Tell me about my family, Nelly. I haven't heard from them for ages."

A worried look flitted across Nelly's soft features, but she passed it off with a forced smile. "Oh, much the same as usual, I expect. We all keep on."

"But—" Elizabeth started to press for a clearer answer but was interrupted as Vina entered the room wiping the perspiration from her forehead.

"Getting those kids to bed is the biggest job of the day. Corralling a flock of geese'd be easier any night." She flopped into a brown, upholstered chair, arms and legs extended. "Your turn, Grams. They're waiting to say their prayers with you."

Nelly patted her daughter as she left the room, and Elizabeth put her doubts away to visit with her friend about farm and children.

When Nelly drove her back to the campus shortly before dorm hours, Elizabeth knew that nothing had really changed. And yet that respite, that brief escape into another world, a world of home and children that she had always taken for granted would follow her teaching career— and now realized might never happen for her—had calmed her spirit so that she could think and pray calmly.

And pray she did—but not always calmly. *Lord, help me bear it* was the theme that ran through most of her prayers. Here was one situation—it seemed that life held so many—that hard work couldn't resolve. So she would just have to bear it. With God's help.

Two days later when she and Gladys slipped, shoes in hands, from the dorm and walked the two blocks to where Lawrence had his car sequestered, she knew she could face the weekend even if Eliot and Ilona should go so far as to announce their engagement.

At 2:00 A.M. they arrived, shivering with cold, at the appointed spot.

It was another hour before Eliot and Ilona arrived with Elsie, Edna, and some others. In the excitement of eluding the juniors and awaiting the rest of their classmates everyone drew together. With cheers of "Well done!" whenever another breathless clutch sneaked in under the cover of darkness, the tension that might have existed with the pairing-off evaporated.

Velda, Bernard, Alice, Roger, and one other were the last to arrive just as the sun was coming up. They piled into cars and were off—the seniors had sneaked.

The fish hatchery was on the road to the mountains, and after less than an hour of driving upwards through sagebrush covered hills, they reached the pine forest. It was a beautiful drive through the early May morning. Birds sang in the evergreens that lined the road and stretched up the mountainside. Off to the right the bank dropped steeply to the Payette River, running full and white over the boulders in its bed.

The sweet, orangey scent of syringa greeted them when they arrived at the lodge.

"Oh!" Elizabeth cried and stood spellbound as a streak of brilliant blue flew across their path.

"Mountain bluebird," Lawrence said. "Beautiful, huh?"

It was. Everything was beautiful. And Elizabeth was determined nothing was going to spoil it. The twelve girls ran up to the two large rooms that had been reserved for them. They were in the mountains, so they could go casual in just skirts and blouses.

After a lunch well-organized by Enoch, who was in charge of provisions, the boys took off for a plunge while the girls played volleyball. Then it was the girls' turn to swim. When Elizabeth saw Ilona's willowy form in her bathing costume that stopped well above her knees, she was glad for the college rule that forbade mixed bathing.

Enoch outdid himself for the evening meal. It was no accident that the class member who worked for a butcher had been put in charge of providing food. The rumored steaks were no mere rumors. And they were grilled to perfection.

"I really can't believe how much better these taste than hot dogs!" Lawrence held the tip of his T-bone and sucked the last morsel of meat.

"Yes, but I do miss the potato soup." Elizabeth ducked as three napkins sailed across the table at her.

The main feature of the lodge was a two-story fireplace that filled one end of the room, built of rustic lava and granite and filled with huge pine logs. The pitch in the logs snapped and crackled, sending sparks up the chimney as the two dozen seniors who had managed to hold on and study, pray, and pay tuition through the depths of the depression sat around singing choruses and reminiscing.

In spite of the golden streaks of sun climbing over the mountain behind the lodge and filtering through the tall pines, the air was chill and damp next morning, so everyone donned sweaters before going out for the morning worship service led by Dr. Gilchrist.

"This is my Father's world . . ." Elizabeth sang from the heart, her true soprano voice rising on the clear, mountain air to join the chorus of birds in the trees above them.

Dr. Gilchrist's words followed the same thoughts as the song. No matter how uncertain the future looked—and as exciting as graduation was, the future was still very uncertain, frightening even—they could always trust in the fact that they served the God who had made the world. Then they closed with the last verse of the song, "Oh, let me ne'er forget that though the wrong seems oft so strong, God is the Ruler yet."

Elizabeth couldn't say for sure that Eliot and Ilona getting together was *wrong*—that it was out of place in the eternal plan of God. She just knew it hurt her with a pain she couldn't bear when she let herself think about it—so she refused to think.

There was little time for contemplation anyway, as everyone scrambled to pack water bottles and sandwiches and put on their sturdiest shoes. The plan for the morning was a hike, and the most stout-hearted would attempt to reach the top of the mountain.

They set out as a group, but it wasn't long before Alice, who would rather smell the flowers, and Velda, whose mind was on her wedding to Bernard, which was to follow right after graduation, fell behind along with several others, including Bernard and Roger. A middle group including Gladys, Elsie, and Edna marched along in time to a song one of their members started.

Elizabeth looked over her shoulder and grinned when she noticed Enoch helping Gladys over a fallen log. It was amazing how popular Gladys had become since the debate. Not just because she had saved the reception, but because she now entered into everything without fear of rebuff because of her poverty.

Ironically, Elizabeth, Ilona, Larry, Eliot, and two other men made up the leading group. Because they were more serious about their hiking, they spent little energy on talking, which was just as well, because Elizabeth couldn't think of anything to say to Ilona beyond an occasional comment on something like the startling beauty of a clump of mountain bluebells.

By the time they stopped to eat their lunches, the six leaders were so far ahead they couldn't even hear those behind them. They sat on rocks and fallen logs by the mossy bank of a tiny stream tumbling downhill to reach the river.

Eliot walked a little apart from the group to a small clearing and gazed at the summit. "About another hour should do it. You all game?"

Ilona produced a green and white bandana from her pack, tied it on a sick and waved her flag. "First one there gets to plant this on top!" She grabbed her pack and took off. The mountain was too steep and the way too clogged with rocks and fallen trees to run, but she set a fast pace.

It wasn't long, however, until Eliot and Harvey, followed closely by Norman, pulled ahead. When they disappeared around a bend in the trail, Ilona darted forward. "Hey, we can't let them get away with that. Come on!" With her usual grace she put one hand on a fallen log and sprang over it. Feeling awkward, Elizabeth clambered over, snagging her stockings.

"Whoa! I can't let you girls beat me!" Lawrence scrambled up the side of the mountain, cutting off a curve in the trail, and sprang onto the path in front of them.

They gave a startled cry. Ilona shouted, "Oh, yeah?" and took off like a mountain goat, leaping from boulder to boulder where a landslide had covered the trail.

Whether Ilona slipped or whether a rock turned under her foot was never clear, but a sharp cry of pain alerted the others as she fell.

Lawrence from above her and Elizabeth from below were at her side in a moment. She didn't cry, but from her rigidly held features, Elizabeth could see she was in pain.

"Here, Lawrence, go dip this in the stream." Elizabeth handed him Ilona's brave banner, now fallen.

While he was gone she eased off Ilona's shoe and ungartered her stocking. The ankle was already beginning to swell. "Don't put any weight on that. Here, lean on me— it's too rocky to lie down right here."

Lawrence was back in a minute, the bandana dripping icy water.

Elizabeth bound her friend's ankle with it. "Do you think you can get her back down, Larry? You'll have to carry her. She really can't put any weight on it. Here, I'll carry your packs."

Ilona was tall but fine-boned and slim. Lawrence picked her up like a child.

Elizabeth was amazed at the tenderness on his face as he gazed down at his charge, and at the answering confidence in Ilona's as she put an arm around his neck to steady herself. Ilona must be in great pain, and yet Elizabeth had never seen her look more content. What was going on? she wondered as she followed them all the way down the mountain.

When they reached the lodge, Bernard, Velda, and Alice were just getting ready to leave since Bernard was in charge of the service at the North Side mission that night.

Lawrence, with Ilona still firmly in his arms, squeezed into the back seat. "Don't worry, Ilona, we'll have you to the hospital in no time."

Elizabeth caught her breath. She had never heard him use that intimate tone of voice.

"Elizabeth, you bring Ilona's things down with you this evening—OK?"

"Sure." His voice to her had been very matter-of-fact, and he had hardly waited for her reply before turning all his attention back to the girl in his arms.

"I think we should have a blanket—and a pillow or two," he ordered without taking his eyes off Ilona, who smiled at him bravely.

Elsie ran into the lodge and was back in a minute with the required items. Then they were off. Elizabeth and Elsie waved them down the mountain, but Alice and Velda were the only ones who waved back.

"Well, what do you make of that?" Elsie turned to Elizabeth. "I thought Eliot and Ilona—and you and Larry—"

"We're all just good friends," Elizabeth assured her with far more emphasis than she felt. She didn't know what to make of it either.

It was almost an hour later when the energetic hikers returned. "What happened to you?" Eliot asked Elizabeth. "We made it to the top and didn't have the flag to plant."

Elizabeth took a deep breath. She had to be the one to tell him. She didn't want to see the pain on his face when she told him about Ilona and Larry, but he had to know, and it might as well come from someone who cared about him.

"Ilona turned her ankle. Larry carried her down. Bernard's driving them to the hospital." She said it all on one breath. Bad news shouldn't be dragged out.

His first response was simple concern. "How's Ilona? Is it just a sprain?"

"I think so. I'm sure she'll be all right."

"Well, that's good." He thought for a moment. "Ilona and Larry, you say? How'd he take that?"

How should she answer that? It was clear what he meant. "Eliot, I think he really likes her. Really, I mean. I've never seen him like that before. And, and—she seemed to respond. I . . ." She should say, 'I'm sorry,' but she wasn't.

And neither was Eliot. He threw out his arms and gave a yip of delight. "Hooray! That's the way it should have been all along."

"But I don't understand. I thought you—er—you and Ilona . . ."

"Yeah, we were sort of leaning on each other." He pulled stiffly away from Elizabeth. "After all, we understood how the other one felt because the person we liked wasn't paying any attention to us."

"Huh?"

He shrugged. "Well, you've hardly spoken to me since the debate. You haven't even come to class meetings—to avoid me, I suppose. And then you've been spending your time with Larry . . ."

She couldn't believe her ears. She backed up a few steps to where a wooden swinging bench hung between two trees and sat down. "The only person I've been spending time with is my supervising teacher—and twenty-four very wiggly fourth graders. If you hadn't been spending so much time with Ilona you'd have noticed." She finished the last on a note of challenge.

"Only because she was breaking her heart over Larry, and he wouldn't notice her. She told me all about it. She never forgot him when she went home to work. That was the main reason she was so determined to get back." He sat on the bench beside her and gave it a shove with one foot. The chains creaked.

Elizabeth smiled. "Well, he's noticed her now."

They sat for a long time, swinging their feet back and forth in time to the protests of the rusty chain.

When Gladys came out to tell Elizabeth it was time to get packed, they were holding hands. Gladys paused for a moment, then grinned at them. "Er, yeah. Great."

They laughed as she turned back to the lodge, then joined the others for the return trip.

Lawrence and Ilona announced their engagement at the end of the Glee Club concert the night before graduation.

Long afterwards, through all the ceremonies, speeches, and emotions of graduation day with Baccalaureate in the morning, a hurried lunch with her family at noon, and Commencement in the afternoon, Elizabeth remembered three moments best.

Through all four years of her college career, she had never once been able to sing the college hymn, "Hallelujah! Amen!" without choking up. And graduation was no exception. Especially the verse "They passed through toils and trials and, though the strife was long, they share the victor's conquest, and sing the victor's song" and then "Through grace I soon shall conquer . . ."

The next memory that she cherished was of her mother, eyes shining, hugging her. "My daughter. I'm so proud. The first one in our family to graduate from college. So proud!"

Then Eliot, hurrying because his family was waiting for him, "Elizabeth, I don't know what to do—I just got word—I've been accepted to the U of I law school." And before she could congratulate him he hurried on, "But I can't afford it—there's not a hope."

Above all was the buoyant but frightening feeling that the days of preparation had ended. The earlier struggles had been only preparing for the real ones ahead. "Through grace we soon shall conquer." There was more than hope; there was assurance—assurance of grace. She turned to tell Eliot, but he was gone.

17

Now it seemed to Elizabeth that the whole world revolved around the process of job-hunting. She was back on the farm living with her family after four years of struggle. She had reached her goal. She had her diploma. But had anything changed? Had it been worth it?

Besides filling out forms and interviewing with every school board in the Boise Valley that had an opening in its slate of teachers—and those were few enough, because anyone who had any kind of job in the summer of 1933 kept it—Elizabeth worked mornings at various clerking, stocking, and bookkeeping tasks at the Kuna Mercantile and tried to be a help to her mother at home. It seemed that Kathryn had taken on ever more responsibility for the farm as Merrick, more handsome than ever with his thick black hair streaked with gray and apparently as strong as ever as he struggled with the daily hardships, was noticeably tired and slowed by evening.

Then a seeming miracle happened. Faith Chisholm, who had taught third grade in the red brick Kuna Elementary school for close to twenty years, bought a shiny black Ford from a Boise dealer. The community was agog. How could anyone, especially a maiden schoolteacher, save up enough money to buy a new car?

That unanswered question was soon forgotten in the more amazing aftermath of the story. Miss Chisholm married the automobile dealer—a good five years her junior—who had sleek black hair and played a saxophone in a swing band.

The departure of Miss Faith Chisholm to the bright lights of Boise opened up fairy tale possibilities for another besides Faith. Elizabeth knocked on the door of the newest member of the Kuna school board before noon the next day.

"Mr. Brewington, when your mother told me you'd been elected to the school board I had no idea I'd be applying to you so soon." She held out her neatly typed credentials.

"Thank you, Elizabeth." He took her papers. "The chairman of the school board has called a special meeting for Friday night. Of course there will be several applicants, but I'm sure they will look favorably on a local girl who has such a fine record as yours."

That night Elizabeth wrote a joyful note to Eliot. She was almost embarrassed to be so joyful and optimistic when she knew he was discouraged over his own future.

If anything, it seemed that things had gotten worse for him since he settled on his career goal. Turning down the place offered to him in law school had been one of the most difficult things he had ever had to do. Now he was continuing with the job he had held through his college years—working for James Kirkland, Esquire.

Elizabeth knew that in one way this was a good job for him—any job was good these days, and it at least seemed to be close to his goal—but that very nearness was the difficulty. To be daily working as little more than an errand boy in the profession he longed to enter as a fully qualified practitioner was a bitter pill for one who had always succeeded so easily at anything he undertook.

But tonight she couldn't contain her joy at apparently having her own goal within her grasp.

Her joy lasted for three days.

She was singing when she came in from the barn where she'd been helping Boyd milk the cows Thursday evening when her father held out the newspaper.

"Better sit down, daughter. It's not pleasant reading."

"Is Favoritism to Dictate School Board Decision?" On the second page of the paper a heavy black headline topped Cyrus Griswold's lead editorial. The article went on to detail the two generations of friendship between the families of the newest school board member and the front-running candidate for the coveted opening for the position of teacher at Kuna Elementary. "Those with long memories will realize that the principal actors in this local drama are even relatives by marriage, as Isaiah Jayne, second husband of David Brewington's mother, is Miss Allen's great uncle."

"But that's ridiculous!" Elizabeth slammed the paper onto the kitchen table.

"Of course it is," Merrick agreed. "But the fact that something was ridiculous never stopped it having an influence on people."

Merrick's cynicism proved to be prophetic, for the school board chose a thin, nervous young man from Caldwell as its new teacher. Elizabeth's only consolation was that it helped her understand even better how Eliot felt.

There was now no question as to the fact that they were steady dates, and Elizabeth felt that she lived from one weekend to the next, when Eliot always managed somehow to borrow a car. Free of the institutional regulations of chaperones, double dating, and applying for social privileges, they could spend their time together as they chose. Church socials, picnics on the banks of Indian Creek, and hand-holding quiet walks down country roads constituted most of their outings.

One Saturday morning in mid-July, however, even the Kuna Mercantile, which usually kept open long hours in order to be of service to farmers who drove to town from long distances, closed its doors, and Elizabeth headed west of town to a brown expanse of sagebrush for what was to be anything but a quiet date with Eliot—especially since Boyd was so excited he continually popped his head and shoulders between them from the back seat. He shouted so as to be heard above the rattle and bump of the ancient Ford Eliot had borrowed from his landlady to drive to Kuna to see the barnstormer show.

"Look! Ahead!" Boyd almost knocked off Elizabeth's perky little hat with its three pheasant feathers as he pointed to the skyline ahead of them. "That's a Curtiss Jenny!"

The biplane circled and dipped as gracefully as one of the many eagles that made their home along the river just beyond the section chosen for the air show.

"Can't this crate go any faster?" Boyd pushed forward on the seat.

Eliot grinned and shook his head. "Sorry, but we're not airborne."

"Did I tell you I saw Lucky Lindy when he came to Boise in '27?"

"You've told him three times, Boyd." Elizabeth adjusted her hat, whose brown felt was turning gray with dust.

But no matter how much they might laugh at Boyd's enthusiasm, or Elizabeth might remind her twenty-year-old brother to act his age, it was impossible not to be drawn into the excitement of the crowd. Like the rest of the nation, Idaho was captivated by the air age—especially since Boise's Varney Airlines had been awarded the first contract in the nation to carry air mail.

Well over a hundred cars and buggies were parked behind the roped-off area. People sat on the running boards of their cars and in the beds of their wagons eating picnic lunches while the two planes that were to put on the show warmed up over the desert, awaiting the arrival of the last of their audience.

Elizabeth noted the ambulance and fire engine parked at the edge of the field. She hoped they wouldn't be needed. "Will there be a parachute jump?" she asked Boyd.

"I don't know. Two years ago in Nampa they had a seventeen-year-old girl who held the world's record for jumps—I'd sure like to see her."

Shaking her head, Elizabeth fanned away a cloud of dust and handed Eliot a ham sandwich.

Boyd, however, was far too excited to eat. "Say, that's a DeHavilland!" he cried and took off at a run toward the field, dodging cars, children, and dogs.

In spite of the discomfort of the heat and the dust, however, when the show started Elizabeth felt herself being drawn by the excitement of the daring young men as they flew their war surplus airplanes in loops, rolls, dives, spins, and stalls.

Earlier she had hoped, as she did every time she and Eliot were together, that they might make some plans, however tentative, about their future. Or, since that seemed impossible, she hoped as always to find some way of encouraging Eliot. He seemed ever more discouraged about reaching his goals.

As the crowd cheered a breathtaking barrel roll, however, she realized the impracticality of any such undertaking for that day.

Nick Ralston, the most famous of the barnstormers performing, crawled out on the wing of the Jenny piloted by Gus Homier, lowered a trapeze, and climbed down the rope ladder. Elizabeth gave one small scream, then watched the rest of the performance with her gloved hand clapped firmly over her mouth as Nick did gymnastic stunts on the bar.

When the show was over, the reality of farm chores returned and most of the spectators departed. Elizabeth and Eliot sat for some time, chatting about the activities of the week and the thrills of the air show, avoiding the topics of their dismal career prospects, as they waited for Boyd to return.

"Where could he be?" Elizabeth looked at the thinning crowd. "Surely he wouldn't have gone home with someone else and not told us?"

"Maybe he's going to take a ride." Eliot pointed to the clutch of spectators awaiting their turn as the two planes ferried paying passengers for an aerial sight-seeing ride over the valley and the Snake River. For those who lived near-by, they dipped low enough to startle the cows in their own pastures, although few farmers would want their cows to be frightened into a run so near milking time.

"I'm sure he'd love it. But isn't it awfully expensive?"

Eliot raised his eyebrows. "Two dollars and fifty cents."

Elizabeth was still shaking her head over the cost of such an adventure when Boyd ran toward them, leaping over the sagebrush bushes. "Come on! We're next!"

"What?"

"Our rides. Come on. I've already paid. We're next!"

"Boyd, you're crazy! I'm not going up in one of those contraptions. Besides, where would you get that much money?"

"Borrowed it from a friend." He was already opening her door and pulling her out.

Protests that she had no desire to fly, that she had promised Father she'd be home in time to help with the milking, and that it was far too expensive went unheard.

She noticed Eliot didn't protest at all. "I'll pay you back, Boyd," was all he said as he leaped from the car.

Suddenly the gleam of delight in their eyes communicated itself to Elizabeth. She sensed Boyd's enthusiasm that had been bounding over the desert all day and Eliot's quieter, but no less real, thrill at experiencing a little of what the eagle knew daily, of what Lindbergh felt flying the Atlantic, of what the brave pilots had experienced flying over France during the war. And she wanted to do it too.

"Right. Last one to the rope flies alone!" She set out running but was easily outdistanced by the men.

In the end, however, she didn't fly alone. As the forward cockpits of both planes carried two passengers, she and Eliot donned goggles and helmets and clambered aboard the Curtiss JN, flown by Gus Homier, leaving Boyd to experience the DeHavilland with Nick Ralston.

The plane bumped out nearly a thousand feet over the desert on a runway cleared only of the larger sage bushes. Elizabeth was aware only of the rush of the wind and the noise of the engine and propeller. Then suddenly they weren't bumping anymore. She looked over the side of the plane. The sagebrush sank beneath them. She grabbed Eliot's arm with both hands. "We're up!"

From that moment she was entranced by the adventure. They flew out over the black lava walls of the Snake River Canyon, the river a curving brown strip beneath them. She tried to remember what it had been like picnicking far beneath those canyon walls and looking up to the top. If anyone had told her then she would one day be flying farther above those walls than the eagles flew she would have thought it a great flight of imagination, better than Flash Gordon or Buck Rogers, who peopled the comic books at Janicke's Pharmacy.

But here she was. She leaned over the side of the cockpit to identify the islands below Swan Falls where they had picnicked so long ago.

As their pilot turned the plane in a wide circle to head back toward the field, Elizabeth looked down on the tiny dirt track of road leading across the desert, then on to the miniature cars and horses marking their landing spot. The people were barely visible. And beyond that the mountains. Even they looked small from this perspective.

Perspective—that's what the view gave her. How infinite God's creation was; how small things on earth. What a pinpoint in the scheme of things were the problems that threatened to swamp her. From up here they seemed so small as to be almost nonexistent. She hoped she would always remember that. Perhaps it would help her feel less overwhelmed.

She hadn't thought to be frightened once on the entire flight. Not until they began approaching the landing strip— and the engine coughed.

She grabbed Eliot's arm and looked back at the pilot. The engine caught, and Gus gave her the thumbs up sign. She relaxed.

Then it did it again. Eliot's arms came around her and held her tight. The engine caught again, and the flying seemed smoother, but she didn't lift her face from Eliot's chest. Nor did she quit praying.

On the third cough, the engine did not come back to life. It was incredibly quiet. Only the rush of wind as the pilot maneuvered the little biplane the best he could without power toward the makeshift runway.

Please, Lord, please. Help us. Elizabeth put her arms around Eliot as well.

It seemed a lifetime. She knew it well could be her life. She felt the thud of the wheels on dirt, heard the tearing sound as bushes grabbed at the underside of the plane. She closed her eyes even tighter as the plane jarred over chunks of lava.

The impact she was holding her breath for, and praying would not come, hit with a flinging of fury all around her. Explosions of light broke against the dark of her closed eyes buried in Eliot's chest. The sensation of being flung forward and upside down as the plane went tail over nose was like the time, as a very young child, she had pitched headfirst down the cellar stairs. But never once did Eliot's arms slacken around her.

Then the front of the fuselage crumpled, and they came to rest lopsidedly, propped by a broken wing.

Black smoke billowed from the engine. She heard screaming, or was it a siren? Smoke stung her nose and made her cough. She felt a blast of hot wind, then nothing.

The light was so bright, but it was all fuzzy. She couldn't see anything. She groped with her hand on the sheet.

"Sis! You're awake." Boyd's strong, warm hands grasped hers. "Oh, sis, I'm so sorry. I shouldn't have made you go up. It's all my fault."

"I can't see."

A woman's voice she didn't recognize drew nearer. "You're OK, Miss Allen. We just have gauze over your eyes to protect them from the light. Shall I remove it?"

Elizabeth nodded.

In a moment she was blinking against the light, but blessedly she could see. "Boyd. What happened?"

"You crashed. I'm so sorry. Probably something in the fuel line."

She struggled to sit up, but he pushed her firmly back down. "Eliot?" It came out weakly, so she repeated, with more desperation, "Eliot!"

"He's in the next room."

She relaxed. He was alive. She opened her eyes again. They were in Samaritan Hospital. One of the rooms she had scrubbed every Saturday morning last year. "How is he? Can I see him?"

The nurse, a small blond girl with a badge that said Joyce Nelson on it, stepped back into her view. "You can't get out of bed until the doctor says. He should be here in about an hour. Then we'll see."

"But how is Eliot?" She pulled at her covers and struggled to get up.

"He's still asleep," the nurse said. "I'm sure Dr. Mangum will be here pretty soon. He can tell you more."

"Boyd . . ." she pleaded.

He shook his head. "I tried. They wouldn't let me in."

"Oh, the pilot. Is he—?"

"He's fine. A few cuts and bruises, a sprained ankle." Boyd patted her arm. "Don't you worry about anything. Mom and Alex were here this morning, but Aunt Nelly took

186

them home. They'll be back tomorrow. Everything's going to be all right."

"But how long have I been here? What day is it?"

"The accident was yesterday afternoon. You've been here about eighteen hours."

"I'm so thirsty."

The nurse held a straw to Elizabeth's lips. She drank, then dozed off. She didn't know how long she spent slipping in and out of consciousness, but finally Dr. Mangum came.

"Well, you've had quite an adventure, young lady. Want to be an aeronaut, do you?"

Elizabeth shook her head with as much energy as she could manage.

The doctor smiled as he examined her. "No, after that I shouldn't imagine you would. But I would say you're very lucky. This shoulder where you were thrown against the side of the plane is going to be very sore for some time, but nothing was broken. You've mostly suffered from shock and smoke inhalation—and not as much of that as you might have. That young man next door seems to have done a pretty good job sheltering you."

"And the Man upstairs." Even though she didn't really like that expression, it seemed to follow.

Dr. Mangum's kind eyes crinkled at the corners. "Yes, indeed. He was watching over you just fine." He continued his examination. "Have you eaten anything yet?"

Elizabeth shook her head.

"Well, we'll get you some soup and gelatin. If you keep that down all right I expect you can go home tomorrow—provided you take it easy for a few days.'

"Yes, fine. But how is Eliot?"

Dr. Mangum perched on the edge of her bed and lay a hand gently against her upper arm. "With God's help we can hope that he'll be all right in time. But I'm going to tell you the truth. It's not going to be easy."

"Tell me."

"His left arm is badly smashed, right here." He patted Elizabeth's arm where his hand lay. "That will heal in time, perhaps somewhat crookedly, but he'll have quite good use of it, I'm sure. The right side of his neck and face were burned. We're applying heavy saline baths. They'll heal. But there will be scarring."

She took a deep breath and relaxed. Was that all? A crooked arm, a few scars? He would hate that. He was always a bit vain about his elegant looks, but he would be all right. She would have her Eliot back. She hadn't realized until that moment—hadn't let herself think about it—how unthinkable life would be without him. They had worried so about their careers, about security, but now she knew that the only security she needed for her future was Eliot.

"Oh, thank you, Doctor."

"Wait. That's not all. Those are the externals."

She caught her breath on a little gasp.

"We can't be sure until he wakes up, but he took an awfully hard blow to the side of his head." Dr. Mangum shook his head. "It's impossible to tell about those things —time and the hand of God. We must trust the Great Physician."

"I want to see him."

Dr. Mangum looked like he was going to argue with her, then shrugged. "Well, I don't suppose it will do any harm. Eat your soup. Then if you're feeling strong enough." He looked over his shoulder. "Nurse Nelson?"

"Yes, Doctor."

"You can help her next door in case she's still a little woozy."

Elizabeth didn't even notice that the chicken vegetable soup was scalding hot. She just knew that if she got it down, followed it with a glass of milk and a few bites of strawberry Gel-set, she could go to Eliot. By sheer force of will she would not have a queasy stomach, nor would she allow her knees to wobble. She had to be strong for both of them, because Eliot, who had protected her from the burning plane, couldn't be strong.

In spite of her most determined efforts, however, it was still some time before Nurse Nelson had duly recorded her pulse and temperature and declared her fit to walk the twenty or thirty feet to Eliot's room.

Elizabeth thought she had complete control of herself, but the sight of the still, gauze-bandaged form on the bed almost overcame her. "As silent as the tomb" was the phrase that filled her mind, but she would not think about tombs.

The nurse's hand on her elbow steadied her. She took a deep breath and walked forward. "Eliot. I'm here, Eliot." She wanted to sob at his lack of response but steeled herself. "May I sit for a while?"

Miss Nelson moved a dark wooden chair to the edge of the narrow bed, and Elizabeth sat. When she seemed satisfied that no harm would come to her patients from the present arrangement, the nurse tiptoed from the room.

Elizabeth started to reach for Eliot's hand, then drew back. Dr. Mangum hadn't mentioned that his hands had been burned too, but apparently they had, for they were swathed in bulky white gauze. She lay her hand along his right arm, about where the doctor had indicated his left was so badly broken.

Oh, God. God. She had never felt her love so strong before. It was as if it were a thick blanket she could wrap around Eliot and hold him close to her heart.

She couldn't imagine what the future held for them. She could barely think beyond this moment and this room. But she knew one thing with overwhelming certainty. Whatever was out there in time or distance, no matter how long or short their future was to be, she didn't want to go into it without Eliot. The scars didn't matter, the weakened arm didn't matter, even—no, she wouldn't think about the possibility of brain damage—nothing mattered but that they be together.

189

With the tacit understanding that they would settle their careers before they thought about marriage, they had talked much about work and little about their relationship. Now she knew that, no matter what, she didn't want to take a chance on anything happening to either one of them without their becoming husband and wife.

The words of the marriage ceremony could never have meant more to any bride at the altar than they did to Elizabeth sitting in that dim, still hospital room. "For better or worse, for richer or poorer, in sickness and in health . . ." Life with Eliot might be the worse of each pair, but she wanted it more than anything else in the world.

18

Eliot still had not wakened when Kathryn came to take Elizabeth home the next day. "You promise you'll call the minute anything happens—*the minute?* It's number 5." Elizabeth gave them the phone number of the mercantile store, knowing they would get a message to her.

The sun seemed so bright. The crops in the field looked so heart-breakingly healthy—viewing them as she did with the knowledge that they would produce only a few cents per bushel. It seemed to Elizabeth she had been gone weeks rather than days. And whenever anyone asked, her answer was always the same, "I'm fine, thank you. And Eliot will be fine." She always said it with her head up.

The verse that had held her steady through so many hard days in college now came back with new meaning. *Who shall separate us from the love of Christ? shall tribulation, or distress . . . or peril, or sword?* She now hardly gave any thought to famine and nakedness—the symbols of poverty she had so worried over in college. In her mind she often found herself quoting the last word as "fire" rather than "sword" as through many sleepless nights she relived the engulfing smoke and heat that had come upon her before she blacked out—except that now she didn't black out, but lay wide awake back on the sleeping porch with Alex breathing rhythmically beside her.

She had lost track of how many such nights she had endured when the gentle swish of the door and a creaky floorboard told her someone was there.

"Mother?" she whispered.

Kathryn knelt by her bed. "I thought you might be awake. The black circles under your eyes told me you haven't been sleeping well." She lay a cool hand on Elizabeth's forehead. "When we came to the desert I didn't sleep well. My papa quoted the Psalms to me." She brushed Elizabeth's thick black waves back from her face, and a gentle breeze rippled in the screened window.

"The Lord is my shepherd, I shall not want . . ." Elizabeth closed her eyes. "Yea, though I walk through the valley of the shadow of death, I will fear no evil . . ." Elizabeth felt long-held tension leave her body, and she began to drift.

She slept late the next morning so was surprised to see her father still at the breakfast table reading the newspaper when she entered the kitchen. She poured herself a cup of fresh-perked coffee and sat beside him.

Merrick shook his head without looking up. "I don't know. Things sure look bad in Europe."

Europe? Elizabeth gulped a mouthful of strong, hot coffee. What was happening in Europe? She had been so intensely involved in her own life—her own life that revolved around those in this house and a lonely figure in a hospital room fifteen miles away from which a phone call had not yet come—that she had forgotten there was a world beyond. "What's happening?"

Merrick shook his head again. "The German army leaders have sworn personal allegiance to their new chancellor—that Adolph Hitler. Churchill is urging England to rearm—but it doesn't look like anyone will listen to him."

Elizabeth blinked, trying to put it all in perspective, wondering what importance events so far away could have to them. "Why should England rearm? What's wrong with Germany being loyal to its chancellor?"

"Maybe nothing. But the point is that the allegiance is to Hitler as a person, not to the office or to the nation. That places a lot of power in the hands of one man."

"So you think Churchill's right?"

"I've always thought a lot of Winston Churchill. My cousin Robbie fought under him in the War. Well, not directly, but Robbie was in the Royal Navy, and Churchill was First Lord of the Admirality."

"But now he's out of office, isn't he?" Elizabeth struggled. She felt as if she would be hard put to name the president of the United States at the moment.

Merrick nodded. "Out of office and few people listening to him, but I wonder . . ." He took a sip of coffee. "Maybe I'm just prejudiced because Cyrus Griswold's so pro-Hitler. 'A real leader for Germany,' he editorializes here."

Elizabeth had gotten up to slice some bread for toast when a stomping of boots on the back porch made her turn. "Clarey!" She flung out her arms.

He backed up, holding out his hand. Then she saw she was still brandishing the bread knife. She tossed it aside, and they fell into a hug, laughing. "I haven't seen you for ages!" she cried.

"Don't know whose fault that is. I've been here most every day lately."

She pulled back and looked at him with a frown. "Why?"

He shrugged. "Took the water off the corn on the Hendricks place so not much to do there. I came to help out. Almost time for the third haying. Plenty to do here."

Water off the corn? Third haying? That meant it was almost time for school to start. And she didn't have a job. But then a red-haired, freckled-faced four-year-old burst in, and Tommy took everyone's attention.

"Did I tell you Mavis's expecting?" Clarey made an obvious effort to sound nonchalant.

"Oh, Clarey! Congratulations. It's time Tommy had a playmate." She didn't go on to say that it was also time

Clarey and Mavis had a home of their own, no matter how hard times were. Living with her parents in their tiny two-bedroom farmhouse would surely be intolerable when another baby came. And Clarey looked so discouraged when he relaxed—sometimes he seemed almost as old as their father.

But now he grinned. That made him look like the brother she had known. "Yeah," he said, "we always had a lot of fun growing up together, didn't we? Swinging on the derrick, swimmin' in the creek. Remember the time Dad told us not to slide on the new haystack?"

"And I got buried when it all came down on top of me! Better not let Tommy hear that—he'll get ideas." She turned to get her nephew a glass of milk. Which he promptly spilled—all over his grandfather's newspaper.

It was when she was sopping it all up with a towel that Elizabeth noticed the two-inch long article on the bottom of the back page. "Oh, look. It says that Miss Elmira Simmons who taught the lower grades at Mora School ever since it opened in 1910 has resigned to care for her widowed mother in Meridian."

Clarey laughed. "Since 1910? Can you imagine teaching squirmy youngsters for that long? The woman must be a saint."

But Elizabeth's mind was working in entirely another direction. "It doesn't say here that they've filled her position. May I take the car this afternoon, Father?"

It took her some time to find out who was chairman of the Mora school board and drive to his farm with her credentials. It took two more days of waiting while the board met and considered. Then they called her in for an interview. And one week before the opening of school Miss Elizabeth Allen signed a contract to teach grades one through four at Mora School.

The impressive red brick schoolhouse with its Spanish tile roof, elevated portico over the arched front door, and matching gazebo at the front of the schoolyard, had been built with right-of-way money from the Oregon Short Line Railroad, and it lacked for nothing. The finest slate chalkboards, a drinking fountain outside each room, an auditorium and lunch room downstairs, sturdy outdoor bathrooms, and—only a short walk away—a cozy teacherage.

John Voorhees and his comfortable wife, Frieda, who kept the tiny kitchen of the teacherage smelling of Dutch cheese rolls and cinnamon twists, lived in the tiny house. Elizabeth had a single room in the back, where she cooked, slept, and prepared her lessons. There was barely time to settle into her compact quarters, filling one wall with makeshift book shelves and the little dugout cellar under her room with colorful jars of Kathryn's canned fruit and vegetables, before school began.

"Good morning, Miss Allen." Thirty-two shiny faces smiled at her over hands folded on the desktops in front of them.

"Good morning, class." She wondered if any of their knees were knocking as hard as hers. "Please stand and put your hand over your heart for the Pledge of Allegiance."

". . . One nation, indivisible, with liberty and justice for all." With a scraping of feet and creaking of seats (she would have to see about oiling those hinges) the students sat down again, and she reached for her Bible.

There was no question in her mind as to what she would read to them that day. "The Lord is my shepherd . . ."

Somehow she got through her first morning. She supervised the girls' bathroom at recess, and John Voorhees watched the boys. At noon all the children pulled their sacks from their cubbies in the cloakroom and marched downstairs to the lunchroom. When lunch recess was over one of the boys from the big room turned the wheel on the big iron bell on the back stairs, and everyone lined up to march inside.

Now came what Elizabeth was sure would always be her favorite time of the school day—reading to her students. She had chosen to start with *Hans Brinker and the*

Silver Skates, a favorite she remembered her teacher's reading to her. Then art. The third and fourth graders would weave baskets from strips of brown and gold paper while the first and second graders cut out round red apples to put in the baskets. When finished, they would make a colorful border tacked above the chalkboard for the lithographs of George Washington and Abraham Lincoln to smile down on.

"Dick. Jane. Sally." She held up the big picture charts and pronounced each name clearly. Her first graders looked at her dully. The first adjustment she would make to her lesson schedule would be to move first grade reading to the morning. Hopefully more of them would be awake then. At her direction two of the older boys opened the windows that lined the front of the room. Some fresh air might help. At last three o'clock came.

"Yes, Sara," she responded to a waving hand.

"May Molly and I clean the erasers this week?"

Elizabeth agreed readily and thanked them—then remembered just in time to have everyone fold his seat up. It would make her job of sweeping the room much easier. After they left, however, she noted with dismay that she had failed to have them pick up all the scrap paper around their desks.

Sara and Molly returned from the schoolyard with a satisfactory amount of chalk dust on their faces and clothes to show they had done a vigorous job. Then they left the room with the customary "Good-bye, Miss Allen," and Elizabeth could sink into the chair behind her desk with the sigh she felt she had been holding for hours. Next she wanted to follow it with a shout. She had done it! Her first day. And no disasters. She was a teacher.

And she had done it all being only half there. For her heart and much of her mind was, as always, in the shaded quiet of a room in Samaritan Hospital where Eliot's burns and broken bones were slowly healing, although he had not regained consciousness.

His father and married sister called regularly from Spokane. Dr. Mangum assured them everything possible was being done. There was no need for them to come until he woke up.

But Elizabeth would not be put off by any such assurances. She drove in every weekend to sit in the bare room and talk to Eliot. For no matter how certain the doctor and nurses were that he couldn't hear her and had no awareness of her presence, there were times when she felt a link of communication.

When she ran out of daily news about her teaching, she read the Bible to him. Always, when she came to particularly comforting passages, she felt him relax. It may only have been that she credited her own relaxation to him, but she felt something.

And since everyone assured her Eliot couldn't really hear her anyway, she said all the things to him she had wanted to say for so long but had held back from expressing. She told him outright how she longed to be his wife, how she now realized that anything else mattered very little to her, how she wanted to marry him if they could never live in anything but a shack together—if he could never be anything more than a lawyer's clerk, although she was perfectly confident of his success once he and the economy were both recovered.

She always got the same answer when she looked questioningly at Dr. Mangum: "We never know in cases like this. Sometimes they wake up in a few days or weeks as bright as if they've just had a good night of sleep. Other times . . ."

She nodded. She knew.

Then she went back to her students. One day in late October she found to be particularly stressful. Perhaps it was the unusually oppressive heat for that time of year that made it even harder than usual for her students to sit still, or perhaps it was the fact that she realized Eliot had now been unconscious for nearly three months. There were a few possibly hopeful signs—he occasionally muttered as if trying to express a coherent thought, his eyelids had fluttered a few times as if he would open his eyes, and twice she had thought she felt the slightest response when she held his hand from which the bandages were now removed. But at times the ache in her heart to have the old Eliot back all but overpowered her.

"See Puff."

"See Puff jump."

"See Spot."

"See Spot run."

Morning recess time at last. She led her students down the broad back stairs and released them to the freedom of the playground. She was supposed to stay with them every minute, but the sun beat hot on her head, and their shrill voices were giving her a headache. The comparative cool and quiet of her room beckoned. She surveyed the yard. The children were playing well. No fights. No name-calling threatening to explode into a fight. She turned and walked back up the stairs.

She had been at her desk, head resting on folded arms, less than three minutes when she heard shrieks. She ran to the door. Little Ellen Taggart, a second grader with the curliest blond hair in the school, sat in the dirt beneath the swing set howling, blood all over her face.

Without thought for the wide white collar on her dress, Elizabeth scooped the child into her arms and fled up the stairs. She didn't even have a first aid kit in her room. The big room was still reciting, but there was nothing else to do. She knocked on the door.

John Voorhees took one look at the situation. His gentle blue eyes smiled at the terrified child. "Ah, cut your lip, have you? I'll wager you walked too close to the swings."

Ellen's curls bounced when she nodded her head.

"Todd, bring us the bandages," Mr. Voorhees said to an older boy.

It was the work of a few minutes to wash off the blood and dust at the drinking fountain—the cut was a small one for the amount of blood it produced—and swab it with iodine. The sting from the yellow-brown liquid brought louder howls than the initial injury, but John followed it quickly with salve and gauze, all held on with a bit of adhesive tape.

"There now, young lady. You'll be right as rain in a day or two, but stay out of the path of those swings, you hear?"

When Ellen had gone, Elizabeth knew she could delay her confession no longer. "John, I—er—I'm afraid it's my fault. I wasn't on the playground."

A wave of brown hair fell over his high forehead when he nodded. "And are you so sure you could have prevented it if you'd been there? It's best not to ascribe too much power to ourselves—or too much fault, either." Spoken in his soft Dutch accent the words held special comfort.

The rest of the morning and lunch passed without incident, but so slowly Elizabeth felt it surely must be dismissal time when she marched the students in for the afternoon. At least they were up to her favorite part of the day.

"I have a new book for us today, class." She held up her own childhood copy of *Heidi*. "Put your heads on your desks. Now picture in your minds the tallest mountains in the world, all green, dotted with sheep and goats and wildflowers—and a small cabin set in a sheltered spot." She began reading. The beloved story filled her own mind with pictures brought back from when she was the age of the children in front of her. She could almost hear her mother's voice reading to her.

The ten minutes allotted to reading aloud stretched to twenty, then thirty. The children were still and quiet, listening, she hoped, but perhaps some dozing. A soft, warm breeze blew in through the windows, wafting the scent of the potted geraniums blooming there.

Elizabeth glanced out the window at the sound of a car on the road in front of the school, then faltered over a word when it turned into the graveled drive and braked to a stop in front of the building. A trim lady in a navy blue, businesslike suit got out and adjusted her hat. Mrs. Vance. The District Superintendent was making a surprise visit. And her students were all asleep or daydreaming well past the time that they should have been deep into geography and history.

She snapped her book shut with a bang that awoke the sleepyheads. "Fourth grade, take out your Idaho history books and review Chief Joseph. I will hear you recite first."

The heavy front door creaked open.

"Third grade. Chapter five in geography."

A purposeful tread echoed from the bare wooden floor of the hall.

"Second grade . . ."

By the time her door opened, Elizabeth was into a well-ordered penmanship lesson with her first graders. "Oh, Mrs. Vance. What a nice surprise. Lucy, would you like to share your book with our visitor?"

Mrs. Vance walked forward, pulling off her short white gloves. "That won't be necessary, thank you. I wish to speak to you, Miss Allen."

Elizabeth gulped. Surely the superintendent couldn't have heard of her lapse in playground supervision already? She looked at Ellen, chewing intently on the end of her pencil as she pondered an arithmetic problem.

"Boys and girls, I have come with some very good news for Miss Allen."

Elizabeth let out the breath she had been holding.

"Some of you may know that your teacher and a friend of hers were hurt at the air show this summer—"

Three hands shot up, ready to tell about their own experiences, but the room blurred to Elizabeth. *Good news. She had said good news. Oh, please, Lord.*

The superintendent went on to explain to Elizabeth and the whole room that the hospital, anxious to reach Elizabeth with the news that Eliot had regained consciousness, had called the school district office because it had the nearest telephone. And Mrs. Vance herself, she announced as she removed her hat, would be their teacher for the rest of the day so Miss Allen could visit her friend in the hospital.

Elizabeth had the vague idea that her class applauded, but it might have been the pounding of her heart. For the second time that day she interrupted the big room lessons. John Voorhees was only too glad to loan her his car.

"Eliot. Oh, Eliot." She had determined not to cry. She had not cried since the first night after she knew how seriously Eliot was injured—well, she hadn't cried much. But now the tears flowed silently down her cheeks, pushed out by all the things she wanted to say, the things she wanted to do—like throwing herself into his arms and kissing him wildly. But instead she sat lightly on the edge of his bed and lay her face next to his on the pillow, getting them both wet with her tears.

"Oh, thank God," she said at last. "I've prayed for this moment for so long. Oh, Eliot—" She held back, but then, because she had said it to him so many times when he couldn't hear her, she said it now when he could. "Oh, Eliot. I love you. I love you so much."

His right arm came around her; his left moved a little. "I'm so weak. I want to hold you tight, but I can't." He choked on the word. "Oh, Elizabeth, I love you too. I have for so long, but there was always so much in the way."

"I know. But now I can't even remember what those things were—they don't seem at all important now, do they?"

He turned his head on the pillow. "Not in the least. I'm alive, and you're here. That's what matters." He paused.

Elizabeth could feel him swallowing hard as if there were a great lump in his throat.

"But Elizabeth, I looked in the mirror . . . and my arm—"

She sat up and held his head in her hands, a gentle, white palm aside each cheek. She looked long, her eyes full of love. Then she bent forward and kissed the angry red scars on his right cheek and down his neck. "Eliot Hudson Taylor Hamilton, don't talk nonsense."

His right arm was quite strong enough to pull her back down on the bed.

19

"Yes, Eliot's back at work full time now." Elizabeth sipped at the tea her mother had given her and pasted her bravest smile on her face. She hadn't endured the ride to Kuna over rutted March roads in the back of a rickety pickup—the only ride she could catch when she decided she couldn't stand another weekend alone in the teacherage —just to pour out all her troubles to her family.

Indeed, she had thought she could help her mother with the work and perhaps cheer up Alex and Boyd with stories of her students' antics. Boyd would certainly have more sympathy than she did for the paper missiles they constructed in imitation of Buck Rogers and flung around the room behind her back.

But now, with evening coming on and a cold wind flinging snow against the house, she was finding it increasingly hard to keep up her brave front.

As soon as Eliot was strong enough to sit up for long periods and carry heavy law books around the room he had begun working again for James Kirkland. "Of course, he can't do the errand running and filing work that he used to do, but there's plenty to do researching cases, and that's the part he likes best anyway." She smiled again as Kathryn refilled her cup.

"He was so thin the last time I saw him. Has he gained any weight yet?" Kathryn asked.

"Well, some, but he's still underweight. He needs lots of rest and exercise."

"How's his arm?" Boyd asked the crucial question.

"Getting better. You'd hardly notice it. It really doesn't hamper him at all. His hand works fully." She took refuge in a long sip of tea. The truth was that the arm was shriveled and pulled in awkwardly at the elbow. He couldn't lift anything heavy.

Not that it mattered at all to her. But she knew it would to an employer. And jobs were so scarce. In spite of the best efforts of the National Recovery Administration, one-third of the work force of America was still unemployed. Kirkland paid a fair wage for a clerk—which was just enough for Eliot's own room and board. And now there were hospital and doctor bills to pay. All thoughts of saving for law school were abandoned. Neither of them even spoke of it anymore.

"But when are you going to get married?" Trust Alex to probe.

Elizabeth could only shake her head. That was something else they never spoke of anymore. A pall of hopelessness seemed to hang over their times together. Sometimes she would close her eyes and relive those wonderful moments in the hospital when Eliot first came to and everything had seemed within their grasp. Now it seemed their dreams were moving farther and farther away.

"I suppose we'll think about that when the hospital bills are paid. If they're ever paid." She couldn't quite suppress her sigh. "You know, when you're little, you think it's all so simple," Elizabeth said. "You think you just fall in love and get married and live happily ever after. It sure isn't like that."

Kathryn laughed. "No, my dear. It surely isn't. But love and a good marriage built on God's direction are the best things I know for getting one through life's difficulties. The older I get the more I realize that your family and your relationship to God are all that really matter in life."

She paused, and Merrick continued. "That's why your mother and I have been so thankful that you found Eliot—such a fine young man." He looked to Kathryn for her to go on.

"Yes, my dear. And that's why we want to help you. We've suspected for some time that medical bills were at the heart of your problem. Your father and I have talked a lot about this—"

"Help us?" Elizabeth couldn't imagine what they meant. How could they help? They barely had money and energy to keep things going here.

Kathryn got up and went into the bedroom. She returned in a minute carrying a brown velvet box. "Have you ever seen these?" She lifted the lid to reveal a set of pale blue-green, sparkling aquamarines set in old-fashioned filigree silver mountings.

Elizabeth frowned, trying to remember. "Once, I think. There was a party. You were so beautiful, Mother. I must have been about nine years old."

Kathryn smiled and nodded. "That's right. It was a party to celebrate the end of the Great War. We drove in to the Dewey Palace." Her eyes grew soft. "What a lovely night that was, Merrick. We . . ." With a little shake she came out of her reverie. "And then two years later the bottom fell out of farm prices, and I never wore them again. They've been in a safety deposit box in the bank all these years. I was always so glad they were there—just in case."

Merrick picked up the ornate brooch and held it in the palm of his hand. "Remember when they were stolen on our honeymoon, Kathryn?"

"How could I ever forget! Maybe that's one reason we've been so slow to part with them."

"It was good knowing we had them, if there was ever something we just couldn't pay for any other way."

205

"But there never was." Kathryn's voice carried a spark of triumph undoubtedly spurred by memories of chopping sagebrush and plucking chickens late into many a night. "But we've talked about it a lot, and we think this is the time."

She held the case out. Merrick placed the brooch beside the earrings, then passed it to Elizabeth. "They would have come to you on your wedding, anyway. So why not a little before? Your Great-Grandmother Phyllida passed them on to your father early because of special need too."

Elizabeth stared at the jewels blinking at her from their bed of satin. "I never knew we had anything this valuable in the family. They seem so . . . so . . . ."

Kathryn laughed. "So incongruous?"

"Yes! Totally out of place on a depression-ridden desert farm. They look like something one would wear to the White House."

"They are out of place. They're from another world," Merrick said. "I don't know how valuable they really are—aquamarines aren't diamonds—but they are genuine antiques. A Boise dealer ought to be able to help you."

"You mean you want me to *sell* them?"

"To give you and Eliot a start. We want you to be as happy together as we've always been." Kathryn slipped her hand into Merrick's.

Elizabeth thought. She couldn't just waltz up to Eliot and say, "My parents want us to get married, so I'm going to sell the family jewels to pay your bills." He wouldn't take money from her before they were married. And he wouldn't even ask her to marry him before the bills were paid. Thoughts chased each other around like squirrels in her mind.

At last she hugged her parents and tried to thank them, although no words seemed adequate. "Thank you, thank you. This means so much to me—but I don't know. Here, Mother, you keep them while I think what to do." Then she kissed her parents and went to bed, planning to think, pray, and plan long into the night. But instead, she fell immediately asleep.

The next morning they had a guest speaker at church. Miss Lottie Richardson, the missionary speaker whose special services at NCC had brought Eliot's search so sharply into focus their first year in college. That seemed a lifetime ago.

Today Miss Richardson was speaking on behalf of the work of Samaritan Hospital, which had graduated a class of nurses and medical missionaries every spring since Dr. and Mrs. Mangum turned their beautiful home by Kurtz Park into a training sanitarium.

"There are now hundreds of men and women ministering to the souls and bodies of needy people on foreign fields, using the training they received at this institution."

But now the hospital faced a crisis. Ten years ago construction had begun to build the best in fully equipped modern hospitals. Today, only $5,000 short of their goal, the work had ceased. This spring fifty nurses would graduate. Without new equipment this would likely be the last class. With the new hospital, the number could be doubled.

"Think what such an army of well-trained missionaries can mean to the Lord's work." Miss Richardson glowed with the vision. "But I'm not asking you to give money." She smiled as her audience relaxed. "I know that's next to impossible for everyone these days. And although I know that with God all things are possible, I think He's sometimes pleased to have us use our ingenuity and creativity. That's why I'm here to ask you to give what you can. Surely almost everyone in this fine audience has some possession he could spare for the sake of lost souls. I have been leading this special drive all over the valley for months now, and people have given wedding rings, purses, watches, typewriters, fountain pens, and even a cow—all to be converted into bricks and mortar for the glory of God.

"I want you all to stand now and sing to His glory. If you have something with you to give now, I want you to march right up here and lay it on the altar—we'll have a great old-time hallelujah march. If what you want to give is at home, bring it tonight, for we'll have another, even greater, march tonight. Let's stand now and sing 'Hallelujah, Amen!'"

Elizabeth didn't need the words of her favorite hymn to prod her. She knew what she must do. Eliot had wanted to be a missionary; God had other plans. But the jewels that had been given them for their future could be given to God to train others who would go to China and all around the world with His word and healing touch.

Still, it wasn't easy. She couldn't imagine herself ever wearing such jewels, but their sentimental value was enormous. They had been in her family for generations. Had they been a wedding present to her great-grandmother? Perhaps from *her* father? Would Elizabeth herself someday have a daughter she would want to hand them down to?

Their monetary value meant little to her except for what it could accomplish. Would she be acting foolishly in giving away her one chance to pay off Eliot's bill? How else could it be done? And what would her parents think? They had given the jewels to her for her life with Eliot, not to respond to a missionary call. Would they understand?

Through all her questioning, however, one fact remained crystal clear. No matter how little she understood why God was telling her this, there was absolutely no doubt in her mind that He had spoken. She could not do other than to obey in blind faith.

She went to talk to Kathryn.

That evening she never gave a thought to how they were to pay off Eliot's bill as she marched forward and placed the brown velvet case on the altar. "If it's God's call, you can't do anything else—my papa taught me that." Kathryn had confirmed what Elizabeth already knew.

She sang with the others, "My soul takes up the chorus and pressing on my way, communing still with Jesus, I sing from day to day." Tears of joy ran down her face as she returned to her seat.

March and April alternated brief snowstorms and quick thaws, which left the roads muddy and all but impassable. Weeks passed when Elizabeth's only communication with Eliot was a hastily scribbled note, which she would write before falling asleep at night. And he answered her as a break from his research.

But finally spring came. The weather turned warm and dry, and the desert sprang into flower. Birds sang, crickets chirped, and the tiny ground squirrels the school-children called whistle pigs burrowed busily under the sage bushes. Elizabeth, reveling in the lavish display, was glad the flowers and little creatures didn't know there was a depression going on.

With spring came the event of the season, the annual grange box social.

"Oh, Elizabeth, that's the most beautiful box I've ever seen!" Since the hot plate in the teacherage wouldn't be adequate for the feast Elizabeth planned to prepare for her box, she had gone home Saturday to Kathryn's kitchen where Alex had lined up their boxes for a critical assess-ment. "How did you ever have the patience to make all those tiny paper flowers?"

Elizabeth smiled. She was proud of the green tissue-paper-covered box wound with trailing vines of pink rose-buds. "All right, I'll confess. It was a spin-off of a class art project. They made ropes of these vines to put above the blackboard and were thrilled when I told them what I wanted to use this length for."

"You've got a whole classroom of little romantics, haven't you?" Alex grinned, then turned to her box. "I don't know, I thought I was so clever to put a doll on mine, but yours is much better."

"Nonsense, the way her scalloped skirt covers the whole lid is great. Who do you want to buy it?"

"Oh, no one special." But Alexandra's eyes gleamed in a way that told Elizabeth there was someone *very* special. Elizabeth just smiled and turned to spread thick chocolate icing over her sour cream chocolate cake before wrapping Frieda Voorhees's crispy Dutch rolls in waxed paper to add to the cache.

A few hours later, dressed in Kathryn's cleverly updated version of her white graduation dress with the big pink flowers on it and carrying her heavy box under a concealing white towel to preserve the mystery that made the bidding such fun, Elizabeth ran to answer Eliot's knock at the door.

"Oh, it's so good to see you!" She would have liked to fling herself into his arms, but their long times apart the past months made her shy. "You look so good."

She could see her words pleased him, although he turned the scarred side of his face away. The gesture hurt her. The red of the scars had faded until they were hardly noticeable, especially to Elizabeth. She had always thought him the most handsome man she'd ever seen—especially tonight with his white shirt starched and ironed stiff and a white handkerchief in the breast pocket of his dark suit.

"You look better than good. You're gorgeous."

Now it was her turn to draw back. She knew she wasn't beautiful, but she so wanted Eliot to think it. She almost wished he wouldn't look at her again for fear he'd revise his opinion. But she fought her instincts to turn away, called good-bye to her family, and went out into the spring evening on the arm of the man she loved.

The grange was packed with people Elizabeth hadn't seen for years. Edith, still as sweet as ever, was there with her Rupert, talking a mile a minute about her three children, and especially happy to compare notes with Mavis as their infant daughters were born just a month apart. Celia and Walter had even come from Boise to attend the event with Celia's parents. Elizabeth wondered if she would have noticed Celia's brittleness and Walter's roving eye if

Celia hadn't confided in her two years before. But it was good to see her old friends again.

"And what am I bid for this beautiful box?" Mr. Oldham, serving as auctioneer for the evening, held up a large round box decorated with a clown face. He sniffed deeply. "Ah, fried chicken *and* roast ham. This box is heavy, gentlemen. Who's really hungry for some of the finest cooking in all of Boise Valley?"

Clarey opened the bidding at fifty cents, but a sharp look from Mavis told him that wasn't her box, so he dropped out, and after a spirited round of competition Rupert bought the box, which turned out to be Edith's, for $1.75, and the bidding continued.

The only bad time Elizabeth had was when she saw Cyrus Griswold eyeing her. What if Mr. Griswold bought her box, and she was obliged to eat dinner with him? But her fears had arisen without considering Mrs. Griswold. The newspaper publisher was forced to pay a fancy price for the privilege of eating from his own wife's gold lamé wrapped box.

Jules Sperlin bought Elizabeth's box, Eliot bought Aunt Nelly's, and then Elizabeth lost track of the bidding. But afterwards when the Sperlins, Jaynes, and Allens took a table together, it somehow happened that the boxes got shifted and Eliot had as much of her fried chicken as of Aunt Nelly's hot potato salad with bacon, while Eliot grinned good-naturedly at jokes about his sparking the teacher.

Elizabeth noticed with satisfaction as Alexandra and Howie Manchester bent their blond heads together over the box her little sister had spent so much time on. Fifteen-year-old Alex hadn't admitted to having a boyfriend, but the sparkle in her smile told Elizabeth that Alex was growing up.

Then she looked at the crowd of young men around Grace Sperlin at the piano. She couldn't help wondering why Boyd wasn't among them. More than once Grace had looked their direction in a manner that made Elizabeth think Grace might be thinking the same thing. But Boyd seemed satisfied to do his valiant duty entertaining Miss Ponsonby, although, since he had cared as little about commercial subjects as about farming, Elizabeth wondered what he found to talk to their old teacher about. Maybe Miss Ponsonby harbored a secret fondness for airplanes.

The evening ended with a community sing of old favorites and the newest hits such as "Red Sails in the Sunset," "Chapel in the Moonlight," and "Moon over Miami."

Mora wasn't Miami, and the little gazebo in front of the schoolhouse wasn't a chapel, but it was in full moonlight when Eliot took Elizabeth back that night. They parked the old car beside the school and strolled hand-in-hand over to the gazebo.

"I've been waiting for hours to get you alone and still," he said at last as they sat on the little bench against the low stone wall of the structure. "I've got such news I didn't even want to tell you while I was distracted by driving."

Elizabeth held her breath. "What?"

Instinctively they leaned forward, and he clasped her hands. "I don't know where to start." He gave a shout of laughter that was the most like the old Eliot he had been for almost a year.

"Oh, Eliot! It's so good to see you happy!"

"It feels good too. Just wait till I tell you. Dr. Mangum came to see me today."

"Oh." She pulled back.

"No, no. Not a medical call. Business. I still can't believe it. But he said their fund-raising campaign—did you know about the one Lottie Richardson is heading up?"

She nodded. She hadn't told him what she'd done.

"Well, it's been so successful they have more than enough to finish the hospital. Can you believe it—someone gave a whole set of antique jewelry! So they want to return some of the generosity people have given to them. They're forgiving some of their bills." He jumped to his feet and flung out his arms, the left one only a little ways from his side. "Elizabeth, I'm a free man—forgiven—getting out of debt is like getting out of jail—you can't imagine—" He came to the seat beside her and clasped her hands again. "My dearest, you're crying."

Elizabeth dashed at her eyes with the backs of her hands. "I—I know—I'm just so happy. Oh, Eliot!" Someday she would tell him about the jewelry, but she couldn't manage the words at the moment.

He kissed her forehead. "But that's not all. I've been talking to Kirkland. He's always known how much I want to be a lawyer. Of course, that's why he's kept me on even when I don't think he could really afford me sometimes, but he's decided he'll take me on."

"Take you on? You already work for him."

"As a student, I mean. He said he's thought about it for a long time and hesitated because it's an awful job—for both of us—but he says I can read for the law under him."

"I don't understand. What does that mean?"

"It means I'll go to law school in his office. He'll train me in everything I need to know to pass the bar exam. It'll take a long time. I'll have to work all day and study all night for years, but it can be done."

"Oh, that's wonderful." She really meant it—it was just that she was so overwhelmed with everything happening so fast. She didn't mean to sound lacking in enthusiasm.

"Oh no, Elizabeth. What have I said wrong?" He suddenly dropped to one knee in front of her. "I didn't mean I'd really have to study *all* night. I mean, we can still get married."

She gasped. Had he really said that? "Eliot!"

"Er—I mean, if you'll say yes. Oh, Elizabeth, please do. I love you so much." He was no longer on his knees. He threw his arms around her and pulled her to her feet. And before she could say yes he gave her fullest, deepest kiss that could have been given under any moon anywhere.

At last, when they were both out of breath, he kept one arm around her and they strolled around the side of the gazebo to stand fully in the moonlight. "Well?"

"Well what?"

"You haven't answered me. I said please. In college you always said I never asked, just gave orders. Now I'm asking."

She kissed him back for her answer.

20

It seemed impossible that anything could happen to dampen Elizabeth's joy that summer as she and Eliot planned for their future. She would teach at Mora for at least one more year while they put every effort toward getting the two things they would need most—a place to live and a car. Then perhaps she could get a teaching job in Nampa, and they could set the date.

No matter how determined she had been that material considerations wouldn't dictate their future, it was inescapable—they had to have a place to live. But if all went well, she could be Mrs. Eliot Hudson Taylor Hamilton by this time next year.

Their most careful plans, however, were to no avail. That was the year of the great drought. For years Idahoans had heard of farms drying up and blowing away in Oklahoma, Texas, and throughout the Midwest. Indeed, many families had moved to Idaho's more favorable climate from these regions. In Boise Valley the well-laid irrigation systems below Arrowrock Dam had continued to water prime crops—even if they then received only a few cents per bushel for the crops in the end.

But suddenly the unthinkable happened. Reports had warned for several years that water levels were dropping. Now the dam was empty. There was no water; there could

be no crops. The accumulated winter snowfall in the mountains and the brief period of rain that spring produced less
than 65 percent of the normal precipitation, and weather
stations began reporting the driest year in southern Idaho
since they had started keeping records in 1909.

By midsummer, Governor Ross declared, "This is the
worst drought in the history of the white man in this territo-
ry. Rivers and creeks are drying up which in previous years
furnished irrigation. Thousands of springs that have been
used for watering livestock in the mountains are dry." The
governor sought federal assistance to keep their cattle herds
alive, but it was slow in coming.

For weeks on end, Elizabeth went about her work,
helping on the farm and planning for the future without
worry. It had been dry before.

"When we first came to the desert, the air was so dry
we could drape our laundry over a sagebrush bush at nine
o'clock at night, and it would be dry in fifteen minutes."
Such recollections by Kathryn and Aunt Nelly made their
situation seem much less desperate.

Elizabeth recalled that just the summer before she
had gone to college the drought scare had been severe.
Rain had finally come—with disastrous results in her case.
But this time there was no cloudburst to bring relief.

"They've cut our allotment again." Merrick's shoulders drooped as he read his letter from the water district.
The first cut a month ago had reduced the amount of water
each parcel of land received. Now they were cutting the
number of allowed waterings. Merrick shook his head.
"Crops we've watered every eight days, now only get water
every fifteen. If these temperatures stay in the nineties our
beans can't survive."

Elizabeth longed to be able to give her father a comforting reply, but there was nothing to say. Instead she
walked beside him in silent companionship as he went to
the barn to do the milking.

Three weeks later the final blow fell. Indian Creek ran dry. The New York Canal ran dry. The newspaper carried a photo of Arrowrock Dam—empty. Now even Cyrus Griswold's crops shriveled, for there was no water for anyone, no matter what his rights were.

Elizabeth, Boyd, and Alex worked long hours carrying water from the cistern in a desperate attempt to keep the livestock alive, and Kathryn lovingly carried every drop of used domestic water to the five rose bushes she had nursed through so many years of winter cold and summer heat.

Merrick got out the old water barrels that Kathryn's father and Uncle Isaiah had long ago stored in the back of the barn. They all had splintered staves that needed replacing, and two of them needed new rims from the blacksmith, but soon they were watertight, and faithful Rosie O'Day began hauling water from the Snake River several times a week. At least she could drink all she wanted from the river while she was there, even if the fifteen-mile return trek across the parched desert was nearly enough to dehydrate her.

Kathryn did all she could to keep her family's spirits up, even to playing the organ after supper, when they could open all the doors and windows and enjoy the cool of a desert evening. Although everyone did his best to enjoy these moments of respite, Elizabeth couldn't ignore the toll the drought was taking on her family, especially on her father.

"I'm so worried about Daddy," she said to Kathryn one night when the others had gone to bed. "He seems to be shriveling and drying up just like the crops and cattle."

Kathryn nodded. "I know. It tears at my heart, but there doesn't seem to be anything to do." She reached for her Bible sitting atop the organ and opened it to Psalm 63. "'O God . . . my soul thirsteth for thee, my flesh longeth for thee in a dry and thirsty land, where no water is.' I read the words, and I know it's telling me I should take refuge in

God, but it's as if the channels to heaven have all dried up too. I try to be strong for your father, but all my efforts are dust."

Elizabeth held her mother's hand in the dark.

Autumn wore on, and their hopes for any crops died with the last dried bean plant, but still they struggled to save the animals.

Elizabeth's concern for her father increased. He had always been so strong, so vigorous, in spite of the fatigue the depression had brought to his lined face. But now his frailty was alarming.

Elizabeth began her second year of teaching at Mora, living in the teacherage and filling her life with her students. But this seemed a far different place than it had just a year ago. Even her students looked dry and dusty, and she could hardly reprimand them for coming to school unwashed when she knew there was no water at home in which to wash.

Often she felt she was as dry inside as any brown weed around her, for in this desperate situation she saw less and less of Eliot.

Then came Thanksgiving. Elizabeth tried desperately to be thankful, especially when she went home for Thanksgiving dinner.

"There, isn't that nice?" She knew her brightness sounded forced as she placed a paper cornucopia and papier-maché fruit centerpiece on the table.

"It's lovely, dear. Your students do such nice work," Kathryn agreed.

But Alexandra just stared at it with red eyes and turned her tear-streaked face away. "Now we're going to get the speech about how much luckier we are than most of the country—at least we have each other and food on the table. But how lucky do you feel that you and Eliot can't get married?" Alex stalked across the room, then paused at the door. "At least he's still in the valley."

Kathryn remained silent while the banging door echoed in the room. Elizabeth needed no more invitation to pour out her heart to her mother. "It's simple economics, Mother. The drought, always the drought. Kirkland has plenty of running water in his office, but when he can't get paid because none of his farmer clients have any money, he can't pay his clerk. Eliot's agreed to a cut in salary rather than look for another job. Besides, there probably aren't any other jobs."

"Is he still reading for the law?"

"He does what he can, but it all seems farther and farther away every time I ask him how he's progressing. I haven't even asked for weeks. And if we don't talk about taking the bar exam, we don't even think of talking about getting married."

Kathryn employed her time-honored technique of listening sympathetically, talking to her daughter, praying with her, and then putting her to work. But Elizabeth's sixteen-year-old sister didn't respond as readily to this formula as Elizabeth herself had always done.

"What is it, Mother?" Elizabeth watched Alex obediently take the egg basket and head to the henhouse.

"We just heard yesterday. The Manchesters lost their place. Bank auction is Monday. They're going to California."

Elizabeth gave her attention to the potato she was peeling for dinner as she tried to remember. "Manchesters —they had the sheep ranch."

Kathryn stirred her spicy-smelling corn chowder. "That's right. Lila and Benji Young were my students when I taught Sunday school. I'm sure you've heard me tell the story about the time I found Benji in the Kuna cave."

Elizabeth nodded. "Yes, and then he was killed in the War."

"That's right—gassed in France. Everyone thought Lila was trying to somehow replace her brother when she broke off her engagement to Davey Brewington to marry that dashing young war hero Howard Manchester. They took over the farm when the Youngs moved into Boise." Her eyes took on a faraway look, and a small smile curled her lips. "That was the year before Alex was born. I guess it's not surprising she and Howie Manchester should fall for each other—they were born just two weeks apart."

"Oh." Elizabeth put down the paring knife and dried her hands on a flour sack towel as the full implication of their conversation sunk in. "So Alex is in love with Howie —or thinks she is. She's only sixteen."

Kathryn nodded. "Yes. That's the size of it. Sixteen is young, and she may well get over it—no matter how firmly she declares she'll never date another boy. But I don't know—they did seem perfect together. And I was only a year older than she is when I first saw your father—I never got over that."

Then Alex returned with a few small eggs in her basket, and they changed the subject.

Elizabeth was sorry for her sister—Alex, who had always been so sunny with her golden curls. She was sorry for the Manchesters, who lost the farm that had been in Lila's family for two generations. She recalled her parents' stories of how the Youngs had shared water from their well before the canals were completed. Elizabeth remembered Lila best, however, from when she achieved notoriety for being the first woman to walk down the streets of Kuna in a pair of anklets. Elizabeth must have been about ten years old then, and the impression was indelible.

Elizabeth was sorry for all who suffered so desperately, especially at this holiday time. But no matter how she regretted the plight of others, she simply couldn't keep her own spirits down—for Eliot was coming for Thanksgiving. He had saved for weeks to buy gas to put in Mr. Kirkland's Ford so they could have Thanksgiving together.

Even the trapped look in Clarey's eyes and Mavis's hollow cheeks didn't extinguish Elizabeth's spirits, although she worried more about that situation every time she saw them. If it was true, as she had long suspected, that they had been intimate before marriage, then certainly they had been wrong—very wrong—to do so. But Elizabeth couldn't help feeling that Mavis's parents were equally wrong in continuing to hold Clarey hostage for that mistake, as she also suspected. And she was certain Clarey and Mavis had no chance of achieving a happy marriage until the Hendrickses left them alone. But, just as with the drought and the economic situation, there seemed to be little anyone could do about it.

Nor was there much anyone could do to find a way she and Eliot could get married. So she would just have to make the most of their all-too-short time together. As soon as the last crumb of pumpkin pie had disappeared she jumped up to do the dishes.

"No," Kathryn commanded. "There's not room for everyone to work in the kitchen, and you did more than your share of the cooking. Out you go." She shoved Elizabeth and Eliot toward the porch where coats hung on hooks. "A nice brisk walk—that's what you two need."

It was exactly what they needed. Because the present was so dismal, and the future looked so dim, as they walked hand-in-hand down the sagebrush-lined dirt road they talked about happy memories of their past, recalling times they had enjoyed together at college and sharing events from their childhoods neither had told the other before.

"Did you have Thanksgiving in China?" she asked.

"When we were in the compound the Americans celebrated. But the Thanksgiving I remember best was being in some small village in northern China with my father. I think I've told you how he always rode his bike from village to village with an accordion on his back—that way he could go through the streets playing it and attract a crowd. That time I accompanied him on a drum.

"It didn't take long to get the attention of every person in that village—especially the children. They scampered along behind us until we had a great parade that wound back to the tent the other missionaries had set up. It held six hundred people, but we had it crowded out. My mother taught the children, and I helped her.

"By the next Thanksgiving she had become too ill to stay on the field and brought me back with her." He gave himself a little shake, as if he realized he had violated their unspoken agreement to remember only happy things that day.

"And did you get a Thanksgiving dinner?"

"Well, sort of. Father had preached in that village before, so there were Christians there. They invited us home with them to eat. When anyone asked my father what he wanted to eat he always asked for millet. It was the cheapest, most plentiful food in that part of China—and the hardest to spoil by cooking. He became known as 'the one who can hold much millet.' That must have been a year of abundance, because I remember we also had sweet potatoes, peanuts, and cabbage."

"You remember from that long ago?"

"I don't forget important things." And the way he looked at her when he said that made Elizabeth shiver deliciously. So did the kiss he followed it with.

Elizabeth always remembered that Thanksgiving as an especially happy one, perhaps because of what came after. By the time she came home for Christmas, her father, who was already thin, had noticeably lost weight, and his whole body shook every time he was taken with a racking cough.

"Has he seen a doctor, Mother?" Elizabeth asked.

"He refuses." The flatness in Kathryn's voice told how worried she was.

Elizabeth shared her concern with Eliot. "Let me see what I can do," he offered.

Eliot had ridden to Kuna with Vina and her family on their way to visit Nelly and Isaiah, and Elizabeth had promised to drive him back. When the time came he convinced

Merrick to join them for the ride. From that step Elizabeth was never sure how Eliot persuaded her father to enter Samaritan Hospital, but within a few hours Merrick was under Dr. Mangum's competent care.

He never left the hospital.

It was a bitterly cold day in February with the sun shining and a mocking, piercing brightness in the clear air when Elizabeth once again stood beside her mother at the Kuna cemetery.

Many times, through the brief graveside committal that followed the church funeral service, Kathryn squeezed Elizabeth's hand until it hurt. But when they left, although her eyes glistened, her cheeks were dry. Elizabeth knew her mother would not cry until she could do it in private. She couldn't be so certain of her own composure as a lifetime of fond memories of her father engulfed her.

"He's with our little Eldon now," Kathryn said as they walked across the rough, frozen ground toward the car. "And with my papa. They always liked each other so much. I know Papa will be so happy to have Merrick in heaven with him. That must be the richest reward of all for soul-winning—sharing heaven with the people you introduced to Christ."

Later at home, eating Aunt Nelly's fried chicken—just as she had on her second day in the desert after Aunt Thelma's funeral thirty-two years before—Kathryn started to recount that memory to her children and grandchildren gathered around her. Then she stopped. "No, I have it wrong, don't I, Nelly? It wasn't fried chicken."

Laughing with the release of grief that often follows a funeral, Nelly said, "Land sakes, no. We didn't have a chicken worth eating that summer. That was jackrabbit."

Under cover of the conversation flowing around them, Elizabeth turned to her big brother. "Clarey, I haven't talked to Mama much yet, but I know she wants to stay on the farm. Can't you move over here now and help her? I know you've been wanting to make a change for a long time." That seemed to be the gentlest way she could put it.

But Clarey shook his head with a hardness she hated to see in the eyes of the brother who had always been so gentle. "I suppose I could come. But Mavis wouldn't. She and her folks are in ironclad agreement on this—I got her in trouble, so I can stay there and take care of them all." It was the first time Clarey had bluntly spelled out what Elizabeth had always suspected.

"But that's so unfair—" Elizabeth started to protest, but it was useless. The fact of the matter, as she had always known, was that, although able-bodied, Mr. Hendricks was lazy. So he had seen the chance and grabbed it to enslave sweet, capable Clarey. He wouldn't give up no matter who got hurt—even his own daughter and grandchildren.

But with the arrival of the mail the next day it didn't matter anyway.

Elizabeth, who was spending the weekend at home before returning to Mora on Monday, was the one to bring in the mail. At first she thought the envelope engraved "Bank of Kuna" in heavy black letters was a routine statement from her parents' checking account. It reminded her of all the business and legal things that would need to be seen to, and for at least the millionth time she was thankful Eliot was there to help them. Not a lawyer yet, but he knew what had to be done and how to do it.

"Here, you'd better add this to your stack." She handed it to him.

A moment later his sharp outcry made her jerk up from the sympathy note she was reading. "Do you know what this is?" He held the stiff paper between two fingers as if it were hot.

"Bank balance? Overdrawn, I suppose."

"You better read it."

She trembled as she took the paper from him. "In The District Court of The Fourth Judicial District of The State of

Idaho, In and For The County of Ada . . ." She read in a voice devoid of comprehension. "Notice of Sheriff's Sale!" She reached a part that made sense. Terrible sense. How was this possible? "Under and by virtue of an Order of Sale issued . . . above entitled Court on a Judgment and Decree of Foreclosure . . . in favor of the above named Plaintiff . . ."

Elizabeth looked back up the page to confirm what she knew. The Bank of Kuna had foreclosed on their farm. The thing her parents had feared, had worked and fought to avoid for years, had happened. The day after her father's funeral.

Maybe this was the time she should just go put her head under the pillow and cry. But she couldn't do that until she understood. "But how can this be? I don't know much about it, but don't there have to be notices and things first? How can they just say we're going to sell your farm and everything you own in—" she looked to the back page where the date of the sale was fixed "—in one month's time?"

Eliot shook his head. "They can't. Believe me, I've seen enough of these. This whole process takes close to three months. Notice of default, summons and complaint, judgment . . ."

"And could it all happen without our knowing anything about it? Without Mother or Daddy doing anything, I mean?"

Eliot shook his head, and a lock of sleek, blond hair fell across his forehead to be brushed back by his long fingers. "Without their doing anything, yes. The process would just plod through the steps if the defendant failed to respond. But they would have to have been given notice." He began searching through the drawers and cubbyholes of the rolltop desk in the corner of the living room where Elizabeth had watched her father do his bookkeeping since she was a tiny girl.

It didn't take Eliot long to find a stack of legal-sized envelopes stuck in the top drawer. "Look," he held up a thin envelope. "He read this one. It's crumpled and dog-eared."

"That would have been the notice of default?"

Eliot nodded again and produced a sheet of scratched notes and figures. "It looks like he tried everything he could think of to take care of this."

Elizabeth looked at the date. "Right after Thanksgiving. No wonder he went downhill so fast."

"The worry sure wouldn't have helped any. Explains why he put off going to the doctor for so long too."

"Medical bills?"

"That, and he didn't want to be hospitalized. Why didn't he tell me? I could have at least responded to these things for him." Eliot held out several unopened envelopes. "He was in the hospital by the time these came."

Elizabeth shook her head. "Boyd probably just stuck them in there because he didn't want to worry Mother. He probably had no idea they were so important."

They were both silent for a few moments. Elizabeth sighed. "Isn't there anything you can do—or Mr. Kirkland? Get the judge to hear the case again or something?"

Eliot considered. "I doubt it. This stuff all looks absolutely proper. Of course the bank might reconsider if we could pay the loan up—get out of default."

Elizabeth threw up her hands. "There isn't a hope. You know that. Everyone I know would be delighted to loan Mother the money, but nobody has enough to buy more than next weeks' groceries—or feed for their cattle, which is much more important."

They sat in stunned silence, Elizabeth looking around the beloved room that held so many memories. She tried to imagine what it would be like seeing this place sold, not being able to call it home and—far worse than for her—what it would be like for her mother, when Boyd walked in looking for one of the books his cousin occasionally sent him from Scotland.

"Boyd, have you seen these? Do you know what they are?" She waved the letters at him accusingly.

"Oh, that's stuff that came since Dad got sick. He told me just to put it in the desk. He'll deal with it when he can." He stopped and blinked. "Oh. Yeah. He can't now, can he? I keep forgetting he's dead. It doesn't seem possible."

"I'm afraid no one can do anything now."

Eliot responded to Boyd's blank look by explaining what had happened.

Elizabeth couldn't believe it when a slow grin spread across Boyd's face. She had the feeling he had to restrain himself to keep from clapping his hands and jumping in the air. "No more farm? You mean it? It's gone?"

Eliot, who was sitting so that he couldn't see Boyd's face, responded with sympathy. "That's right. I wish I could tell you some other way—something more hopeful. But this looks absolutely definite."

"No more farm? No more cows to milk? No hay to stack? No clacking chickens to feed?"

Eliot rose and clapped a hand on Boyd's shoulder. "I'm so sorry, Boyd. I know this must be the worst for you—next to your mother. You've worked so hard."

At mention of his mother, Boyd's face fell. "Oh, that's right. It will be hard on Mom. Terribly hard." He turned to Elizabeth. "Forgive me, sis. I was being selfish. It's rotten for you too, I know. I really am sorry—but, still . . ."

She rose to take his hands. "Boyd, I had no idea you hated the farm this much. You didn't hide that stuff on purpose, did you? Just so you wouldn't have to—no, I'm sorry." One look at the shock on his face at such a suggestion told her that she knew better than that. Honest, open Boyd would never be capable of doing such a thing, if he could even have thought of it. "Sorry," she repeated.

"I'm sorry too. Really, I am. I'm sorry for everything—for all of you, but see—" He drew a much-worn letter from the billfold he carried in his hip pocket. "I thought there could never be any hope—"

He held out the letter bearing a Scottish stamp, and Elizabeth read it. Then she looked up. "Ian's turning ten acres of the estate in Selkirk into an aerodrome, and he wants you to come over and go into business with him? I don't understand."

"We've written to each other for years—daydreaming about something like this. He knows how crazy I am about planes, and how there's no chance of my doing anything like this here."

Elizabeth nodded, not really taking it all in. "So you want to go to Scotland and—and—" she glanced through the letter again "—and fly airplanes and give flying lessons with your cousin? But you've never met him. You don't know anything about the place. You don't know how to fly. The only time you were ever up in a plane was the time—" She choked, recalling the horror of the smoke and flames. "Boyd, you can't."

"Yes, he can. He must."

They all turned at the sound of Kathryn's voice. No one had seen her come in. "How long have you been there, Mother?" Elizabeth asked.

"Long enough. I knew something was worrying your father terribly. He wouldn't tell me—wanted to protect me from all the worry he was bearing." She swallowed hard. "But Boyd is absolutely right. This frees him completely. There's nothing for any of us here now." She crossed the room to hug him. "It's a wonderful opportunity for you. I wouldn't have you miss it. Besides, where else would you get a job?" Her eyes went soft again, as they so often did when she recalled days long ago.

"It's beautiful there in Scotland. You've never seen anything like the way the sun sparkles on the Ettrick Water. And the salmon jump—I'd go with you if I could."

Boyd held her at arms' length, a huge smile on his face, but she shook her head emphatically. "No, no. I have far too much to see to here. Perhaps someday I shall come visit you, though."

"But Mother. He doesn't know how to fly," Elizabeth repeated.

"Almost I do. I've studied every book ever written on the subject. Ian's been sending them to me for years. He's been taking lessons at an aerodrome in Edinburgh. He'll teach me."

Elizabeth wanted to protest that it wasn't safe, but she knew that would only spur his enthusiasm. And his going would mean one less mouth for their mother to feed. Where would Kathryn and Alex live when the farm was sold one month from today? It was unthinkable. But she had to think.

21

SHERIFF'S SALE.

The pale yellow placard with the glaring black letters hung limply from the picket fence next to the winter-shriveled shoots of the climber rose. Last night it had been soaked in a March rain. The rain, bringing hopes for relief from last year's drought, was much welcomed by everyone. But it was too late for the Allens.

The sign detailed the time and terms of the sale. One o'clock tomorrow. Exactly twenty-four hours from now. Kathryn and Alex were busy loading their personal belongings, "effects" the sheriff's order had called them, into the car.

They would spend the night with Aunt Nelly. Then what? A few wealthy families in Boise still maintained a household staff. Kathryn had thought of seeking employment with a family as a cook. But it was unlikely anyone would be willing to provide room and board for her and Alex both—no matter how delectable her pies were.

Elizabeth, who had arranged to leave school early in order to help her mother, still couldn't believe it was happening.

"You're so calm, Mother. How can you go about this as if you were packing for a weekend vacation?"

With her square jaw set, Kathryn took her old blue and white gingham sunbonnet off the hook on the back porch and put it in a bag. "I've always taken life as it came. Every day has its own challenge. I try to meet it the best I can, knowing God's helping me."

"I suppose you know, most women—probably men too—would have fallen apart if they had to face half of what you have in the past month."

Kathryn set her bag down and reached for the coffeepot on the stove. She poured two mugs and set them on the table, then sat and took a sip of one. "I doubt it. I think most people just do what they have to do. Those of us who've learned to rely on the Lord have a real advantage, of course."

Elizabeth sat down and picked up the other mug. "But have you always been like this?"

"I'd like to tell you I fought some great spiritual battle and came out with a peace I've never lost. In a way that's true—life's a battle, and the longer you live, the easier it gets because you can look back on all the hard times before and realize you made it through. So you figure you'll probably make it through this one. But basically, I think the Lord just created me with the ability to trust Him easily. Faith seems to come more easily to some than to others. Whatever it is, I thank Him for it." She took another sip of coffee. "That doesn't mean I've never gotten worried or upset, mind you. And it certainly doesn't mean I don't grieve for your father—except I am glad he was spared this."

Elizabeth squeezed her mother's hand. "I know. And I'm certainly thankful God made you as He did. Your example of calm is a wonderful heritage. I try to learn from it—use it as a model when I feel turmoil inside."

She paused. "I just can't help feeling it's my fault, though. If I hadn't given the jewels . . ."

"Daughter, you gave them to the Lord's work. Don't you *ever* regret what you give Him. Now no more of that."

They were interrupted by a knock at the door. The front door. In a farming community almost no one bothered with the formality of walking around to the front door, especially in the middle of the afternoon when anyone in the house would be in the kitchen. "Must be Rev. Brown. He said he'd try to drop by."

Elizabeth went to the door with a smile. She always found comfort talking to their tall, thin pastor with the beaky nose and fringe of gray hair that made him look like a tonsured monk. Maybe he could add some insights to the conversation they'd just had. She swung the door open. "Welcome, we were—" She froze.

"Good afternoon, Elizabeth." Cyrus Griswold removed his hat.

Elizabeth stepped back. It wasn't fair to say he leered at her. She just felt that way whenever she saw him.

"Is your mother at home? I'd like to see her on a little business matter."

Elizabeth felt like saying, "She doesn't want to renew her newspaper subscription," but instead led the way wordlessly to the kitchen. Elizabeth left them alone and went out to the back porch to finish the packing her mother had left undone. The door was open, so without meaning to eavesdrop she heard the conversation that followed the sounds of briefcase straps being unbuckled and papers being shuffled.

After a brief introduction, which was undoubtedly meant to put his hearer at ease, Griswold explained how he had obtained the sheriff's permission to make the offer he was now prepared to make. He went to some length to explain how he had moved the sheriff to sympathy by explaining the plight of the newly widowed woman and dependent daughter being forced out of their home.

So he proposed to buy the property from Kathryn today, before the auction. She, of course, would have to give the money to the bank. Then, although the property would be his, since he had no immediate use for the house Kathryn could continue to live there.

It was all Elizabeth could do to restrain herself from stomping into the kitchen and pouring her cup of cold coffee over that weasel's head. Her mother was still a very attractive woman, and Alex was beautiful. Did he think he was setting up a private harem for himself?

Kathryn's voice was much calmer than Elizabeth knew her own would have been had she been the one to reply. "I can understand your wanting the property, since it borders yours, Mr. Griswold. But why don't you just buy it at the auction tomorrow?"

In Elizabeth's mind she could see Griswold leaning toward her mother, all but grasping her hand. "I had hoped to spare you the anxiety and embarrassment. And this seems so much more businesslike, doesn't it? An auction is such a public spectacle."

Kathryn's laugh was brittle. "And so much less predictable, isn't it? You would undoubtedly be required to pay a much higher price, wouldn't you?" Her chair scraped against the floor as she rose. "Besides, I don't think Alex and I would be comfortable living under the conditions you suggest. We are not a charity case."

"Oh, my dear Mrs. Allen, I had no idea of suggesting such a thing." There were no sounds to indicate that Griswold had taken her hint to rise, however impolite it was for a man to remain seated in a lady's presence. "You could certainly pay me a modest rent if it made you feel better."

"It will make me feel better to see to my own arrangements. Thank you, Mr. Griswold." Steps sounded as she walked toward the door to the living room.

There was no answering male tread. "All right, Mrs. Allen. It pains me to have to proceed in this direction, but you seem to leave me no choice. As you suggest, I do want to acquire this property for the best price possible. Your continuing to live here is a matter of indifference to me, but I mean to have the property, so listen carefully."

Kathryn's steps moved slowly back toward the table. "If you will not sell to me . . ."

As much as Elizabeth wanted to hear Griswold's threat —what had begun as happenstance had by now turned into whole-hearted listening by the door—she felt she must summon help for her mother. She turned to see Clarey, who had been coming over to do the heavy work since Boyd left for Scotland two weeks ago, emerge from the barn. She slipped from the porch and ran across the barnyard to him.

By the time Elizabeth had blurted out her story and they raced hand-in-hand back to the house, Kathryn was alone in the kitchen, sitting with her head in her hands, an unsigned bill of sale on the table in front of her.

"Mother, what happened?" Elizabeth and Clarey spoke at the same time.

"Clarey, sit down. I hope you don't mind if I ask your sister to stay too. This affects us all."

"You aren't going to sell to him, are you, Mother?" Elizabeth interrupted.

"That's up to Clarey." She turned to take her son's hand. "My dear, why didn't you tell us about Tommy? Surely you didn't have so little faith in us as to think we'd reject the child for his parents' misbehavior? And here you've been living under this burden of secrecy for six years now —but if it means that much to you, I'll give in to Griswold's blackmail."

"Blackmail?" Elizabeth reacted before her brother did. "What's he trying to pull?"

"If I don't agree to sell to him he says he'll print the full truth about Tommy's parentage on the front page of the next issue of the paper."

"But he can't. Isn't that libel or something?" Clarey asked.

Elizabeth, who had picked up some understanding of the law through her conversations with Eliot, answered. "It's not libel if it's true. Mother, I've known for years that

Tommy was conceived before Clarey and Mavis were married. You must have guessed—he was born so early." She turned to her twin. "Clarey, I know it's a terrible embarrassment, especially for Mavis, but you don't want Mother to do this, do you? I mean, most people must have guessed at the time anyway."

Clarey dropped his head in his hands. "Oh, what a mess I've made of things. You and Dad raised us right, Mother. I always knew you'd be so hurt to know I'd broken God's law. But I made it right with God years ago, and I'll spend the rest of my life trying to make it up to Mavis and her folks. Now that you know, I don't care who else knows —let him publish his smut."

"Wait a minute," Elizabeth said. "He has to have proof to publish. What could he possibly have? He wasn't at that graduation party. He didn't see you go off that night."

"I don't know what you're talking about, Elizabeth," Kathryn said. "But I believe he has the proof he claims. You see, Tommy's grandmother knew. Before the Rudolphsons moved last summer she set up a trust at the bank. She wanted her only son's only son to inherit something from his real family."

There was a stunned silence in the kitchen.

Finally Elizabeth spoke. "Mrs. Rudolphson—his *grandmother?* "Mother, are you saying Tommy *isn't* Clarey's?"

"I thought you said you knew."

"I knew he was born too early. I didn't know *Rudy* was the father."

"I didn't know either."

Two heads spun to look at Clarey's white face.

"Are you absolutely sure, Mother?" His lips barely moved as he spoke.

"As sure as I can be without having seen the document. You know Griswold's on the board of directors of the bank. I don't think he was in on setting up the trust. I gather he just found the document in the bank's files."

"Snoop!" Elizabeth spit out the epithet.

Kathryn and Elizabeth were silent, almost holding their breath, while Clarey continued to sit immobile. Suddenly he slammed his fist down on the table, jumped to his feet, threw his arms over his head, and gave a great shout. Then he snatched the bill of sale off the table and tore it top to bottom three times.

"I'm free!" He pulled his mother to her feet and kissed her, then his sister.

"Clarey, you're insane!" Elizabeth pushed him back.

"No, no, I'm not. I'm truly sane for the first time in years. What's that verse in the Bible, Mother, about you shall know the truth and the truth shall make you free? That's it. I've just learned the truth. And I'm free."

Suddenly Elizabeth understood. "Oh, I see. Yes, you are!" And she hugged Clarey and kissed him.

"Will you two please explain to me what's going on?" Kathryn sat back down.

"Well, you see, for years, Mavis's parents—"

Clarey interrupted his sister. "They've been blackmailing me. They said I got their daughter in trouble, so I had to stay there and work for them to make it up to them—ruined her chances for an education, a rich marriage—whatever—they went on and on."

"But you didn't ruin her—you rescued her!"

"Yes, and now I can move home and farm for you, Mother."

Their euphoria melted as reality flooded back.

Kathryn nodded. "What a shame we learned too late." She took Clarey's hand. "Of course what you did was wrong too, my dear. But you've certainly more than paid for it. We must all trust the Lord to work everything out from here."

"I wonder if Griswold will really publish that," Elizabeth said. "It's only purpose would be to be vindictive after the auction's over, but I wouldn't put it past him."

Kathryn rose. "Well, that will have to be his decision.

Nelly is expecting us for supper. I don't think we should keep our hostess waiting."

The next morning Elizabeth could tell that even her mother's iron composure was close to breaking as they drove back to their farm for the last time. There was almost an hour before the auction was to start, but already a large crowd had arrived. Although Saturday was a regular work day for most people, it seemed that many stores and offices in Kuna would be seriously understaffed, for businesspeople, teachers, and shopkeepers enlarged the crowd of farmers one would expect to attend. If it hadn't been such a solemn occasion, this could have been a very good party. It seemed to Elizabeth that everyone she knew for miles around was there.

Except Griswold. Elizabeth stood on an upturned crate and surveyed the crowd carefully. She was sure she wasn't overlooking him. Did he have the tact to be scared off by his own threats? That seemed unlikely. The thought that he might be using force on Kathryn gave her a jolt. Then Elizabeth looked to her left and saw her mother visiting with Marie Sperlin, so she relaxed.

Where was Eliot? He had promised to be there that morning. She knew there wasn't anything he could do—but she didn't want to go through the ordeal without him. It wasn't like him to be unreliable.

She noticed Jules Sperlin and Uncle Isaiah moving purposefully through the crowd, speaking to each one there, receiving a nod, shaking hands, then moving on. She was wondering briefly what was going on, when something much more important happened.

Eliot arrived. She went to him, and he folded her wordlessly in his arms. She would have stayed in that protecting embrace for hours if she could have. But even Eliot couldn't keep reality out for long. Jules walked over to shake hands with him. They looked each other in the eyes, nodded, then Jules walked off.

"What's going on?" Elizabeth asked.

Just then the sheriff arrived with the auctioneer, and everyone turned toward the podium set on a hay wagon in front of the barn.

"Ladies and gentlemen . . ." The auctioneer began his accustomed chant.

The stock, considered good bidding items, were to be offered first—a technique to warm the crowd up. Elizabeth's eyes prickled as a deputy led dear, gentle Rosie O'Day in a circle beside the wagon.

"Now, what am I bid for this fine horse? An excellent children's pony—never been known to kick—doesn't eat much—obedient in the harness . . ." The auctioneer went on and on.

"Seventy-five cents!" Isaiah Jayne shouted. Nobody laughed at the low price. And nobody bid against him—no matter how hard the auctioneer begged.

When the best milk cow went for ninety cents and the chickens for ten cents apiece—fifteen for the rooster—the auctioneer changed his tactics. This obviously wasn't a good day to sell livestock. He began offering the farm machinery, mopping his brow with a bandana every time the sheriff scowled at him as another valuable piece was knocked down for a dollar or two.

Elizabeth couldn't understand it either. "But Mr. Eastly's a history teacher—what does he want with a hay derrick?" she asked when he grinned proudly over his new purchase. She was even more amazed when, for $1.50, Mr. Oldham bought the tractor that had been Merrick Allen's pride and joy. And Mrs. Oldham and their children seemed so pleased—surely the school superintendent couldn't be thinking of going into farming?

Strangest of all was that no bid was ever raised. Auctions, even forced ones, were considered great entertainment. There was a psychology about them. Elizabeth had often heard talk about the idiotic purchases someone had made at an auction just from the sheer excitement and competitiveness of bidding against a neighbor. But today the psychology was lacking. No one bid against anyone else.

Finally when little Mr. Janicke from the pharmacy pushed his wire-rimmed glasses up on his nose and shouted out a bid of "Ten dollars—and an Oodles bar" for the land, Elizabeth knew that either the entire community had gone mad—or she had.

Eliot beside her was enjoying it all enormously. She turned to him in fury. "What's the matter with you? How can you be laughing about this? My father put his life into this place, and my grandfather, and my mother, and all of us. This is good stuff. And nobody's willing to pay anything but peanuts. It's an insult."

"No, wait. You don't understand."

"You're the one who doesn't understand." She was so upset she feared she'd disgrace herself by crying. "I don't care whether the sheriff gets ten cents or ten dollars. But I care about the animals, about our things."

She choked, then went on. "Do you have any idea how hard my mother worked to get that living room rug? And the blacksmith bought it for thirty-five cents. Do you think he'll take any kind of decent care of it? He'll probably put it on the dirt floor in his shop. People won't take care of things they don't pay anything for."

Before Eliot could respond, the auctioneer gaveled the whole fiasco to a close, mopped his brow a final time, and jumped off the hay wagon—which Miss Spinar, the English teacher, had purchased for fifty cents.

Not until the sheriff and his deputies left with their few coins rattling in their tin cash box did all the Allens' friends and neighbors gather around Kathryn and present her with the duly processed bills of sale for all her possessions.

"I don't understand." Elizabeth shook her head.

"Nothing to understand." Eliot grinned. "Absolutely legal sale. Carried out to the letter of the law under the eagle eye of the sheriff. This is the property of these good people. If they want to make a gift of it, who's to stop them?"

"You mean—it was all planned ahead?"

"Well, the laws on collusion aren't quite clear. I wouldn't want to point any fingers at these good people. But I have heard of such things happening in other communities."

In the midst of all their rejoicing nobody noticed the cloud of dust streaking toward them from the direction of the Kuna-Meridian road. It wasn't until a formerly shiny green Packard braked to a halt and an angry voice followed on the sound of a slamming door that Elizabeth gave a thought to Cyrus Griswold's conspicuous absence.

But he wasn't absent now. "What? Whaddayou mean, it's all over? Auctions take hours and hours. Should only be done with the cows by now. I didn't want those anyway."

"All done, Mr. Griswold." Eliot stepped forward. "Pity you had to go to Boise this morning. Did you get your money all right?"

Elizabeth appreciated Eliot's covering her ears so she didn't have to hear Griswold's reply.

"Ladies present, Mr. Griswold." Jules clapped a heavy hand on a shoulder of the man whose head reached barely above his elbow. "I heard rumors about a run on the bank. Was it true?"

Griswold didn't stay to reply, but later, after the women of Kuna produced the picnic hampers they had kept discreetly out of the sheriff's sight and everyone was busily emptying their plates of fried chicken, potato salad, and cinnamon rolls, the story went around the yard.

Elizabeth suspected this final touch had been Eliot's special contribution to the success of the day.

He grinned when she put it to him. "All right. I'll admit that I suggested everyone take their cash out of the Kuna bank—just so they'd have plenty on hand to bid with, you understand—not with any idea of starting a run on the bank or of depriving Mr. Griswold of the cash he might need, seeing as how all sheriff's sales are cash on the head."

He took a drink of cherry punch, then grinned again. "But even I couldn't have orchestrated the situation in Boise. I hoped he'd have to drive in there to get cash, and I had heard rumors of a run on City National, but even if I had known he banked at First Security, how could I have predicted the lines there that would delay him so long?"

Elizabeth laughed at his look of wide-eyed innocence, then gave her attention to his account of the story that had just been reported from Boise on the six o'clock radio news. Apparently fearing that the run on a neighboring bank would cause the same thing to happen to his, the manager of First Security had hung a huge red, white, and blue banner from the second story windows of his bank:

For the Benefit of Our Patrons This Bank Will Be
OPEN UNTIL LATE TONIGHT
If You Want Your Money Come and Get It!

The bold tactics had prevented the threatened run but had so jammed the bank lobby with inquirers and sightseers that it had taken hours to transact any business. To the enormous frustration of one particular client.

22

That night Elizabeth couldn't believe she was back in the creaky, old iron bed on the sleeping porch, with Alex breathing rhythmically beside her, just as she had slept for most of the nights of her growing up. After all they had gone through—the certainty of having lost the place and having mentally abandoned it—surely the fact that she was still here was a dream. She moved her hand on the stiff cotton sheet. It was real.

Another thing that added to her sense of unreality was the many old friends she had seen that day—teachers from high school, merchants who had had stores and offered services in Kuna ever since she could remember, young people her own age she had lived near and gone to school with all her life: Edith and Rupert, who had bought and returned Kathryn's dishes; Millie and Franklin, who brought their three children and bought and returned the very bed she was lying on . . .

She thought of how much her life had changed—far more than for those who had married and stayed right there in Kuna after high school. Since the days when Kuna High and these people had been the whole focus of her life she had known the wonderful people and experiences of college—friends who had moved all over the country but would still keep in touch at Christmas—and now, the new people, new challenges of her job with the community at Mora. She knew that in the years ahead there would be many more changes, many more new people.

But always as a stable anchor was her family. Its members changed too—moved, died, married, had children, but they were her family—loving her, supporting her, always there to come home to. It would have been so even if this home hadn't been here. The family would always be.

What her mother had once told her, now she understood for herself. That was the truly important thing in life —after her relationship with God. Her family. Only one thing was missing. Eliot wasn't yet part of her family. Once they were married, her relationship with him would be the closest of all. And she was determined to wait no longer. She would tell him in the morning. Even without a house or car. This June. She couldn't wait any longer. Yes, she would tell him. In the morning.

She rolled over and scrunched her eyes tight closed. But it didn't help. She couldn't get to sleep. And if she didn't sleep, morning wouldn't come, and she couldn't tell Eliot. It was like being five years old and waiting for Santa Claus.

At last she got up and put on her old chenille robe. Eliot had accepted Kathryn's invitation to stay the night and was sleeping just two rooms away on the sofa.

But she didn't get that far. They almost ran into each other in the kitchen.

"I've got to talk to you!" they whispered simultaneously, then laughed so hard they had to cling to one another for support.

Finally Eliot led her into the living room and lit the kerosene lamp.

"Let's get married." They both blinked at what seemed to be an echo. "Right away." They dissolved in laughter as they again spoke at the same time.

Finally, brushing away the tears streaming down her face as the tensions of the past month washed away, Elizabeth attempted sensible conversation. "What I've been thinking is that life's so uncertain. We've been waiting until we had a bit of security to get married. But we might never have financial security—look how close Mother came to disaster today. I don't want the fact that I never have a house or a car to mean that I never have you either."

"Yes, that's exactly what I was thinking."

After a long, very secure kiss, Elizabeth continued. "Why does it always take near disasters to bring us to decisions? It was the airplane crash that pushed us into getting engaged—now the drought, Daddy's death, the foreclosure, and we decide to get married."

"Perhaps it's because crises make us clarify our values—get rid of the peripheral stuff so we can focus on what's really important."

"Must be, because I know what's really important to me—you."

"And you to me." And he kissed her again.

They set their wedding date for June seventeenth. The church that Elizabeth's grandfather Adam Jayne had started, first with brush arbor meetings, then as a tent Sunday school, had long outgrown its original meeting place and launched a building program more than a year ago. Done entirely with donated materials and labor, it was truly a miracle that the enlarged building was to be completed just in time for the wedding.

Somehow Elizabeth managed to keep her students on track while she saw to the details of her wedding plans. Ilona wrote an ecstatic letter from Seattle that she and Lawrence would be delighted to be attendants. Eliot's sister, Shirley, and her husband would drive down from Spokane bringing Eliot's father with them. Elizabeth was so pleased. She wasn't sure she would feel properly married if Rev. Hamilton didn't pray at their wedding. Alex would be maid of honor, radiant in the blue taffeta two-piece dress Kathryn had already begun sewing for her. Ilona would look like a long-stemmed daffodil in yellow.

Then Elizabeth considered. It had been easy for Eliot to choose his three attendants: Wilson, his brother-in-law; Lawrence; and Clarey. But Elizabeth wasn't sure who should wear the pink gown in her rainbow procession. Gladys was teaching school in another part of the state. She would be happy to see her former roommate again, but they hadn't kept in close touch since graduation. Celia, her best friend from high school, still lived in Boise, but it seemed Celia had avoided her—probably out of embarrassment—ever since she had confessed the truth about her own marriage. Shirley would be an appropriate choice, but, although she had had some very warm letters from her, Elizabeth had never actually met her future sister-in-law. That left Mavis.

Mavis had at first been defensive, then shy, around Clarey's family after he had faced her and then her parents with the facts about Tommy's parentage. But Clarey continued to demonstrate his love for his wife and her son, while declaring his independence of her parents. And neither Kathryn nor Elizabeth changed their friendly attitudes towards Mavis. She had gradually warmed toward them. Clarey and Mavis were now living with Kathryn, sleeping on the boys' porch with their children, while Clarey built an addition onto the house. Elizabeth had already decided on Tommy as ring-bearer. Yes, she would ask Mavis.

At last the school year ended, and Elizabeth could concentrate on preparing for the rest of her life. She and Eliot decided—it really didn't require a decision because there were no alternatives—to share his basement rooms in Kirkland's home. Hardly ideal accommodations, but at least they would be together, and Eliot would have no transportation problems for getting to work. Elizabeth interviewed with the Nampa school board. They had three vacancies to fill and close to twenty applicants.

But she had little time to worry as she spent every available moment sewing on the yards of white satin that were to make her sleek, long-sleeved bias-cut gown with chapel train. When her need for a wedding dress had finally become a reality, Kathryn had returned to the farm woman's eternal solution—egg money—to buy the fabric.

Elizabeth and Kathryn joked that the treadle on Kathryn's New Home sewing machine was kept in such constant motion that it probably went of its own accord when they were asleep. Elizabeth thought to tell the Lord a special thank you for Rev. Brown, the kind friend who had bought the sewing machine at the auction and returned it to them.

A few days before the wedding a beautiful silver bowl arrived from Scotland accompanied by a card from Boyd, Ian, and Ian's parents, Robert and Rowena. Kathryn's eyes took on a glow as mellow as the ornate bowl as she ran her finger around the grape and vine pattern.

"This stood on the buffet in the dining room. You can't imagine how overwhelmed I was when I went to your father's home as a new bride—all the furnishings were as elegant as this—I'd never seen anything like it. But they were so kind to me. Even when they rejected Merrick, they were kind to me. Oh, my dear—" she hugged Elizabeth "—it all seems so very long ago, and yet the memory is so clear. What wonderful memories I have of my life with Merrick. No one could ask for a better life—in spite of all the struggles. Or maybe *because* of all the struggles. Anyway, I wish nothing better for you, my dear, than that your marriage be as happy as mine was."

The joyful sunshine of Elizabeth's wedding morning seemed to herald promise of just such bliss. Alex was out of bed first—a rare occurrence.

"Roll over and sleep. Don't you even think of touching an egg this morning—I'm off to gather them now."

When Elizabeth went into the kitchen some time later she saw that Alexandra had gathered not only the eggs— which she did allow Elizabeth to touch in sunny side up state—but also had filled every available container with fragrant, pink and lavender sweet peas from the vines covering the back fence. "Oh, Alex, they're wonderful!"

"I'll be off to the church pretty soon. Grace has borrowed enough long white cloths to cover every table at your reception, and we'll have a big bouquet of sweet peas for each table."

"That's perfect. Thank you, Alex."

Soon after that Aunt Nelly and Uncle Isaiah drove over with an armful of Talisman roses and baby's breath, tied in trailing satin ribbons for the bridal bouquet, and a little basket of pink petals for her youngest granddaughter, who would be flower girl.

At precisely two o'clock that afternoon Elizabeth stood at the back of the beautiful new church—the first bride to be married there—and watched little Flossie Sperlin in a lavender taffeta dress walk up the aisle beside grinning, red-headed Tommy Allen, carefully dropping a single rose petal with every step, just as she'd been told to do.

Elizabeth raised her eyes to the front of the church where tall Rev. Brown and tiny Rev. Hamilton stood in their black suits, each clutching a Bible.

And then she looked at Eliot, tall, sleek, shining. *Oh, God, thank You. I never asked You for anyone so wonderful. I couldn't because I couldn't have thought him up. But You did. And You gave him to me. Thank You, thank You.*

"I love you truly . . ." Elizabeth's mind repeated the words as Grace sang, and her heart swelled with joy.

Grace sat down quietly after her solo, and, after the briefest of pauses, Marie brought the congregation to its feet with the opening chords of *Lohengrin.*

Elizabeth had often heard her married friends say what a blur their wedding day was in their minds, and she was determined hers would not be that way. As she walked slowly down the aisle on the arm of Isaiah Jayne, her great-uncle, she noted the face of each person she passed, meeting eyes and returning smiles. This day would live forever in her mind. She savored every moment. Especially Eliot's warm, sure clasp of her hand and long, loving look when Isaiah handed her to him at the altar.

"Dearly beloved, we are gathered here before God and these witnesses . . ."

Yes, Lord, thank You, thank You, her heart sang in response to every word Rev. Brown pronounced.

If most of their guests hadn't had cows to milk, the bride and groom might have been very late indeed getting off on their honeymoon. James Kirkland had provided a brief trip as his wedding present to his clerk. With the loan of Kirkland's car they drove to Boise for a night at the Idan-Ha Hotel.

Elizabeth hadn't been there since the long-ago day Aunt Nelly took her and Kathryn there to lunch—the day the cloudburst had almost ended her dreams of college. But now there was no harsh interruption of her dreams as she floated in on the arm of her new husband.

Mrs. Eliot Hudson Taylor Hamilton, she said to herself in the oval-framed mirror as she brushed her hair, then turned to his arms.

It was the middle of the night when she awoke gently, aware that she was smiling in her sleep. Eliot lay beside her, propped up on his good elbow, looking at her in the dim light of the room and stroking her shoulder as if he couldn't believe there was anything so precious in the world. She stretched her arms around his neck and pulled him down for a kiss.

After a leisurely breakfast the next morning they continued with their plan to spend a day sightseeing at Arrowrock Dam, now in its twentieth anniversary year.

They left Boise and wound their way up the narrow road. As they clung to the edge of the hill above the tree-lined river, Elizabeth's mind ran in two directions. She was savoring every moment, and she was also looking forward to getting to her new home and beginning real married life.

It didn't matter one bit to her that the apartment was merely a single room in a basement. She had already purchased red and white checked fabric from Woolworths. It would take her no time at all to make matching curtains and tablecloth. And the dim linoleum floor she had seen once would look so much better when she had it properly scrubbed and waxed. She sighed in anticipation.

"What are you thinking about?" Eliot took a hand off the steering wheel to pull her closer to him.

She laughed. "Oh, you'll never guess. I was thinking about scrubbing floors. I know it's silly, but I can't wait."

Then the scene outside the windows became even more gripping than that in her mind. They passed Diversion Dam, and Elizabeth remembered her mother's account of attending its opening before she was married. Elizabeth thought it ironic that now, the year following the worst drought in recorded history, should be the anniversary of the centerpiece of the greatest irrigation project ever engineered. Fortunately, late snowfalls in the mountains had done much to brighten the outlook for the coming summer.

The whole car shimmied and rattled over the washboardy road, and Eliot was obliged to keep both hands on the steering wheel. Elizabeth was gazing at the bright blue sky with its fleecy white clouds above the rocky hills when Eliot executed a particularly sharp turn in the road, and Elizabeth exclaimed, "Oh, this is it! Oh, my goodness!"

Eliot pulled to the side of the road, and they got out. Placid green water pooled at the base of a great sweeping curve of concrete wedged between lava-jutted hills covered with sagebrush, greasewood, and an occasional pine tree. An American flag fluttered at the far end of the semicircular sweep of the dam lined with round-globed streetlights.

Birds twittered and called, a raucous crow cawed, bees buzzed through the air, and fish jumped in the water. The sun warmed her head, and love for Eliot warmed her heart. He put his arm around her, and she leaned against him. He felt as strong to her as the great cement embankment before them. Perhaps he couldn't always hold back life's problems as the dam held back the waters of the reservoir, but she knew she could always count on his strength.

As thrilling as the dam was, however, the best part was when they hiked up a little winding road through a draw in the mountain. Water from a spring trickled alongside the dirt track, while wild raspberries, pink rambling roses, and yellow and purple wildflowers bordered it. Clumps of mountain syringa bloomed everywhere, covered with flocks of white and yellow swallowtails and other butterflies of every size and description: black with white-bordered wings, orange with brown spots, and clusters of tiny, bright blue flutterers. They spread a blanket in this wonderland and ate their lunch from a hamper provided by the hotel.

Late in the day, with evening falling across the valley before them, they drove slowly back down the twisty dirt road. Elizabeth closed her eyes and smelled again the sweet syringa and saw the amazing rainbow cloud of butterflies. This too was a day that would live forever in her heart.

The next afternoon they pulled into the driveway beside a big white house on Twelfth Avenue in Nampa.

"Welcome home, Mrs. Hamilton." Eliot kissed her in the car, then once again after sweeping her off her feet and carrying her over the threshold into their room.

"Oh, Eliot, I'm so happy! I have such confidence. It's—it's like nothing more can go wrong now that we're finally married."

23

But she was wrong. Elizabeth had determined that her memories of her wedding would remain sharp, and they did, but ever after it seemed to her that the closing years of the 1930s blended in a blur of struggle. And it started the day they got home from their honeymoon.

James Kirkland, looking as polished as he always did with his well-clipped mustache and smoothly brushed brown hair, adjusted the yellow bow tie that accented the crispness of his starched white shirt and welcomed the bridal couple with what he considered good news.

"Well, they've been at me for a long time, and I've finally given in. With success, you may just be living in the house of a celebrity."

"Oh, congratulations, sir. You've decided to run, have you?"

Apparently Eliot knew immediately what his employer was talking about. But it took Elizabeth some time to sort out the fact that they were discussing James Kirkland's decision to accept his party's urging that he run for county prosecutor.

"It'll mean more work for you, you know." He clapped Eliot on the shoulder. "But assuming I'm elected, and I intend to work hard enough to see that I am, I plan to take you into the prosecutor's office with me."

Before Eliot could finish saying thank you, Kirkland went on. "It shouldn't mean much cut in salary—might not mean any. I'll do the best I can for you."

Elizabeth caught her breath. Cut in salary? He was getting so little now, and she hadn't yet been assured of a teaching position.

But Kirkland's next words were more worrying still. "Only thing is, and I am sorry about this—but we all have to make sacrifices for the public good—I'm afraid that as prosecutor I won't have time to direct your law office study."

Elizabeth clutched Eliot's arm and squeezed it tightly —unclear whether it was for his comfort or her own. She knew how much reading for the law meant to Eliot. She knew the long night hours he had put into his studying after his work days were ended. She knew this was his last chance. The end of his dream.

But when Kirkland had finally gone and left them alone, Eliot didn't want to talk about it.

The end of Eliot's hopes, however, did not mean an end to hard work for the newlyweds. Eliot did some low-key campaigning for Kirkland, making speeches for the candidate when Kirkland's own schedule wouldn't allow him to be in two places at one time, and more and more the work of the office fell on Eliot. Even though he lacked a degree, his practical experience made it possible for him to research and draft briefs and prepare documents that only needed Kirkland's signature before filing.

And just two weeks before the opening of school, Elizabeth was notified that the woman chosen for the coveted position of third grade teacher at Lakeview School was going to have a baby—a condition that immediately disqualified her to stand in front of impressionable young children—and the job was awarded to Elizabeth.

Now her days were filled with attending teachers' meetings, riding the city bus across town to prepare her room, and staying up late at night preparing lesson plans.

That November Kirkland was elected Canyon County prosecutor by a narrow margin, even though he did not belong to the popular party, and Eliot moved with him to the small, dark office in the Canyon County Courthouse. Commuting to Caldwell, the county seat, lengthened Eliot's working day, but Elizabeth, who always had papers to grade and art projects to prepare, had no trouble occupying herself companionably in the chair next to his as he worked late into the night.

It was amazing to Elizabeth how moving only a few miles to a town of a few thousand people and having her husband involved with politics merely at the county level seemed to broaden her horizons. At least three newspapers littered their apartment daily—and, living in one room, having a single newspaper out of place meant that the whole apartment was a mess.

But she enjoyed the sense of knowing what was going on in the world—being a small part of it even. Even if such things as Italy's continued occupation of Ethiopia and Churchill's warnings of German aggression worried her, and she felt that she should apologize to the world for that dreadful American woman Wallis Simpson—especially when King Edward VIII gave up his throne to marry the American divorcée.

The lively eight-year-old girls in her class, however, certainly found nothing worrying or embarrassing in the newspapers the next May. For days and then weeks, it seemed that every little girl in America talked of nothing but "The Little Princesses," as every newspaper and magazine in the land published pictures of eleven-year-old Elizabeth and six-year-old Margaret Rose, whose daddy had been crowned King of England and who had gone off to live in a real palace with their pet dogs and horses. It was even better than Shirley Temple because, of course, her stories were just pretend, although it was a subject hotly argued through many a recess.

Then it was summer. Summer in the desert always meant concern for water, but this year it came in a new form.

"Biggest case to hit the prosecutor's office since Kirkland was elected." Eliot tossed a stack of files on the table as he came in after work. "And it's all mine to prepare for trial."

Elizabeth wiped her hands on a kitchen towel, then moved herself into position in her husband's arms now that they were free from legal documents. "I'd beg you to tell me all about it, but I know you will anyway." She kissed him, then turned back to the stove to stir her stew. "How about stacking those files on the floor until after dinner?"

Eliot moved the papers and began setting the table as he talked. "You've read about the Deer Flat water rights dispute in the paper?"

Elizabeth nodded. Irrigating the rich but arid farmland in the Deer Flat area south of Nampa had been one of the major projects to bring prosperity to the area twenty years ago or more. Now there was a scandal brewing.

"Something about possibly forged documents, isn't it?"

"That's right. It seems that Frank Wellington, who has several hundred acres of sugar beets out beyond the lake, has discovered that the amount of water his land should receive was apparently illegally reduced when his neighbor's father forged a bill of sale. Seems the senior Wellington was too sick at the time to notice."

"So Wellington is your client?" Elizabeth put a plate of biscuits on the table next to the steaming bowl of vegetables and meat.

Eliot nodded as he pulled out his wife's chair for her to be seated. "Wellington's claiming eleven years' damages from Ives for lost and reduced crops." He sat across from Elizabeth. "And I get to research all the records and interview all the parties involved."

It was engrossing work for Eliot, but best of all were two side benefits. Because the assignment would require so much travel beyond the reaches of the bus lines, Kirkland, who was buying a new car more suited to his rising position, would sell his old one to Eliot on terms so easy even he could afford them. And because the Deer Flat area was about halfway between Nampa and Kuna, this would be an excellent opportunity for Mr. and Mrs. Hamilton to pay an extended visit to her family.

Clarey had finished building his addition to Kathryn's house with a large room for him and Mavis and a smaller one for their two children. That left the former boys' sleeping porch available for her and Eliot.

"Not what one might want for guest quarters," Kathryn said as she set her daughter's valise on the small bedside table.

"Oh, Mother, it's lovely to be back on the farm. We've had a very good year in Nampa, but when you're born and raised on a farm even a small town like Nampa can feel crowded—especially living in a basement apartment."

"My dear . . ." A frown crossed Kathryn's face. She seemed uncertain how to continue.

"Oh, no, Mother, no problems—I've never been happier." She paused to kiss Kathryn's cheek. "Truly. Except for one thing—I don't think Eliot will ever be really content not being a lawyer. And it's so unfair. He works so hard and does such a good job—but he's really nothing more than an errand boy."

Kathryn led the way back into the sitting room, and Alexandra brought in iced tea.

"Oh, thank you, Alex. Isn't it wonderful to have electricity?" Elizabeth addressed both her mother and sister.

"I love it." Alex plopped on to the sofa beside her sister. "But mama says the lights are harsh. I wish we could afford a refrigerator. This old ice box leaks."

"But I see Clarey put in a washing machine." Elizabeth nodded toward the round white appliance in the kitchen.

"It's wonderful for Mavis, with two children to wash for," Kathryn said. "But he nearly burned the house down doing it."

In response to Elizabeth's alarmed look she told how he had somehow miscalculated when he ran the vent for the washer onto the porch, and a spark ignited inside the wall. Fortunately they had discovered the smoldering flames before much damage could be done.

"Oh, Mother. You could have lost everything!" Elizabeth cried.

"Yes. How many times that's been true. But the Lord has always spared us. Mr. Griswold's still hoping, though."

"What? Is he still causing you trouble?"

"Nothing we can really put our finger on. I just feel a little like a wounded calf with a buzzard perched on the nearest boulder."

"Buzzard is right." Alex spat the words. "And it's so unfair that he always seems to have more water than anyone else. His hired man doesn't work nearly as hard on his land, but his crops are always greener."

Just then the back screen door banged, and Clarey came in. "Well, hello, little sister."

Elizabeth jumped up and hugged him soundly, ignoring the dust and sweat that seemed an eternal part of any farmer.

"Heard you talking about buzzards—that must mean Griswold." With one hand he took the glass of iced tea Alex offered him; with the other he picked up that week's *Kuna Times.* "Seems to me he may do the most harm of all with this newspaper of his. I remember years ago Pa worried about his isolationist editorials—now look what he's taken up."

Elizabeth looked at the headline Clarey held out to her. "'The Nazi salute is the coming salute for the whole United States.' What! Does he mean that?"

"He hides behind the fact he's quoting other speakers, but he means it all right. Of course, lots of people think Hitler's just great, but this American Nazi propaganda Griswold's pushing is sure too much for me. 'Adolph Hitler, the real Messiah'—that's sacrilegious, if you ask me."

Elizabeth started to agree with him when Mavis came in with the children, who had been feeding the chickens and lambs.

"Mail just came." She handed a letter to Kathryn after greeting her sister-in-law.

Elizabeth observed Mavis as she sat on a chair close to Clarey while Tommy climbed up on his lap. She smiled. The move had obviously done wonders for the whole family. And the truth hadn't damaged their relationship.

"Let me read this to all of you." Kathryn held out her letter. "We hear from Boyd so seldom. Oh, he mentions he saw the statue of Fletcher the Warrior in Selkirk. He says, 'I've walked past it lots before, but Ian pointed it out to me the other day and just casually mentioned that we were sort of descended from him. I don't know whether that's another of their legends—every hill and rock here seems to have one—or whether it's true, but I think I'll claim the old guy for an ancestor.'"

Kathryn put the letter down. "I can't believe I never told you that story. Tommy, I shall put you to bed with it tonight—a fine, fierce warrior he was." Her eyes took on their far-away look. "Merrick contributed five pounds toward building that statue. I'm so glad to know it got done. My goodness, I haven't thought of that for years."

Elizabeth wasn't sure whether or not her mother wiped a tear away.

When Eliot came in hot and tired from a long day of going through the dusty, poorly organized records of several Deer Flat farmers, Elizabeth warmed up some supper for him and recounted her thoughts about Griswold. "What do you think about Alex's comment? Could there be anything to the idea that he got more than his share of water—like they're accusing Mr. Ives of?"

Eliot considered. "Guess anything's possible—especially with a character like Griswold. Getting hold of the evidence would be the problem."

"Could you look into it—as part of what you're doing for Kirkland?"

Eliot frowned. "We'd have to work through the Ada County prosecutor's office. If I had evidence of fraud I could request permission—I don't know, we'll have to see what turns up. I didn't find much today."

It was a week later before Eliot returned home from his tedious work elated at having found something of interest.

"What did you find?"

"Will you win your case?"

"Is it evidence against Griswold?"

The family crowded around him.

"Better than that." Eliot tossed his brown felt hat on the rack by the door, then crossed to take Elizabeth's hands. "I've found a house."

"For us? One we can afford? Oh, Eliot! Is it possible?" She took her hands from his grip and flung her arms around his neck.

"Yes to all three. But—"

"Uh-oh, what's the catch?"

"No catch. It's just obvious—a house we can afford can't be up to much."

Elizabeth calmed down and sat on a straight-backed chair. "Tell me all about it."

Kathryn and Alex turned back to setting the table for supper, and Mavis took Tommy and Susie out to wash their hands at the pump.

"Well, it's on the farm where I was investigating today. He'd built it for a hired man, then the man quit. It's not far from Deer Flat Reservoir—"

"So are there trees?"

258

Elizabeth couldn't believe their fortune when Eliot nodded.

"A few locusts out back."

"Oh, that's wonderful! A car and now a house!"

"Well, maybe I was a little hasty calling it a house. It's more of a shack, really. Just one room, covered with tar paper."

Before Elizabeth could reply, Kathryn laughed from the kitchen. "Oh, aren't you the lucky ones! What I would have given for tar paper to keep out the dust when we moved to the desert." She came in and hugged her daughter. "Forgive me, I couldn't help hearing. It sounds awful, but so very much like the way your father and I started out." Then she turned serious. "I'm sorry. I wish you could have it easier than we did. And yet I wouldn't trade those memories for anything. There are lots worse things than living in a one-room shack. And at least you won't be swarmed by flying ants."

Elizabeth agreed, smiling at the memories of her mother's stories.

Just two weeks later Elizabeth and Eliot moved into their tar paper shack with no less excitement than the Little Princesses could have felt at moving into Buckingham Palace. Elizabeth spent the rest of the summer making it as cozy as she could. She remembered how Alice and Velda had made printed tablecloths and parchment lampshades for their domestic arts class and imitated their patterns.

When school started that fall she returned happily to Lakeview School, driving in to Nampa with Eliot, where he and Kirkland then rode the interurban train to Caldwell.

The water rights case progressed slowly, but by mid-October Eliot thought he had enough solid evidence that Kirkland could bring charges.

"But what about Griswold? Didn't you find anything against him?

"Well, the closest I've come is finding that his bank did finance Ives—so there could be some connection. Getting the proof is another matter. I can't go to the Ada County prosecutor with nothing but suspicions."

The more unlikely it seemed that they would be able to get hold of convicting evidence against Griswold the more Elizabeth wished they could.

As 1937 turned into 1938, however, they became more involved in their jobs and the small community church they attended, as well as enjoying as many quiet evenings together as possible in their little home. And Elizabeth attempted to put other troubles out of her mind. One thing that contributed greatly to their evenings was Eliot's Christmas present to her: a radio.

Thursday evenings became one of their favorite times of the week as Kate Smith's cheery "Hello, everybody!" sailed into their living room/bedroom/kitchen. The antics of Amos 'n Andy, and Edgar Bergen and Charlie McCarthy brought many bright spots to the routine of Elizabeth's days. She especially needed a bright spot when Eliot brought home the huge file of the water case.

"I'm going to give this one more going over. Maybe I'm missing something. If I could find just one clue that we could apply to Griswold . . ."

But he didn't. It was long past midnight when he closed the file with a sigh. "I hate injustice. I hate to see cheats and liars getting away with it." He ran his fingers through his blond hair, shiny in the lantern light. "That's why I wanted to be a lawyer—to work for justice. It just seems like the harder I work the less progress I make." The lamp highlighted the silvery web lines of his scarred cheek.

Elizabeth felt love for him wash over her like a wave. She put her arms around him and pulled him toward the old iron bedstead in the corner of the room. She recalled something she had heard her mother say long ago. "I can't do much about the unhappiness and injustice in the world. But I can love those around me. It's not much; yet it's everything."

24

Their radio became increasingly important to Eliot and Elizabeth as hostilities around the world filled every news report. Stories of Japan's occupation of China were particularly painful to Eliot as he recalled places and people he had known there and they learned of the persecution of American missionaries.

"We'd be there now if you had gone as a missionary when you wanted to." Elizabeth reached out her hand to her husband.

He took it, and together they breathed a silent thank you for God's protection.

Then Elizabeth remembered something she had never told Eliot—about donating the jewels for the training of missionaries.

Eliot dropped the hand he was holding so he could pull her into his arms. "I'm so glad you did. Those jewels may have provided someone's last chance to hear the gospel."

And they bowed in another prayer of thanksgiving.

That summer and fall Hitler's troops marched to the border of Czechoslovakia.

In September they followed news commentator H. V. Kaltenborn's marathon coverage of the eighteen-day Munich crisis while British Prime Minister Chamberlain met with Hitler. Kaltenborn was skeptical that the pact would result in lasting peace. Churchill was outraged, calling the agreement "a total and unmitigated defeat."

Cyrus Griswold was ecstatic.

The weekly Kuna newspaper came out three days ahead of schedule with two-inch headlines declaring "Peace in Our Time" and reporting on the "gracious, magnanimous" attitude of Adolph Hitler, who had attended the meeting only because his friend Mussolini had asked him to do so.

The "peace in our time" lasted five months. In March 1939 Hitler violated his Munich agreement and occupied Prague.

In September he invaded Poland.

On September 3, Great Britain and France declared war on Germany.

This produced a spate of "America First" editorials in successive issues of Griswold's paper. "America should steer clear of any entanglement with the foreign world," and "America, situated two broad oceans away from foreigners, should remain aloof from European quarrels." So ran the sentiments of the editorial page. The front page quoted at great length from Senator Borah, who, when the declaration of war was followed by a lull in hostilities rather than the decisive battles everyone anticipated, dubbed the European proceedings "The Phony War," a phrase that immediately caught on across America and in England.

As 1939 dragged on, no one hoped and prayed more fervently that the war would remain phony than the American family of Ian Buchanan and Boyd Allen—both volunteers in the Royal Air Force.

Elizabeth was the first to know of Boyd's decision.

"Sis, you'll know best how to break this to Mom and the others [he wrote]. It's probably impossible for you to understand, being so far away—and I thank God that you all are far away—but here we realize that

262

we'll all be doing the goose step and saying "Heil Hitler" if that maniac isn't stopped. Our unit will be going down to Kent next week (you'd love it, they call it the garden of England). From there we'll be flying sorties over the Channel. These Spitfires are the greatest to fly."

He went on to the end of the page about his airplane.

Elizabeth's first impulse was to write back that he was an American and should come home—he didn't have to fight their war for them. Then she realized she sounded just like Griswold. Boyd had always had a special affinity for their father's people in Britain. When she recalled her mother's accounts of being there—of the beauty of the country and the warmth of the people—she knew Boyd couldn't turn his back on them now. And she knew their mother wouldn't want him to.

She would wait a few days to tell her mother. Maybe she would have some good news of her own to offset Boyd's worrying announcement. But the next morning a cramping backache told her she would have no good news this month.

So she drove to Kuna and shared Boyd's letter with her family. Alex cried. Kathryn set her jaw, just as Elizabeth remembered her doing from her earliest days whenever something went wrong. But Elizabeth couldn't help noticing the increased wrinkles above that jawline and the gray in the hair around it. Again she longed to have good news for her mother—and for herself and Eliot.

But as there was none, she signed her contract to return to teaching another year. As much as she loved her students—perhaps because she loved her students so much —her longing for a baby increased. What had at first been a vague wish was rapidly becoming an urgent need.

Perhaps the emotion she felt would have been lessened if she could have discussed it with Eliot. But as his own unhappiness grew, she felt it more and more important that she present a happy face to him. Perhaps the one good thing about her own dissatisfaction was the fact that it helped her understand his frustration at being denied an opportunity to do what he wanted to do—at being stuck in a dead end job.

Just as at first the stock market crash and Great Depression had seemed far away, so did the war in Europe that winter. With so little happening—or at least so little being reported in their newspapers—and their occasional post cards from Boyd amounting to a few lines scribbled on the back of a pretty picture of the French countryside or a cathedral in Paris, it was much easier to think of her brother as being on a pleasure trip than as risking his life in a war. Then in April the Nazi army occupied Norway.

Hitler overran Denmark in a few hours. The Low Countries were next. Holland held for four days against the invaders. Then there was only France between Hitler and England. And now the French fell back, leaving the English army exposed on the beach at Dunkirk.

Elizabeth again spent every possible moment that May listening to the radio. She scoured every newspaper report to try to get some idea of where Boyd might be, what he was going through, whether he was all right. The reports were full of accounts of the valiant RAF pilots providing air cover against the mighty Luftwaffe as British, French, and Belgian troops were ferried across the channel largely by pleasure craft and fishing vessels piloted by amateurs risking their own lives to save their army. The miracle was that the normally choppy Channel was like glass for the three days of the evacuation, then turned rough again.

Elizabeth's eyes stung as she read it. "That gives me goose bumps. It's like Israel and the Red sea, or crossing the Jordan."

The evacuation was cheered as one of the great heroic events of history, but the Allens were not cheering. Kathryn's last post card from Paris came from Ian, not Boyd: "His plane is missing. We're still hoping."

Elizabeth cried as she read Churchill's speech. "I have nothing to offer but blood, toil, tears and sweat . . . to wage war against a monstrous tyranny."

She knew he was right. This evil must be stopped. But she hated a war that took her adventurous young brother and so many young men like him. The heathen were raging, and they had to be stilled, just as God had directed the armies of Israel to do, but she longed for the green valleys and quiet waters of the Psalms. She longed for a baby. She longed for fulfillment for Eliot. She longed for a world where roses could bloom in the sunshine.

That November, Roosevelt defeated Wendell Wilkie and began a precedent-breaking third term as president of the United States. He introduced the Lend-Lease Bill, by which the U.S. would supply armaments and food to England, for which the British would pay later.

This sparked another spate of isolationist editorials from Griswold, liberally seasoned with such accusations as "interventionism" and "warmongering." The rhetoric was just what Elizabeth needed to stiffen her resolution that Hitler must be stopped. Boyd was no warmonger, but he had cared enough for freedom and justice that he had apparently given his life. And now that only England stood against all the Nazi forces, the Atlantic Ocean suddenly didn't look quite so broad.

Elizabeth sighed and rustled the paper.

Eliot looked up from the file he was reviewing for Kirkland, who had been reelected to another term. "More bad news?"

Elizabeth straightened out the newspaper and found her place. She was happy enough to share her reading with Eliot. With each of them feeling so much dissatisfaction in their personal lives, it was a relief to discuss national news. As a matter of fact, it seemed to be about all they did discuss anymore.

Elizabeth loved Eliot as much—even more—than ever, and yet she worried. As usual she took refuge in the news.

"Griswold's editorial again. He claims to see grave dangers in the fact that they are flying the Stars and Stripes on the streets of London in appreciation of Lend-Lease. He says the Italians are right in saying that 'Roosevelt's gesture may cause many unpleasant surprises to England and the United States in the Pacific.'" She looked up. "I wonder what he means by that—in the Pacific. What does that have to do with anything?"

Eliot shrugged and vented his frustration with the file in front of him by shoving the papers farther back on the table. Several sheets fell off, and Elizabeth continued as he retrieved them.

"Apparently Hitler said, 'With or without Lend-Lease, England will fall.' What bothers me is not so much that Hitler said it, but that Griswold seems to be so delighted."

Eliot slammed his hand down on the papers in front of him and shoved his chair back, raking into the linoleum. "I wish Griswold would fall. Someone should be able to do something about that man. I know he's corrupt. If only I could have found something against him on that water case, but it seems like he always stays just inside the law—or covers his tracks too well for us. And what can an errand-boy/clerk do anyway?"

Elizabeth suddenly felt her throat close and her eyes sting as she looked at her husband. He worked so hard. He cared so much. But he felt he accomplished so little. She put the newspaper down, crossed the tiny room to him, and sat on his lap, running her hand over his smooth hair. "Does it help that you're everything to me?"

"Help? Oh, Elizabeth—what would I do without you? I don't know how you manage to put up with all this—" He gestured toward the tar-papered walls. "It sure isn't what I wanted for you."

She smiled and kissed his cheek just in front of his ear. "It's a lot better than what my folks started out in, and I'll bet it's a lot better than anything you lived in in China."

"Hmm," he agreed.

266

"But you know, the more the world falls apart around us, the more I realize how unimportant such things are. Mansions are being bombed every night in London. What good are fancy houses then? God, you, and my family—that's what's important." She kissed him again. "But let me have a look at this file. What are you working on now?" She picked up another paper that had fallen to the floor.

"Oh, it's a request from the Attorney General. He wants information on this pro-Nazi group that's making so much trouble back East—afraid it'll break out here with their amateur storm troopers."

"Are they illegal?"

"Marching around in costumes isn't illegal, but in some areas they've gone beyond that. He just wants to know what's happening around the state, so I'm going through all these dusty files."

"Found anything?"

He shook his head.

"Well, here, let me help." She picked up a manila folder and blew the dust off it. For a while they turned pages companionably in the flickering light of the kerosene lamp.

At last she paused over a newspaper clipping that Kirkland's predecessor had put in a file nearly ten years before. "Hmm—this article about these pro-Nazi, quasi-military camps—a lot of this stuff they were teaching sure sounds like things I've read in Griswold's editorials."

Eliot leaned over her shoulder to read, then became so engrossed he took the clipping out of her hand. The second time he read it he did so pacing around the room, barely staying within the arc of light from the lantern. At last he tossed the file page on the table and pulled Elizabeth to her feet.

"My beautiful, intelligent wife—who somehow manages to love me—you've done it!" After the heartiest kiss he'd given her for weeks he explained. "I think you've just found the key we've been looking for for years—ever since that snake attacked you in his office."

"And you walked in and rescued me."

He started to argue that it was really her father who had rescued her, but she stopped the argument by returning his kiss. Then he continued. "I could never get my hands on anything solid enough to get a warrant to see his personal files. But if I build a case around this very carefully—I just might."

"You mean put Griswold in jail?"

Eliot shook his head. "I don't think that's possible. But we might get enough to disgrace him publicly—county commissioner, bank director, newspaper publisher—he can't maintain all that without the respect of the public."

Then somehow Griswold was forgotten as the lamp ran out of kerosene.

25

Three months later, in the late spring of 1941, Elizabeth knew for certain that she had her good news. She skipped out of Dr. Nolte's office, told the superintendent she wouldn't be signing a contract to teach next year, and went home to welcome Eliot with all his favorite foods for dinner, ending with lemon meringue pie.

She had only one doubt, which she voiced in a subdued tone some time after Eliot had calmed down from his excitement over the news that he was to become a father. "I hate to mention anything negative—but can we get along without my salary?"

She saw the jolt her question gave him, but he covered it quickly. "We'll get along. We'll get along fine. I don't want you worrying about anything. Do you hear? If this file I'm preparing against Griswold is good enough I just might ask for a raise."

"Oh." Elizabeth, preoccupied for weeks with alternating between hopes that one of her dearest dreams was about to come true and fears that she was imagining things, realized that she hadn't asked about his work. "Tell me, what have you found?"

"I thought you'd never ask. You thought you were the only one in the family with good news, didn't you?" He pulled an official-looking document out of his briefcase. "I got it today—a warrant to search Griswold's personal files. It took a lot of doing to convince the Ada County prosecutor to go to the judge, but we got it!"

Elizabeth hugged him with such force that the little wooden chair he was sitting on almost tipped over.

Their joy was mitigated, however, by the daily news reports of bombs falling on London and America's new troubles across the Pacific Ocean. Japan's invasion of China had been followed by an aggressive program of kicking all white devils out of Asia. Germany, Italy, and Japan signed the Tripartite Pact, bringing Japan into the Axis coalition.

The U.S. placed an embargo on American oil and scrap metals to Japan, and then in mid-summer President Roosevelt froze all Japanese assets in America. A delegation of Japanese negotiators came to Washington, D.C., with the directive from Hirohito that they had until November 29 to settle the matter peacefully.

With the press of work in the understaffed prosecutor's office, it took several months for Eliot to get the break he had worked so hard for and waited so many years for. Finally, the Monday before Thanksgiving he came home from work waving a packet of letters he had found in Griswold's files.

"And all because you saw the connection between his editorials and the article about those American Nazi camps." He placed the letters before Elizabeth and kissed her, standing to her side, rather than in front where the baby was a very large presence.

She read for several minutes. "Wow! Personal letters from the American Nazi leader himself. Of course, we never doubted he was a committed Nazi, but can you put him in jail for that—even with such hard evidence?"

"Of course not. He has the right to think what he wants to think—and so do all his friends and neighbors when these become public."

Elizabeth felt as if she spent days holding her breath waiting for the story to break. When it finally did, she had one of the biggest disappointments of her life. The papers that even bothered to print the story gave it small headlines and little space somewhere on page two or three. Those who did happen to read the item gave it little reaction.

Late that week Aunt Nelly picked her up in her rattly Ford to go out for some fresh air. They stopped at Janicke's Pharmacy for phosphates and Oodles bars before going on to visit her family.

The conversation around the soda fountain was typical of attitudes across the valley. One farmer shrugged. "I allus knew Griswold held radical ideas."

"Not that I like what that Hitler's doing, mind you," his neighbor at the counter added.

"Well after all, Senator Borah and a lot of others back there in Washington say we should tend to our own business, not Europe's—they probably know more about it than we do," another said.

"That's right, and some pretty important people are thinking twice about the Jews."

The first one finished his coffee and set his cup on the marble counter with a clatter. "I don't know. Griswold might not be so far off base."

So the reasoning went. And when Griswold wrote a long editorial in the *Times* assuring everyone of his loyalty as an American, Elizabeth was sure he would remain a power in the community for a long time to come. She and Eliot had fought a long, valiant battle against corruption in their little community and lost.

She hugged the baby inside her and prayed that the larger battle raging in Europe would not be likewise lost. But the clouds darkened daily. England had stood alone for two years under a deluge of fifty thousand tons of German bombs. Two million British homes had been destroyed, and forty thousand British lives lost. How much longer could they stand? If they fell, America would be alone in the world.

Elizabeth and Eliot loved their little Deer Flat community church and rarely missed a service. Since Elizabeth had quit teaching it was almost her only social contact, as well as their source of spiritual food and opportunity for ministry. But one morning, with the baby due in just a few weeks, she didn't feel like going out in the cold December weather. She urged Eliot to go on without her.

At first he refused, then remembered that he had agreed to read the Scripture that morning. He checked to be sure there was adequate wood in the little stove that served both for cooking and heating, tucked an extra quilt over her feet, and kissed her three times before leaving.

"Are you sure you'll be all right? I don't like your not having a telephone here." He paused at the door.

"Silly. I'll be fine. The baby isn't due for three weeks yet. I didn't sleep very well last night, that's all." She grinned at him. "So you just go on and get out of here, and let me get some rest."

He blew her a kiss and started to go.

"Just one thing—"

Her words called him back. "Turn the radio on for me before you go out. Nice and low. It'll be company."

He did and closed the door gently behind him.

Three hours later he opened the same door in a hurry to get home, but quietly in case she was sleeping. Then he froze. "Elizabeth!" He rushed to her side. "What is it? The baby—is it time?" When her only response was to wipe away the tears streaming down her cheeks he grasped her by the shoulders. "Are you sick? Elizabeth, talk to me!"

She gave a little hiccup and gestured toward the radio. "Didn't you hear?"

He looked at her blankly.

"Oh, I guess you couldn't have. Oh, Eliot, it's so awful!" She leaned into his arms and shook with silent sobs while he held her.

At last she sat up and gestured toward the radio dial. "Here. I turned it off—I couldn't stand any more. Turn it on—you can hear for yourself."

The static that followed the click of the dial cleared. The voice of a frantic newscaster filled the room. ". . . the total so far is eight battleships and three cruisers sunk or damaged. We don't have an update on planes lost, but experts estimate close to two hundred. Well over two thousand American men . . ."

Eliot turned down the volume. "*American* men? What's happening? Where?"

"Pearl Harbor. The Japanese attacked this morning. It's unbelievable. They say the American navy is paralyzed. They say everything is destroyed—just smoke and flame and dead bodies and rubble everywhere."

Elizabeth and Eliot, like everyone else in America, hardly left their radio for the next twenty-four hours. Monday they heard President Roosevelt address Congress to ask for a declaration of war against Japan. "Yesterday, December 7, 1941—a date which will live in infamy—the United States of America was suddenly and deliberately attacked by naval and air forces . . ."

It was more than Elizabeth could take in. The world wasn't simply crumbling around her, it was being violently smashed by bombs. She felt the secure life she and Eliot had worked so hard to build had sunk with the battleships in Pearl Harbor. This was the end of everything: A world of peace and roses for her baby to grow up in, a chance for Eliot to become a lawyer, the happiness she had hoped Alexandra would find, all of Eliot's efforts to bring Griswold to justice—she could have gone on and on, cataloging the despair she felt.

How many more lives would be lost in the coming days? What about Clarey? Boyd was already gone. Would Kathryn lose both her sons? What about the boys Alexandra's age? She had held to her youthful determination not to give her heart to anyone since Howie Manchester left.

But at least she had friends. Would they all be swallowed up in a firey gulf such as the radio announcers described from Pearl Harbor and London?

She had only one consolation. Eliot's stiff elbow. It had been months, years perhaps, since she had given a thought to his scars or the slight inconvenience of his arm, but now she clung to that mild disabling as a lifeline. Surely a weak arm would keep him out of the war. Surely.

But it was such a small glimmer against the darkness all around her.

Even putting a name to her hopelessness seemed too much effort. With a creak of the iron bed she turned her face to the wall. She might have put the pillow over her head, but that seemed like too much effort as well.

Eliot left the Bible he had been reading open on the table and came to cover her, pulling the sheet up smooth over her shoulder and tucking the quilts around her gently. He didn't even touch her, yet she felt soothed, caressed.

He returned to his reading, this time aloud: "Who shall separate us from the love of Christ? shall tribulation, or distress, or persecution, or famine, or nakedness, or peril, or sword?"

There it was, the verse that had meant so much to her so many times through the struggles of the Depression, and now with a new meaning. Earlier she had focused on aspects of distress, famine, nakedness. Now she knew that even the sword—the peril of war—couldn't separate her or her loved ones from the love of Christ. *Thank You, Lord, thank You.* And she realized how long it had been, caught up as she had been in the turmoil of current events, since she had prayed and really trusted the Lord to see her and her family through this new peril.

With as smooth a movement as was possible for an almost eight-and-a-half-months pregnant woman to make, she rolled out of bed and crossed the room to kiss her husband. "Give me a few minutes to get myself organized, then let's drive out to see Mother and the others."

It was almost suppertime when they arrived. A thin powder of snow lay on the fields and sagebrush bushes that glowed with a blush of pink as the winter sunset turned the sky red. The whole house smelled warm and spicy from Kathryn's new-baked apple pies. Alex and Mavis hurried to set two more places at the table as eleven-year-old Tommy played soldier, crouching behind the sofa.

Elizabeth counted the plates. "Oh, were you expecting company? There's an extra place." Then she noticed Alexandra was wearing her Sunday dress. "Someone special, Alex?"

Alex tried to sound casual, but she couldn't hide her blush. "Remember Howie Manchester?"

Elizabeth clasped her hands and squealed. "Oh, Alex, I certainly do. You thought you'd never see him again. Is he—?"

"He's just as handsome as ever—more." Alex ran to her sister and hugged her as far as her arms would go around Elizabeth's bulging figure. "And he came just to see me. He never wrote because he was determined not to until he could offer me something, but he never forgot me. Never."

"And now he has something to offer?"

Alex bit her lip. "He doesn't think so, but he said he couldn't go off to war without seeing me again."

"Oh." Elizabeth put her hand to her throat. "He's enlisted?"

Alex nodded. "In the army. He has to report next week, so he rode the bus all night to get here to see me first." The bang of the porch screen told them someone was coming, so she leaned toward Elizabeth to whisper hurriedly, "And I'm not letting him get away this time, you'll see."

Clarey and Howie entered, and Kathryn started toward them. "Howie, supper is almost—" She stopped with a gasp as she saw the official seal on the paper her son was holding out. "Clarey?"

"What have you done?" It was more the aggressive pride on his face than the document that drew the question from Elizabeth. Someone had to say it, so she did, almost under her breath—yet it sounded like a shout in the frozen silence of the room. "You enlisted."

Mavis gave a muffled sob and ran to her husband. "Why did you do that? You didn't have to."

"Yes, I did."

"But you have two children."

"That's why I had to. I don't want our children growing up under Hitler and Hirohito or any other tyrant that tries to rule the world with bombs. They have to be stopped. And I have to do my part."

Elizabeth stood woodenly. This was exactly what she had been afraid of. She couldn't help agreeing with Clarey's brave words, and yet . . . It was selfish of her to be glad it wasn't Eliot standing there with his orders to report, but she couldn't deny the feeling. At least the war had brought Howie to Alexandra, but at what cost?

Kathryn, however, showed no such hesitancy as she crossed the room and hugged them both. "Maybe they'll send you to France. You can try to find out what happened to Boyd."

"No!" Mavis threw her arms around Clarey. "I've heard about those French women!" And with that the tension in the room dissolved in laughter.

Halfway through the meal Elizabeth looked around the table, amazed. Anyone would think it was a celebration. How could Kathryn, who had already lost one son in the war, be so valiant? Perhaps only Elizabeth, who knew her best, recognized the firm set of her mother's jaw that told how much her determined cheerfulness cost her.

Later, however, when Alexandra announced over coffee that she and Howie were getting married the next day, it took no effort for everyone to be genuinely jubilant. Kathryn moved to the old organ in the corner, pumped up the bellows with her feet, and played the "Wedding March" to everyone's applause, in spite of a few missed notes.

It was the next day, after Alex and Howie had stood before Rev. Brown, pledged their vows, and then departed for a twenty-four-hour honeymoon before Howie left for boot camp, that Elizabeth realized it was possible for even something as disastrous as a war to bring solutions to some problems. This was not the wedding she would have chosen for her little sister, but it certainly was the groom she would have chosen, and without the pressure of going off to war Howie would not have come to Alex.

Further, Elizabeth had applauded Alex's announcement that while she awaited her husband's return from war she would attend NCC. "I think I might like to be a teacher like Elizabeth—until I can do something better—like Elizabeth's doing now." She looked at her sister's pregnant form, and Howie pecked his new bride on the end of her upturned nose.

Elizabeth thought she had never seen a more radiant couple. She prayed that their brief time together wouldn't be their last.

It seemed that was to be only the beginning of surprises. A few minutes later there was a hesitant knock at the door. Eliot went to answer it, then stood aside to usher in Phoebe Griswold. Her usually mannequin-perfect gray hair stuck out in stray wisps from under her black felt hat. She held her black purse awkwardly in front of her, clutched in both hands.

Kathryn rose to greet her visitor as graciously as if she'd been an invited guest. "Mrs. Griswold, won't you sit down? Perhaps you've heard? My youngest daughter was just married."

"Oh. I didn't know. I'm sorry—I didn't mean to interrupt." Elizabeth had never seen the domineering Mrs. Griswold so unsure of herself. "I wouldn't have come, but I don't think there's much time—I don't know. Cyrus's already gone—I don't really know what to do. I couldn't think of who else to go to—Cyrus always talked about our farms being right together—about how good it would be if they were worked as one—so I thought . . ." She started to get up. "I'm sorry. I shouldn't have come." She had taken a long envelope from her purse, which she started to put back in.

Eliot stopped her. "Don't go, Mrs. Griswold. If there's something I can help you with—or any of us—just ask. You're our neighbor."

She looked even more confused. "Thank you. I know Cyrus wasn't always the best neighbor. He wasn't a bad man, not really—maybe I pushed him too hard—I don't know. Anyway, if you want to buy the land, I brought the deed."

Elizabeth gasped, unable to believe what she heard. All these years Griswold had been trying to get *their* land one way or another, and now his was being offered to them.

Eliot took the envelope to look the documents over.

"I don't understand," Kathryn said. "You said your husband is gone?"

The woman nodded. "I guess if you're going to buy the land you should know. He's gone to Mexico."

"Mexico?" they asked in chorus.

Mrs. Griswold nodded. "It's best. Easiest route to Germany now that we're at war. He didn't mean to betray America or anything, you know. He really thought Hitler was right—a strong leader who knew how to organize things. Cyrus always tried so hard to organize everything, but it seemed to get away from him. Anyway, that was the thing he admired most in people.

"But now—with what Japan did, and them being Germany's ally—it was best he go. I know where he—where his family came from—near Dresden. With the money from the farm I'll go too when I can. I don't much fancy leaving

278

America, but we've been married a long while—through good times and bad. Er—that is, if you want to buy it."

Elizabeth looked at her mother. It was Kathryn's decision. Now Clarey would be gone too, and hired hands would likely become harder to get. Would she have the money? Such a short time ago, but for their neighbors, the farm would have fallen under the auctioneer's gavel at a sheriff's sale. Now, she could tell by the look on Kathryn's face, her mother was considering doubling the size of her holdings.

"Farm prices have soared," Kathryn thought out loud. "One hates to say good things about the war when so many lives are being lost, but I've never got such prices as I did this fall. How much were you thinking of, Mrs. Griswold?"

The business talk continued for a considerable time. Elizabeth joined Mavis in taking Tommy and Susie to bed. When she came back to the living room, Mrs. Griswold was gone, and Kathryn was the owner of one hundred sixty more acres—with the generous water rights they had suspected attached to the land.

"Eliot, can you draw this up in proper form? I want to make the new land over to Clarey—" Kathryn paused as her eyes flicked over him "—with it to pass to Tommy and Susie," she added quietly.

Later, when they drove home in the crisp winter dark with a few snowflakes glistening in the headlights and Elizabeth's head on Eliot's shoulder, she thought how just a few days ago she would have believed it impossible to have her cup so overflowing. Even in a world ravaged by war, God could bring evidence of His peace and goodness. Perhaps especially so in a torn world, for then people had nothing but God to cling to.

The realities of war were very present, however. The nation prepared to go on rationing, and complicated systems with books of stamps and coupons were worked out for purchasing items needed for the war effort such as meat, gasoline, and silk stockings.

Elizabeth was glad she had learned how to darn stockings during the Depression, for she would now need the skill again. Already the paper announced a counter at Woolworths where nimble-fingered seamstresses would darn stockings while one waited.

And the area was warned by local wardens to prepare for blackout. No one knew for sure when the first air raid would come, as the siren was installed and thoroughly tested. Elizabeth joined in making blackout curtains, and Eliot hung them securely over the three tiny windows in their shack. That night he went out to be certain no crack of light from their kerosene lamps showed through.

Elizabeth had noticed for several days that Eliot was unusually quiet. At first she passed it off as the pressures of work. But the silences grew. One evening the unthinkable crossed her mind. *Has he found someone else?* And she knew she must speak.

"Eliot, what is it? You're so quiet. You never talk to me anymore."

She held her breath for the answer as he seemed to have difficulty finding the right words. "Well, I've been thinking a lot about my—our—future. Actually, I've been talking with someone—"

"Who?" Her lips were stiff, but she made her voice sound almost natural.

"Well, the recruiting officer, actually." Suddenly it was as if a floodgate opened, and the words poured out. "I could go into JAG—the Judge Advocate General Corps, legal department of the military—work as a clerk, court reporter, that sort of thing.

"Then, when we've dealt with Hitler and Hirohito I can finish reading for the law while clerking for a judge."

His voice had taken on increasing enthusiasm as he spoke, and his eyes sparkled. But suddenly he stopped. "That is —I mean . . ."

At first she couldn't believe what she was hearing. "You mean *enlist?*" How could that be? She thought she was safe from that at least. "I thought—your arm . . ."

"He stuck his left elbow out and glanced at it. "Yeah, I asked the recruiter about it. He said at the moment they're taking anyone who can shoot, move, and communicate. Especially for clerical positions like I want. So everything's fine if—if—"

She took a breath and lifted her head. "You mean, if I won't get hysterical and stand in your way. Eliot Hamilton, have you ever known me to be a hysterical female? Have I ever stood in your way for anything?"

He kissed her cheek. "You are the calmest, strongest woman I know—besides your mother—and everything I've accomplished has been with your help."

She knew she didn't feel nearly as calm and brave as she appeared, but she knew she would get through it with the Lord's help. She couldn't manage a smile, but her voice was steady. "Well, then, you'd better get on with it, hadn't you?"

Still he hesitated. "It's just that—"

"Yes?"

"Well, the recruiting officer said I'll have a much better chance of getting my choice if I do it right away. Like tomorrow morning. That means I might be gone by the end of the week—sooner maybe—right before Christmas—right before the baby—"

"Eliot! Stop making excuses. It's decided." She leaned back against the pillow. "I'm just so tired, so terribly tired. Let me take just a little nap, then we'll talk more."

He tucked the quilt tightly around her, and she slept.

Hours later a strong, insistent cramp woke her.

"Why is it so dark in here? Have I slept all afternoon?"

"You have, my love. Afternoon and evening both." Eliot moved the four steps from his chair to the bed and sat on the edge. "Want something to eat?"

She shook her head. "Just something cold to drink."

Forty minutes later a second cramp took Elizabeth's breath away.

"Eliot." She made an enormous effort to keep her voice calm, but he caught the note of urgency.

"Is it time? Where's your bag? Twenty minutes to the hospital. Less. No problem." He was halfway to the door, shrugging into his coat.

She laughed. "No hurry. We've got hours yet. Probably all night." Then she felt the soft gush as her water broke. "Oh. Maybe not quite that long. Bring me a towel, will you?"

He was halfway across the room when the siren started. High and screeching, the wail rose and fell, surely making all its hearers for a radius of many miles want to cover their ears and hide in the nearest shelter. Eliot froze.

"The blackout curtains," Elizabeth prodded. "Close the curtains."

He did, then turned to her. "Elizabeth, I can't take you out in an air raid. It's probably just a practice, but I can't turn on the headlights. If I ran you into a ditch—I'll go for the doctor."

"No. Don't leave me." The air raid siren continued to wail.

"But the baby's coming."

"I was raised on a farm. You were raised on a mission station. How many births—animal and human—do you suppose we've witnessed between us?" She caught her breath, then forced herself to breathe deeply, rhymically, as another cramp held her in its grip.

"Right. I won't leave you. What do we do first?"

"Clean sheets, I should think."

The contractions were coming less than ten minutes apart when there was a knock at the door.

"Do you suppose it's the doctor? How could he have known?" Eliot turned the lamp to a tiny flicker before he opened the door just a crack.

"Mother!" Elizabeth cried when the shadowy form drew near. "How did you know I needed you?"

"I didn't. I just wanted to spend the evening with you. I was already on my way when that siren started, so I turned off the headlights and came on. It took forever. At least the roads were rutted enough to make driving by Braille possible."

When Eliot had hung up her coat, Kathryn prepared to help welcome her grandchild into the world.

And an hour later, an exhausted but radiant Elizabeth lay propped against her pillows nursing her new daughter. "Stephanie Jayne Hamilton." She caressed the downy red-gold head with one finger, then looked up into the tender eyes of her husband sitting beside them. "Look what we did. Great, huh?"

He shook his head in amazement. "It's hard to believe anything so wonderful."

Kathryn, standing above him, put her hand on his shoulder. "It gives you all that much more to fight for."

Elizabeth had told her, in broken bits between contractions, of Eliot's plan to join the Judge Advocate Corps, and she heartily approved.

"And we'll be fighting here on the home front. Elizabeth, Stephanie, and I will keep the farm going—grow enough to feed a battalion—a whole division even. It won't be the first time I ran a farm alone with another woman."

Her account of her plans were interrupted by the first blasts of the all-clear signal, an off-and-on clacking, equally as loud and irritating as the alarm but bringing with it the blessed release of tensions. For this night at least, the emergency was over.

"Oh, good. Now I can drive home with my headlights on." Kathryn kissed all three of them and was out the door before they could argue that she should stay longer.

When the all clear ended, the quiet in the room was like a great hollow. Eliot reached over and clicked on the radio.

Smoothly, as if on cue, the full-throated tones of Kate Smith filled the room, singing "God Bless America."

Eliot enfolded his wife and infant daughter in an embrace of infinite tenderness and yet as strong as if he would never let them go. The blackout had ended for the moment, but it was still night—a night that could well be a long one. Yet even in the deepest blackout there would always be the light from above.

Eliot dropped his lips to Elizabeth's and held her in a long kiss that would last through all the weary days and dark nights ahead to the end of the war. It was a kiss full of promise for the future when they would build a new and better life together in a world of peace and plenty.

Author's Note

This is a novel—a work of fiction—but one very dear to me because I was able to use so many bits and pieces of my own family history. The intercollegiate debate described actually occurred between Stanford and Northwest Nazarene College in 1934 with NNC indeed winning. I have changed the names of all the participants except Will Rogers, Jr.

My mother was the first recipient of the Senior Sweater at Kuna High School, my father proposed to my mother under the gazebo at Mora School, and they did live in a one-room tar paper shack. My mother was sitting by the radio nursing me when she heard the announcement of Pearl Harbor. The baby born in the area's first blackout was a friend of mine.

My deep gratitude goes to the many excellent local historians, reference librarians, and public officials who have patiently answered questions for me, especially: Edith Lancaster, archivist, Northwest Nazarene College; Arthur Hart, author, *Life in Old Boise;* Lynda Campbell Clark, author, *Nampa Idaho, A Journey of Discovery;* and Annie Laurie Bird, author, *My Home Town.* I also recommend the Time-Life series *This Fabulous Century* for a truly "you are there" sense of history.

DFC

A NOTE TO THE READER

This book was selected by the book division of the company that publishes *Guideposts*, a monthly magazine filled with true stories of people's adventures in faith.

If you have found inspiration in this book, we think you'll find monthly help and inspiration in the exciting stories that appear in our magazine.

Guideposts is not sold on the newsstand. It's available by subscription only. And subscribing is easy. All you have to do is write Guideposts, 39 Seminary Hill Road, Carmel, New York 10512. For those with special reading needs, *Guideposts* is published in Big Print, Braille, and Talking Magazine.

When you subscribe, each month you can count on receiving exciting new evidence of God's presence and His abiding love for His people.

Guideposts is also available on the Internet by accessing our homepage on the World Wide Web at http://www.guideposts.org. Send prayer requests to our Monday morning Prayer Fellowship. Read stories from recent issues of our magazines, *Guideposts*, *Angels on Earth*, *Guideposts for Kids* and *Positive Living*, and follow our popular book of daily devotionals, *Daily Guideposts*. Excerpts from some of our best-selling books are also available.